HOPE AND HISTORY,
AN EXPLORATION

WORLD PERSPECTIVES

Volumes already published

I	APPROACHES TO GOD	Jacques Maritain
II	ACCENT ON FORM	Lancelot Law Whyte
III	SCOPE OF TOTAL ARCHITECTURE	Walter Gropius
IV	RECOVERY OF FAITH	Sarvepalli Radhakrishnan
V	WORLD INDIVISIBLE	Konrad Adenauer
VI	SOCIETY AND KNOWLEDGE	V. Gordon Childe
VII	THE TRANSFORMATIONS OF MAN	Lewis Mumford
VIII	MAN AND MATERIALISM	Fred Hoyle
IX	THE ART OF LOVING	Erich Fromm
X	DYNAMICS OF FAITH	Paul Tillich
XI	MATTER, MIND AND MAN	Edmund W. Sinnott
XII	MYSTICISM: CHRISTIAN AND BUDDHIST	Daisetz Teitaro Suzuki
XIII	MAN'S WESTERN QUEST	Denis de Rougemont
XIV	AMERICAN HUMANISM	Howard Mumford Jones
XV	THE MEETING OF LOVE AND KNOWLEDGE	Martin C. D'Arcy, S.J.
XVI	RICH LANDS AND POOR	Gunnar Myrdal
XVII	HINDUISM: ITS MEANING FOR THE LIBERATION OF THE SPIRIT	Swami Nikhilananda
XVIII	CAN PEOPLE LEARN TO LEARN?	Brock Chisholm
XIX	PHYSICS AND PHILOSOPHY	Werner Heisenberg
XX	ART AND REALITY	Joyce Cary
XXI	SIGMUND FREUD'S MISSION	Erich Fromm
XXII	MIRAGE OF HEALTH	René Dubos
XXIII	ISSUES OF FREEDOM	Herbert J. Muller
XXIV	HUMANISM	Moses Hadas
XXV	LIFE: ITS DIMENSIONS AND ITS BOUNDS	Robert M. MacIver
XXVI	CHALLENGE OF PSYCHICAL RESEARCH	Gardner Murphy

XXVII	ALFRED NORTH WHITEHEAD: HIS REFLECTIONS ON MAN AND NATURE	Ruth Nanda Anshen
XXVIII	THE AGE OF NATIONALISM	Hans Kohn
XXIX	VOICES OF MAN	Mario Pei
XXX	NEW PATHS IN BIOLOGY	Adolf Portmann
XXXI	MYTH AND REALITY	Mircea Eliade
XXXII	HISTORY AS ART AND AS SCIENCE	H. Stuart Hughes
XXXIII	REALISM IN OUR TIME	Georg Lukács
XXXIV	THE MEANING OF THE TWENTIETH CENTURY	Kenneth E. Boulding
XXXV	ON ECONOMIC KNOWLEDGE	Adolph Lowe
XXXVI	CALIBAN REBORN	Wilfred Mellers
XXXVII	THROUGH THE VANISHING POINT	Marshall McLuhan and Harley Parker
XXXVIII	THE REVOLUTION OF HOPE	Erich Fromm
XXXIX	EMERGENCY EXIT	Ignazio Silone
XL	MARXISM AND THE EXISTENTIALISTS	Raymond Aron
XLI	PHYSICAL CONTROL OF THE MIND	José M. R. Delgado, M.D.
XLII	PHYSICS AND BEYOND	Werner Heisenberg
XLIII	ON CARING	Milton Mayeroff
XLIV	DESCHOOLING SOCIETY	Ivan Illich
XLV	REVOLUTION THROUGH PEACE	Dom Hélder Câmara
XLVI	MAN UNFOLDING	Jonas Salk
XLVII	TOOLS FOR CONVIVIALITY	Ivan Illich
XLVIII	ACROSS THE FRONTIERS	Werner Heisenberg
XLVIX	EVIL AND WORLD ORDER	William Irwin Thompson
L	TO HAVE OR TO BE?	Erich Fromm
LI	ENERGY AND EQUITY	Ivan Illich
LII	LETTERS FROM THE FIELD	Margaret Mead
LIII	IN THE CENTER OF IMMENSITIES	Bernard Lovell
LIV	HOPE AND HISTORY	Morton Smith

WORLD PERSPECTIVES *Volume Fifty-four*

Founded, Planned and Edited by
RUTH NANDA ANSHEN

HOPE AND HISTORY, AN EXPLORATION

MORTON SMITH

HARPER & ROW, PUBLISHERS

NEW YORK

Cambridge   London
Hagerstown   Mexico City
Philadelphia   São Paulo
San Francisco *1817* Sydney

909
S 655h

FIRST EDITION

Designer: Sidney Feinberg

Library of Congress Cataloging in Publication Data

Smith, Morton, 1915–
    Hope and history, an exploration.
    (World perspectives ; v. 54)
    Includes index.
    1. Social history. 2. Civilization, Modern.
I. Title.
HN16.S55   909   77–3774
ISBN 0–06–013991–9

---

80 81 82 83 84 10 9 8 7 6 5 4 3 2 1

FOR RUTH NANDA ANSHEN
"THE ONLIE BEGETTER OF THESE INSUING"

Contents

WORLD PERSPECTIVES—*What This Series Means*
—Ruth Nanda Anshen   xi

I. THE CURRENT CRISIS AS A QUESTION OF HOPE   1

II. HOPE AS A FACTOR IN HISTORY   32

III. HISTORY AS A FACTOR IN HOPE   75

IV. THE HOPE FOR HOPE   162

Index   223

ABOUT THE AUTHOR   231

ABOUT THE FOUNDER OF THIS SERIES   232

World Perspectives

What This Series Means

It is the thesis of *World Perspectives* that man is in the process of developing a new consciousness which, in spite of his apparent spiritual and moral captivity, can eventually lift the human race above and beyond the fear, ignorance, and isolation which beset it today. It is to this nascent consciousness, to this concept of man born out of a universe perceived through a fresh vision of reality, that *World Perspectives* is dedicated.

My Introduction to this Series is not of course to be construed as a prefatory essay for each individual book. These few pages simply attempt to set forth the general aim and purpose of the Series as a whole. They try to point to the principle of permanence within change and to define the essential nature of man, as presented by those scholars who have been invited to participate in this intellectual and spiritual movement.

Man has entered a new era of evolutionary history, one in which rapid change is a dominant consequence. He is contending with a fundamental change, since he has intervened in the evolutionary process. He must now better appreciate this fact and then develop the wisdom to direct the process toward his fulfillment rather than toward his destruction. As he learns to apply his understanding of the physical world for practical purposes, he is, in reality, extending his innate capacity and augmenting his ability and his need to communicate as well as his ability to think and to create. And as a result, he is substituting a goal-directed evolutionary process in his struggle against environmental hardship for the slow, but effective, biological evolution which produced modern man through mutation and natural selection. By intelligent intervention in the evolutionary process man has greatly accelerated and greatly expanded the range of his possibilities. But he has not changed the basic fact that it remains a trial and error process, with the danger of taking paths that lead to sterility of mind and heart, moral apathy and intellectual inertia; and even producing social dinosaurs unfit to live in an evolving world.

Only those spiritual and intellectual leaders of our epoch who have a paternity in this extension of man's horizons are invited to participate in the Series: those who are aware of the truth that beyond the divisiveness among men there exists a primordial unitive power since we are all bound together by a common humanity more fundamental than any unity of dogma; those who recognize that the centrifugal force which has scattered and atomized mankind must be replaced by an integrating structure and process capable of bestowing meaning and purpose on existence; those who realize that science itself, when not inhibited by the limitations of its own methodology, when chastened and humbled, commits man to an indeterminate range of yet undreamed consequences that may flow from it.

Virtually all of our disciplines have relied on conceptions which are now incompatible with the Cartesian axiom, and with the static world view we once derived from it. For underlying the new ideas, including those of modern physics, is a unifying order, but it is not causality; it is purpose, and not the purpose of the universe and of man, but the purpose *in* the universe and *in* man. In other words, we seem to inhabit a world of dynamic process and structure. Therefore we need a calculus of potentiality rather than one of probability, a dialectic of polarity, one in which unity and diversity are redefined as simultaneous and necessary poles of the same essence: nature's ingenious balance.

Our situation is new. No civilization has previously had to

face the challenge of scientific specialization, and our response must be new. Thus this Series is committed to ensure that the spiritual and moral needs of a man as a human being and the scientific and intellectual resources at his command for *life* may be brought into a productive, meaningful and creative harmony.

In a certain sense we may say that man now has regained his former geocentric position in the universe. For a picture of the Earth has been made available from distant space, from the lunar desert, and the sheer isolation of the Earth has become plain. This is as new and as powerful an idea in history as any that has ever been born in man's consciousness. We are all becoming seriously concerned with our natural environment. And this concern is not only the result of the warnings given by biologists, ecologists and conservationists. Rather it is the result of a deepening awareness that something new has happened, that the planet Earth is a unique and precious place. Indeed, it may not be a mere coincidence that this awareness should have been born at the exact moment when man took his first step into outer space.

This Series endeavors to point to a reality of which scientific theory has revealed only one aspect. It is the commitment to this reality that lends universal intent to a scientist's most original and solitary thought. By acknowledging this frankly we shall restore science to the great family of human aspirations by which men hope to fulfill themselves in the world community as thinking and sentient beings. For our problem is to discover a principle of differentiation and yet relationship lucid enough to justify and to purify scientific, philosophic and all other knowledge, both discursive and intuitive, by accepting their interdependence. This is the crisis in consciousness made articulate through the crisis in science. This is the new awakening.

Each volume presents the thought and belief of its author and points to the way in which religion, philosophy, art, science, economics, politics and history may constitute that form of human activity which takes the fullest and most precise account of variousness, possibility, complexity and difficulty. Thus *World Perspectives* endeavors to define that ecumenical power of the mind and heart which enables man through his mysterious greatness to re-create his life.

This Series is committed to a re-examination of all those sides of human endeavor which the specialist was taught to believe he could safely leave aside. It attempts to show the structural kinship between subject and object; the indwelling of the one in the other. It interprets present and past events impinging on human life in our growing World Age and world consciousness and envisages what man may yet attain when summoned by an unbending inner necessity to the quest of what is most exalted in him. Its purpose is to offer new vistas in terms of world and human development while refusing to betray the intimate correlation between universality and individuality, dynamics and form, freedom and destiny. Each author deals with the increasing realization that spirit and nature are not separate and apart; that intuition and reason must regain their convergence as the means of perceiving and fusing inner being with outer reality.

World Perspectives endeavors to show that the conception of wholeness, unity, organism is a higher and more concrete conception than that of matter and energy. Thus an enlarged meaning of life, of biology, not as it is revealed in the test tube of the laboratory but as it is experienced within the organism of life itself, is attempted in this Series. For the principle of life consists in the tension which connects spirit with the realm of matter, symbiotically joined. The element of life is dominant in the very texture of nature, thus rendering life, biology, a transempirical science. The laws of life have their origin beyond their mere physical manifestations and compel us to consider their spiritual source. In fact, the widening of the conceptual framework has not only served to restore order within the respective branches of knowledge, but has also disclosed analogies in man's position regarding the analysis and synthesis of experience in apparently separated domains of knowledge, suggesting the possibility of an ever more embracing objective description of the meaning of life.

Knowledge, it is shown in these books, no longer consists in a manipulation of man and nature as opposite forces, nor in the reduction of data to mere statistical order, but is a means of liberating mankind from the destructive power of fear, pointing the way toward the goal of the rehabilitation of the human will and the rebirth of faith and confidence in the human person. The works published also endeavor to reveal that the cry for patterns, systems and authorities is growing less insistent as the desire grows stronger in both East and West for the recovery of a dignity, integrity and self-realization which are the inalienable rights of man who may now guide change by means of conscious purpose in the light of reason.

The volumes in this Series endeavor to demonstrate that only in a society in which awareness of the problems of science exists, can its discoveries start great waves of change in human culture, and in such a manner that these discoveries may deepen and not erode the sense of universal human community. The differences in the disciplines, their epistemological exclusiveness, the variety of historical experiences, the differences of traditions, of cultures, of languages, of the arts, should be protected and preserved. But the interrelationship and unity of the whole should at the same time be accepted. For the time-honored dichotomy between science and value judgments must continue to be challenged and we must now require that science tell us not only what *is* but what *ought* to be; to *de*scribe but also to *pre*scribe.

The authors of *World Perspectives* are of course aware that the ultimate answers to the hopes and fears which pervade modern society rest on the moral fiber of man, and on the wisdom and responsibility of those who promote the course of its development. But moral decisions cannot dispense with an insight into the interplay of the objective elements which offer and limit the choices made. Therefore an understanding of what the issues are, though not a sufficient condition, is a

necessary prerequisite for directing action toward constructive solutions.

Other vital questions explored relate to problems of international understanding as well as to problems dealing with
prejudice and the resultant tensions and antagonisms. The
growing perception and responsibility of our World Age
point to the new reality that the individual person and the
collective person supplement and integrate each other; that
the thrall of totalitarianism of both left and right has been
shaken in the universal desire to recapture the authority of
truth and human totality. Mankind can finally place its trust
not in a proletarian authoritarianism, not in a secularized
humanism, both of which have betrayed the spiritual property
right of history, but in a sacramental brotherhood and in the
unity of knowledge. This new consciousness has created a
widening of human horizons beyond every parochialism, and
a revolution in human thought comparable to the basic assumption, among the ancient Greeks, of the sovereignty of
reason; corresponding to the great effulgence of the moral
conscience articulated by the Hebrew prophets; analogous to
the fundamental assertions of Christianity; or to the beginning of the new scientific era, the era of the science of dynamics, the experimental foundations of which were laid by
Galileo in the Renaissance.

An important effort of this series is to re-examine the contradictory meanings and applications which are given today to
such terms as democracy, freedom, justice, love, peace, brotherhood and God. The purpose of such inquiries is to clear the
way for the foundation of a genuine *world* history not in terms
of nation or race or culture but in terms of man in relation to
God, to himself, his fellow man and the universe, that reach
beyond immediate self-interest. For the meaning of the
World Age consists in respecting man's hopes and dreams
which lead to a deeper understanding of the basic values of
all peoples.

World Perspectives is planned to gain insight into the meaning
of man, who not only is determined by history but who also

determines history. History is to be understood as concerned not only with the life of man on this planet but as including also such cosmic influences as interpenetrate our human world. This generation is discovering that history does not conform to the social optimism of modern civilization and that the organization of human communities and the establishment of freedom and peace are not only intellectual achievements but spiritual and moral achievements as well, demanding a cherishing of the wholeness of human personality, the "unmediated wholeness of feeling and thought," and constituting a never-ending challenge to man, emerging from the abyss of meaninglessness and suffering, to be renewed and replenished in the totality of his life.

Justice itself, which has been "in a state of pilgrimage and crucifixion" and now is being slowly liberated from the grip of social and political demonologies in the East as well as in the West, begins to question its own premises. The modern revolutionary movements which have challenged the sacred institutions of society by protecting injustice in the name of social justice are here examined and reevaluated.

In the light of this, we have no choice but to admit that the *un*freedom against which freedom is measured must be retained with it, namely, that the aspect of truth out of which the night view appears to emerge, the darkness of our time, is as little abandonable as is man's subjective advance. Thus the two sources of man's consciousness are inseparable, not as dead but as living and complementary, an aspect of that "principle of complementarity" through which Niels Bohr has sought to unite the quantum and the wave, both of which constitute the very fabric of life's radiant energy.

There is in mankind today a counterforce to the sterility and danger of a quantitative, anonymous mass culture; a new, if sometimes imperceptible, spiritual sense of convergence toward human and world unity on the basis of the sacredness of each human person and respect for the plurality of cultures. There is a growing awareness that equality may not be evaluated in mere numerical terms but is proportionate and analogical in its reality. For when equality is equated with interchangeability, individuality is negated and the human person transmuted into a faceless mask.

We stand at the brink of an age of a world in which human life presses forward to actualize new forms. The false separation of man and nature, of time and space, of freedom and security, is acknowledged, and we are faced with a new vision of man in his organic unity and of history offering a richness and diversity of equality and majesty of scope hitherto unprecedented. In relating the accumulated wisdom of man's spirit to the new reality of the World Age, in articulating its thought and belief, *World Perspectives* seeks to encourage a renaissance of hope in society and of pride in man's decision as to what his destiny will be.

Man has certainly contrived to change the environment, but subject to the new processes involved in this change, the same process of selection continues to operate. The environment has changed partly in a physical and geographical sense, but more particularly from the knowledge we now possess. The Biblical story of Adam and Eve contains a deep lesson, which a casual reading hardly reveals. Once the "fruit of the Tree of Knowledge" has been eaten, the world is changed. The new world is dictated by the knowledge itself, not of course by an edict of God. The Biblical story has further interest in that the new world is said to be much worse than the former idyllic state of ignorance. Today we are beginning to wonder whether this might not also be true. Yet we are uneasy, apprehensive, and our fears lead to the collapse of civilizations. Thus we turn to the truth that knowledge and life are indivisible, even as life and death are inseparable. We *are* what we know and think and feel; we are linked with history, with the world, with the universe, and faith in *Life* creates its own verification.

World Perspectives is committed to the recognition that all great changes are preceded by a vigorous intellectual reevaluation and reorganization. Our authors are aware that the sin of *hubris* may be avoided by showing that the creative process itself is not a free activity if by free we mean arbitrary, or unrelated to cosmic law. For the creative process in the human mind, the developmental process in organic nature and the basic laws of the inorganic realm may be but varied expressions of a universal formative process. Thus *World Perspectives* hopes to show that although the present apocalyptic period is one of exceptional tensions, there is also at work an exceptional movement toward a compensating unity which refuses to violate the ultimate moral power at work in the universe, that very power upon which all human effort must at last depend. In this way we may come to understand that there exists an inherent independence of spiritual and mental growth which, though conditioned by circumstances, is never determined by circumstances. In this way the great plethora of human knowledge may be correlated with an insight into the nature of human nature by being attuned to the wide and deep range of human thought and human experience.

Incoherence is the result of the present distintegrative processes in education. Thus the need for *World Perspectives* expresses itself in the recognition that natural and man-made ecological systems require as much study as isolated particles and elementary reactions. For there is a basic correlation of elements in nature as in man which cannot be separated, which compose each other and alter each other mutually. Thus we hope to widen appropriately our conceptual framework of reference. For our epistemological problem consists in our finding the proper balance between our lack of an all-embracing principle relevant to our way of evaluating life and in our power to express ourselves in a logically consistent manner.

Our Judeo-Christian and Greco-Roman heritage, our Hellenic tradition, has compelled us to think in exclusive categories. But our *experience* challenges us to recognize a totality richer and far more complex than the average observer could have suspected—a totality which compels him to think in ways which the logic of dichotomies denies. We are summoned to revise fundamentally our ordinary ways of conceiving experience, and thus, by expanding our vision and by accepting those forms of thought which also include nonexclusive categories, the mind is then able to grasp what it was incapable of grasping or accepting before.

Nature operates out of necessity; there is no alternative in nature, no will, no freedom, no choice as there is for man. Man must have convictions and values to live for, and this also is recognized and accepted by those scientists who are at the same time philosophers. For they then realize that duty and devotion to our task, be it a task of acting or of understanding, will become weaker and rarer unless guidance is sought in a metaphysics that transcends our historical and scientific views or in a religion that transcends and yet pervades the work we are carrying on in the light of day.

For the nature of knowledge, whether scientific or ontological, consists in reconciling *meaning* and *being*. And *being* signifies nothing other than the actualization of potentiality, self-realization which keeps in tune with the transformation. This leads to experience in terms of the individual; and to organization and patterning in terms of the universe. Thus organism and world actualize themselves simultaneously.

And so we may conclude that organism is *being* enduring in time, in fact in eternal time, since it does not have its beginning with procreation, nor with birth, nor does it end with death. Energy and matter in whatever form they may manifest themselves are transtemporal and transspatial and are therefore metaphysical. Man as man is summoned to know what is right and what is wrong, for emptied of such knowledge he is unable to decide what is better or what is worse.

World Perspectives hopes to show that human society is different from animal societies, which, having reached a certain stage, are no longer progressive but are dominated by routine and repetition. Thus man has discovered his own nature, and with this self-knowledge he has left the state of nonage and entered manhood. For he is the only creature who is able to say not only "no" to life but "yes" and to make for himself a life that is human. In this decision lie his burden and his greatness. For the power of life or death lies not only in the

tongue but in man's recently acquired ability to destroy or to
create life itself, and therefore he is faced with unlimited and
unprecedented choices for good and for evil that dominate
our time. Our common concern is the very destiny of the
human race. For man has now intervened in the process of
evolution, a power not given to the pre-Socratics, nor to Aristotle, nor to the Prophets in the East or the West, nor to
Copernicus, nor to Luther, Descartes, or Machiavelli. Judgments of value must henceforth direct technological change,
for without such values man is divested of his humanity and
of his need to collaborate with the very fabric of the universe
in order to bestow meaning, purpose, and dignity upon his
existence. No time must be lost since the wavelength of
change is now shorter than the life-span of man.

In spite of the infinite obligation of men and in spite of their
finite power, in spite of the intransigence of nationalisms, and
in spite of the homelessness of moral passions rendered in-
effectual by the technological outlook, beneath the apparent
turmoil and upheaval of the present, and out of the transfor-
mations of this dynamic period with the unfolding of a cosmic-
consciousness, the purpose of *World Perspectives* is to help
quicken the "unshaken heart of well-rounded truth" and interpret the significant elements of the World Age now taking
shape out of the core of that undimmed continuity of the
creative process which restores man to mankind while deepening and enhancing his communion and his symbiotic relationship with the universe. For we stand on the threshold of
a new consciousness and begin to recognize that thought is
as powerful an evolutionary force as teeth, claws, and even
language. Thus, "There is no parting from your own shadow.
To experience this faith is to know that in being ourselves we
are more than ourselves: to know that our experience, dim
and fragmentary as it is, yet sounds the utmost depths of
reality. . . ."*

RUTH NANDA ANSHEN

*A. N. Whitehead, *Science and the Modern World*, London, 1926.

Other works by Professor Smith

The Ancient Greeks. Ithaca: Cornell University Press, 1960.
(With Moses Hadas) *Heroes and Gods*. New York: Harper &
Row, 1965. (*Religious Perspectives* XIII).
Palestinian Parties and Politics that Shaped the Old Testament. New
York: Columbia University Press, 1971.
Clement of Alexandria and a Secret Gospel of Mark. Cambridge,
Mass.: Harvard University Press, 1973.
The Secret Gospel. New York: Harper & Row, 1973.
(With Elias Bickerman) *The Ancient History of Civilization*. New
York: Harper & Row, 1976.
Jesus the Magician. San Francisco: Harper & Row, 1978.

HOPE AND HISTORY, AN EXPLORATION

I

The Current Crisis as a Question of Hope

I

If history is still being written a thousand years from now, and if historians then are fairly well informed about what we call the second millennium A.D., they may pick out, as a turning point in the course of western civilization, the close-up photographs made in 1971 of the surface of Mars. Perhaps those photographs contained little to surprise astronomers, but to the public they brought a new message: "Dead End."

It was the end not only of the fantasies of a generation brought up on Buck Rogers,[1] but also of the tacit assumption behind western civilization, at least since the beginnings of Phoenician and Greek colonization, that there was always more land. All men had to do was go out and occupy it. From the Aegean and Phoenician littorals to the western Mediterranean, from the Mediterranean coasts to the rest of Europe, from Europe to South Africa, Asia, the Americas, Australia and the South Seas, the extension of western civilization by settlers, soldiers, businessmen, and missionaries had both assumed and confirmed this belief and the hopes based on it. There had always been a frontier, and the unexplored, unconquered lands beyond the frontier had been a region of un-

---

[1] Admittedly visitors from outer space are alive and well, and living not only in the comic strips, but also in publications that sell widely to "adults" with the minds of comic strip readers. They, however, belong to a different field of discourse.

known possibilities, an assurance that there was something to hope for. But now, suddenly, there seemed to be no place to go. The rest of the planetary system was uninhabitable, the nearest star was more than 260 billion miles away—more than four years' journey at the unattainable speed of light. And would it have habitable satellites? Probably not. From now on, it seemed, man would have to stay home. The earth could be more fully used: the oceans might be settled, some subterranean settlement would be possible, if tolerable; but beyond the earth there seemed to be nothing available. Here we were stuck. Books like *Spaceship Earth*[2] were prompt to point out the economic implications. If the first appearances proved true, not only human life, but the resources available to maintain it, were practically limited to the earth and the radiation reaching it. The notion of life as perpetual growth, an endlessly expanding process, was made untenable, and we were faced, instead, with a new question: Given the limitation of life to this planet of which the lifetime is limited, what can we hope for?

"This fundamental fact" (the historian in the year 3000 may observe) "was bound, sooner or later, to change the course and nature of the 'western' civilization then predominant. The change came more quickly because the fact was brought to public attention at a juncture when many other causes converged to produce a crisis. Although the general functioning of society went on more or less as usual (in spite of some severe local disturbances), the expectations, estimates, plans, and, more profoundly, the hopes of the ruling classes of the western world were called into question." I should like to know what "other" causes he will list, and how he will arrange them.

In my own list, no doubt distorted by close-up vision from a single standpoint within the field, first place would be given to the growing awareness of ecological problems, an awareness made acute by the oil embargo and its consequences.

---

[2] B. Ward, *Spaceship Earth* (New York, 1976).

Ecological problems confronted us with the necessity of making fundamental decisions, so I should give second place to the extreme difficulty we find in making them, a difficulty traceable superficially to democratic process, but more profoundly and paradoxically to our power to act. Knowing how enormous are the changes we can produce, we fear to face the consequences. This fear again results from our uncertainty as to what we hope for, and I should list, as further causes of this uncertainty, our lack of accepted social standards (both of ideals/patterns for society as a whole, and of standards for personal behavior), and, closely related to this, the widespread rejection of the traditional pattern and value system of western society, which is either discredited by anthropological relativism or, by some minority groups, almost wholly repudiated. Lack of a generally accepted social ideal has made all sorts of private escapism common, so escapism, too, belongs in this list of causes which contribute to the presently prevalent mood of uncertainty and uneasy hesitation, the condition we may fairly call a crisis of hope. Since this list has necessarily been diagrammatic and abstract let me now, in this chapter, try to flesh it out by brief descriptions of each of the causes listed.

II

The ecological and economic problem posed by the constant growth of population and industrialization of society had been long developing and occasionally recognized, but my impression is that it was first brought to general attention by the data published by the Club of Rome, the findings of the Senate Select Committee on Nutrition demonstrating the extent to which world population is outrunning food supply, and the many related documents, all suggesting in one way or another that the human population of the earth may soon be more than the planet can support even for a short time, and perhaps is already over the possible limit for long habitation. (Our imaginary historian in A.D. 3000 will probably refer to the past century as The Age of Waste, when much of the world's limited supply of tin was irretrievably squandered in cans, untold tons of silver went for needless photographs, and areas comparable to continents were deforested to make newspapers. Not to mention the waste in wars.) Admittedly much of the ecological outcry was the work of rich men determined to protect their properties and even their playgrounds, sometimes with cynical disregard of the needs of the city populations—consider, for instance, their attempts to prevent rational development of water and atomic power in order to increase the value of their coal and oil stocks (and the pollution coal and oil will produce). When an isolated black representative at an ecological congress told his colleagues that he was less interested in preserving the bald eagle than in exterminating the common rat, he was thought terribly insensitive. But in spite of the dubious motives of some supporters, the problem was forced on public attention as a general one, not to be met by mere correction of one or another particular abuse. We have already destroyed and are now destroying much that we need to live on; our resources, and those of the entire world, are limited; we should therefore choose carefully what we will hope for and try to achieve. *Non omnia possumus omnes;* we can't do everything.

The resultant crisis is worldwide, but as an American I see it mainly from the American point of view. This may not be wholly a disadvantage. Because of the fundamental role of the United States in the economy and defense of the free world, problems throughout that world have repercussions here, and decisions taken here, or our inability to decide (often more important), may shape the course of events all over the earth. As Rome was for a while the nerve center of the Mediterranean world, as London was of the British and Moscow is of the Russian empire, so Washington and New York have become the centers of the free world's split personality, and the quiet crisis of western civilization through which we are living is particularly an American crisis. The new realization of the limits of human hopes and capacities was felt as a limitation of what *we* could hope for and could do.

This realization was made acute by the oil embargo that followed on the heels of the ecologists' political triumph and effectively set aside many of the ecological reform laws by making their implementation prohibitively expensive. Cities found they could not pay for the power they needed unless power companies were permitted to burn fuels containing sulfur. The proposal to purify automobile exhaust fumes—at considerable cost in efficiency, hence with greater consumption of fuel—ran head on into the increased price of gasoline. Any number of similar examples could be found. The withdrawal of billions from the national economy to pay for fuel imports, the consequent combination of inflation and recession, subjected every budget to critical scrutiny and necessitated at every level, from the smallest household to the national government, a series of difficult choices that brought home to everyone some consequences of our limited powers and gave tangible meaning to the questions of our hopes and our consequent policies.

III

These questions are yet more difficult because, thanks to democracy, our methods of determining our national hopes are cumbersome and open to all sorts of interferences. First, innumerable accidents, personal and political, determine the outcome of elections; then the elected representatives are influenced by private concerns, economic inducements, and pressure groups of various sorts; finally the bodies in which these representatives meet are managed by parliamentary maneuvers that sometimes make it possible for a few members to thwart the great majority. Consequently, even when the decisions arrived at by democratic process happen to resemble remotely the hopes of most of the electorate, the resemblance cannot be taken as proof of paternity. The goddess of liberty has too many lovers—after all, she is a French *grande dame.*

Yet even if we could, as a nation, readily express our hopes in official actions, we should probably do well to hesitate, for fear of the results. We are too powerful. Technological advance has given us the ability to carry through not merely physical operations, but economic and social changes that previous generations merely dreamt of. Therefore we have to consider carefully what consequences would follow from the realization of such dreams. Plato could freely indulge in planning states necessarily imaginary; Roman emperors could legislate with the assurance that little of their legislation would be carried out unless their subjects found it to their own interest. Modern states can supervise their citizens and compel obedience to an extent never before anticipated in countries of comparable size. They can also act at distances and with speed and power hitherto unexampled. Consequently they have unexampled difficulty in deciding what to do. Social, political, and economic theorists now live in danger of seeing their dreams come true—and finding them nightmares.

A conspicuous example of this, and one of recognized importance as a cause of the current crisis, was our difficulty and delay in deciding what we wanted to do about Vietnam. There was never the slightest question of our physical ability to conquer the country—if we were willing to destroy Hanoi, wipe out the dikes of the northern rivers, send an army into the north, risk war with Russia and/or China, and impose on ourselves the discipline and sacrifices necessary to support these measures. But there was never the slightest question, either, of our unwillingness to resort to these measures, let alone accept the necessary discipline and sacrifices. Hence the long, increasingly acrimonious debate, settled, at length, largely because our government decided that the domestic dissent generated by the war was becoming more dangerous and expensive than would be the immediate consequences of losing it. This decision clearly was reached in part because many of our youth were unwilling to support military efforts overseas. A nation that will not fight for its interests cannot long defend them. As soon as our condition became apparent, the oil producers found an excuse to quadruple their prices. Pacifism abroad produced at home the economic crisis already referred to: inflation, unemployment, and the endless series of hard choices by which we must redefine our hopes and reconcile ourselves, so far as we can, to a new and poorer way of life. Presently the government of Panama took similar advantage of the same weakness. Other governments will soon do so. The end is not yet.

IV

The hard choices are made particularly difficult by another aspect of our present crisis: our lack of generally accepted standards by which to choose. This, too, is largely a consequence of technological development. Until the beginning of the present century, the lower classes generally adhered to their ancestral religions. Sins were plentiful, but they were recognized as sins; the traditional standards of each group were accepted by its members. Disbelief and books were middle and upper class luxuries. Then came compulsory public education, comic books, radio, and television. We now have a predominantly agnostic population in which the religious denominations are minority groups, while in the religious denominations believers are again minorities. And even the believers of a single denomination are commonly in dispute with each other as to what they should believe—particularly on questions of moral theology. As a result of this fragmentation the Old and New Testaments have been made ragbags of texts from which one preacher pulls out one slogan, another another, to suit his general tastes and immediate needs. These slogans commonly serve programs determined by practical or personal considerations, and are cited as authorities even in questions to which they are least applicable, questions of social and international policy. Biblical laws, like those of most primitive peoples, were made for small groups living in small communities with strong group discipline; they were to regulate the members' behavior towards each other, *not* towards outsiders. "Thou shalt love thy neighbor as thyself," meant "Thou shalt love thy fellow Israelite as thyself." As rules for the preservation of such groups these laws were successful. As rules for large societies in which group discipline is no longer effective, they tend to produce parasite populations, living on the piety of their neighbors. As rules for international finance and diplomacy they are likely to lead to economic disaster and political enslavement.

By contrast to the Biblical tradition, the philosophic has simply been dropped. No recognized system of philosophy enjoys general acceptance as a guide in moral questions. Hegel admittedly had much influence on Marxism, as did the *philosophes* of the eighteenth century on the development of democracy, but none of their descendants cite them as authorities. Voltaire would be disgusted by America, Hegel horrified by the USSR. As for classical philosophy, can you conceive of an American president citing Aristotle as an authority? The last politician to approach such a temerity was Goldwater, one of whose speechwriters adapted from Aristotle the sensible observation that in the practice of virtue it was right to be an extremist. That was all the enemy needed; "extremist" became a dirty household word, and this imprudent lapse into Aristotelianism helped lose the election. Few modern philosophers have had so much influence on the course of history. The most prestigious of the past generation, Heidegger, supported the Nazis while they were in power and never denounced them after their fall—to all appearances, without effect. For the difficult question of determining our hopes we are left with the guidance of those vague entities "common sense" and "the standards of our society."

Unfortunately, another conspicuous aspect of the present crisis has been the decay of social standards, not only in our society, but in all others. I wonder if any bicentennial speaker had the courage to begin, "Men, Americans, countrymen, lend me your ears. I come to bury the American tradition, not to praise it." If one were to judge from many American cities, the United States would seem not a nation but a public convenience; few of those who use it have any love for it, or any connection with each other beyond their common needs. Even the defenders of democracy are forced, like Churchill, to recognize it as "the worst of systems—except for all others." This defense might suffice for its domestic consequences, but abroad its missionary zeal has been recognizably disastrous. American medical missions must bear a great part of the blame for the population explosion; American diplomatic and military efforts to defend democracy have involved us in needless wars. Our double failure in Vietnam was particularly disillusioning because the generally advocated remedy proved worse than the disease: Intervention led us into a bottomless swamp of military expenditures; by withdrawing we left most of our allies to Communist regimes that used prison camps, torture, and mass murders with a freedom unusual even by Communist standards, and went on to fight each other in wars even bloodier than those they waged against us. Reversing the story of the ugly duckling, the dove of peace has grown up to be a vulture.

These foreign failures have been felt more sharply because of the pervading sense of failure at home, exacerbated by the aftermath of the Watergate witch-hunt. That supercolossal television show has given us a new regime in which presidential patronage of shady figures, the use of executive authority to block investigation of criminal congressmen, and the determination of Congress neither to reform itself nor to face the basic facts of financial life, are all more obvious than they were before. Corruption, admittedly, was long familiar. Anyone who took seriously the screams of moral anguish uttered by Nixon's opponents should have thought those gentlemen so naive as to be unfit for public office. More serious for the disillusionment of many upper class Americans was the revelation, not of the amorality of our highest government officials, but of their inefficiency. But what do we expect of politicians? Perhaps it was Ogden Nash who brought Walter Scott up to date:

> Breathes there the man, with soul so dead,
> Who never to himself hath said,
> "Why in the Hell
> Can't this government
> do anything economically and do it well?"

A short while ago we were assured by President Ford that, "If the U.S. government made beer it would cost fifty dollars a six-pack." I don't believe him. That must have been only the budgeted price. It would cost a hundred.

Not only the moral atmosphere produced by this pervasive corruption and inefficiency, but also the physical environment it has produced, the generally down-at-the-heel, littered, vandalized, broken world in which most inhabitants of most American cities live most of their lives, has made the American tradition material for comedy.

> O beautiful for patriot dream
> That sees beyond the years
> Thine alabaster cities gleam
> Undimmed by human tears!

What satire could match that? The only thing equally funny and pathetic, from the same field of discourse, are Marx's pages about the gradual withering away of government that will necessarily occur in the communist state. Perhaps they are even funnier. True, they lack the concentration of poetry. But they make up for that by displaying the great Victorian German pundit making a fool of himself with all possible pretension to scholarly authority.

When general political traditions have fared so badly it seems hardly worthwhile to specify the particular figures whose disgrace has enlivened the recent decades of disillusionment. In religious affairs the stupendous success of the Second Vatican Council left the Roman Catholic Church in such chaos that even the death of a cardinal in a prostitute's residence, and the necessity of the Pope's appearing on radio to assure the faithful that he was not a homosexual, could have little apparent effect. In business affairs the frequency of individual scandals, the vast amounts often involved, the terrible consequences for many of the victims (for instance, the thousands of old people trapped in nursing homes with the amenities of concentration camps), and above all the regularity with which exposure is commonly followed by continuance —all these testify to the general disintegration of the standards of public behavior, and the consequent growth of apathy and cynicism.

In the face of all this, the attempt to decide what one can and does hope becomes doubly difficult. And when this difficulty paralyzes the class that rules the nation that rules half the world, the situation is serious. Solzhenitsyn put his finger on the point in his Harvard address when, after remarking on the role of American pacifists (among whom many Harvard officials and faculty had been conspicuous) in "the betrayal of Far Eastern nations, in a genocide, and in the suffering today imposed on thirty million people there," and remarking also the indifference of these distinguished liberals to their victims' consequent calamities, he concluded, "To defend oneself, one must also be ready to die; there is little such readiness in a society raised in the cult of material well-being. Nothing is left, then, but concessions, attempts to gain time, and betrayal."[3]

In the present crisis the difficulty of self-devotion has been further compounded by the deserved demise of the "counter culture." The freaks and frauds of '68–'71, their wanton attacks on the universities, and, above all, the pretentious nonsense they propounded, were most disturbing as demonstrations of the failure of university education, and even of the tradition being taught, to win the support of potentially competent students, or even to train them to think clearly, analyze practical problems objectively, and express themselves with good manners and good sense. That the non-students produced by this failure themselves failed in their attacks on the

---

[3] *Harvard Gazette*, June 8, 1978, pp. 18 f.

universities was largely due to their own absurdities, excesses, and inability to produce a program that could hold the hope of their followers. Soon they failed even to maintain their own beliefs. The recent studies of the fate of the "beat generation," recording their gurus, psychiatrists, hospitals, crimes, and suicides, are the pathetic epitaphs of a pitiful hope—a hope foredoomed to failure because of its determined disregard of facts, but itself a fact, and evidence of a failure other than its own. The pointed question, "What is possible?" burst the bubble of the counter culture, but not before it had momentarily reflected a glittering reverse image of the world, swimming with purple and rose, yellow and green and peacock blue. "Whither is fled the visionary gleam? Where is it now, the glory and the dream?" The gray quiet that has descended is itself disquieting—it has too much of disillusionment and despair. "The only trend that seems common to all —or very nearly all—British writers, intellectuals, and artists as the year 1977 draws to its close," wrote Auberon Waugh, "is a tendency to get drunk."[4]

Admittedly, there has been plenty of cause for disillusionment. While the Children's Crusade was producing such contemptible figures as Charles Manson, "Squeaky" Fromme, and the lawyers who scrambled for the publicity to be had by defending them, the great official representatives of alternate political philosophies and ways of life—England, Sweden, China, India, and Russia—were at the same time deeply discredited. In England a labor party devoted to the protection of indolence and an intelligentsia so foolish that it gave away the lands it lived on have dissolved within fifty years the largest and most diverse empire—the most widely extended structure of actual political unity and cooperation—that the world has ever seen. The socialist oligarchy of Sweden was at least creative; it produced an iron-gray welfare state that for some time had the highest moral pretensions and suicide rate

[4] A. Waugh, "The Literary Scene—1977: England," *New York Times Book Review*, December 4, 1977, p. 86.

in the world—interesting evidence of the lethal effect of destroying hope, and hence initiative, by overtaxation.[5] In
China the "democratic" dictatorship became almost a personal theocracy, supported by the hells of the torture chambers and work camps, and the periodic judgments of the
purges. The ludicrous charges and countercharges that followed the deity's demise were all that was needed for the last
act of this tragicomedy—except the greatest desideratum,
that the show should end. Finally Russia, in spite of its repudi-
ation of Stalin and Stalinism, has perpetuated an oligarchic
tyranny less terrible than Stalin's only to the members of the
oligarchy. The exposures of the KGB by Barron and the
Gulag Archipelago by Solzhenitsyn left little pretense possible for determined supporters of Russian communism.[6] They
have to face the terrible irony of history that has consistently
made communist revolutions the means of imposing on unfortunate peoples new aristocracies (i.e., the members of the
communist parties) more numerous, expensive, and oppres-
sive than were the old ones, better organized and defended,
and consequently more secure against revolution. In the face
of these facts, those who continue to advocate communism
are often reduced to open cynicism. One of them, outside
Columbia University, selling tours of the USSR, was approached by a student:

"Can you give me a guided tour of the Gulag archipelago?"

"I wish I could." No doubt a moment of truth. But not
much to hope for.

V

At the opposite extreme from such political developments, but perhaps even more important in the crisis of
hope, are recent changes in standards of personal morality
and of behavior. These standards have been steadily eroded

[5] L. Silk, "The Swedish Disease," *New York Times*, October 10, 1977, p. D1.

[6] J. Barron, *KGB* (New York, 1974); A. Solzhenitsyn, *The Gulag Archipelago*, (New York, 1974–76, 3 vols).

since World War II. Much of the erosion has been due to changes in the political and economic environment. Politically, the unpredictability of the actions of the great powers and the enormous consequences of these actions have made it harder to plan ahead. Within single states the rapidity of technological change and consequent shifts in employment and economic conditions, factors beyond the average man's control and sometimes beyond his knowledge, have displaced great numbers of workers and made planning and long-term hopes difficult for many more. The rising rate of production, stimulated by increase of population, lowering of tariff barriers, and growth of international trade, has created enormous demands for labor and pulled whole tides of men, by the hundreds of thousands, from one country into another—Turks and Greeks, Yugoslavs and Italians into Germany; Portuguese, Algerians, and Moroccans into France; natives of the Caribbean into London and New York, Mexicans into the southern United States, southern negroes into the north, and so on. These floods of culturally displaced persons have augmented those of the refugees created by World War II and by subsequent political events —the million immigrants to Israel and the million refugees from it, the refugees from Cyprus and from Vietnam, and so on. Besides these permanently displaced persons there has been an annual efflux and reflux of millions of tourists, temporarily displaced persons, living momentarily for the moment, the structural framework of their lives temporarily reduced to a series of hotel and flight reservations. *Carpe diem* —live for today—has become the implicit teaching of a substantial section of the social system. Moreover, all these aliens have been released from the restraints of their native societies and have found themselves in new ones where their old standards were not valid and their behavior, even when well meant, often helped to break down the existing standards.

Particularly important for the change in social stability has been the change in the position of women, since women had long been the most important stabilizing element in western society. It was the woman who "made" the home, stayed in it, took care of it, took care of the children, and so perpetuated the family from which the man went out every day to "make" the living, and to which he was expected to return every night, bringing the wherewithal to keep the home going. This was his primary legal responsibility, for this the woman had a legal claim on his person and the proceeds of his labor. The claim was justified not only by the children's need of support, but also by the fact that the home was the principal school of the children and the woman their principal teacher. Her maintenance of the home and the standards she maintained in it were expected to give them not only the criteria of right and wrong and the notions of propriety that would make them acceptable citizens, but also the love of stability and continuity, the need and hope to have a home, that would persuade them to "settle down" and "make" homes of their own, beget and train children of their own, and so carry on the state.

"Making" a home was a full-time job, so long as most of the work had to be done by hand. With electrification and labor-saving devices, women began to enjoy technological unemployment and develop outside interests fostered first by women's magazines, then by radio and television programs designed to appeal to them and sell them various products. With this intensive education about gadgets needed for better homes and gardens, the "standard of living" (as measured by acquisition of gadgets) rose rapidly; so did the pressure on the husband's income and hence on the husband. So did the society's need for labor to produce more gadgets, and for money to pay more laborers. So did the general inflation that bloated the family's expenses. When both husband and income proved insufficient, women began to take advantage of the new market for labor and use their new leisure to get some of the new money for themselves. Homes of course disintegrated, divorce laws were liberalized, and great numbers of women joined the mass of semitransient labor and contributed to the growth of "the loneliness industry"[7]—bars, health clubs, church groups, dating services, small apartment complexes, and similar devices for accommodating single people and enabling them to enjoy transient companionship with other transients. Their children, growing up in streets and day care centers, were educated mainly by radio or television programs, comic books, and each other. Arriving at adolescence with little attachment to home, they soon swelled further the population of *déracinés*, "the uprooted."

The growth of this "lonely crowd" had conspicuous consequences for patterns of behavior, as well as for hope. Many —perhaps most—of its members did not hope to have homes. The men thought of a home as an obligation likely to have expensive legal consequences. Many of the women were divorcées, once burned and twice cautious; others feared the adventure and the possibility of failure; yet others had acquired (from educations designed primarily for boys) ambitions for careers of sorts that left little leisure for marriage. Those with such training who did marry often found their emotional commitment to their homes insufficient to support the sacrifices required, so their marriages broke up. Such experience of home life as their children did get was often unpleasant. But the maintenance of a home and the anticipation of children's careers are the chief natural devices for extending hope beyond day-to-day existence. Admittedly some single individuals form extended plans—for travel, retirement, etc.—while others become involved in some "cause" or plan of research or social structure (ecclesiastical or gangland hierarchy, corporation or political system) that gives continuity and concern to life; but these are the exceptions. Most float.

The size of this emotionally drifting, socially mobile, celibate population has now been enormously increased by "the pill," of which the dangers were at first unrecognized and are

[7] On this see S. Gordon, *Lonely in America* (New York, 1976); further D. Riesman, *et al., The Lonely Crowd* (New Haven, 1950).

at present neglected. (Many women would rather risk cancer than pregnancy; it's more fashionable.) Of course the social importance of the pill goes far beyond its impact on this group; in the long run it may have major political consequences and may even substantially alter the biological makeup of the human race. But its first effect was a matter of short-term hope: it offered "sex without fear," not only to unattached workers, but to all heterosexuals from high school children to middle-aged married couples for whom the advent of another child might mean a serious financial or physical strain.

The consequence was a great increase in sexual indulgence and with it a generally more tolerant attitude towards the expression of sexual interests. For this there were many other contributing causes—psychiatry had long since given it a medical basis, legal reform was moving towards greater protection of individual liberty, the discrediting of puritanic religious traditions (both Christian and Jewish) led to reaction, the influence of distinguished artistic and literary figures counted for something, that of the national magazines, the motion pictures, and television, for much more. The result was a deluge of books and pictures on sexuality, almost all of them treating it as an end in itself, not as a part of the family-building process. The sexual presuppositions of the uprooted were tacitly propagated to the whole population. Accordingly even more adolescents drifted easily, without any moral crisis, into the floating population; the breakup of families became easier—the alternative life was at hand, readily available, widely advertised, and often more attractive.

Often less satisfactory. It did make possible more satisfactions, but it satisfied fewer hopes and those few were less varied; they reflected a smaller range of psychological needs. In the pattern formerly customary sexual attraction led to marriage, family, and, consequently, a wide variety of gratifications (not least, of the need to feel important) among which sexual pleasure, like food, sleep, and shelter, had a necessary but subordinate role for which monotony was no great disad-

vantage. However, when made both an end in itself and readily available, sexual indulgence soon produces a class of dissatisfied sensualists (e.g. Baudelaire), many of whom go on,
in search of excitement, to assorted perversions. Thus ennui,
as well as the general relaxation of sexual controls, has contributed to the increase of homosexuality. Another factor has
been the symbolic value of the acts. Since most adults are
mediocre, they often try to find in sexual achievement an
agreeable career substitute. The sense of achievement is increased by that of defying society.

Unfortunately, homosexual play—usually a harmless collection of contortions—often proves inadequate as a vehicle
for repressed resentment. Once the symbolic satisfaction
wears thin, something worse has to be found, commonly sadism and masochism. And once the ego's censorial power is
undermined, deeper psychological drives come to the surface
and demand actual gratification. Hence the desperate progress of the stupid from entertainment by violence to acts of
violence and from acts of violence to atrocities, in futile efforts
to retain the excitement of novelty. A sadist in Texas some
years ago, after murdering several dozen boys, was reportedly
killed while trying to handcuff, presumably with intent to
murder, the boy who had been his decoy and assistant. Perhaps he felt he had come to the end of that road. No doubt
even murder, reduced to a routine, becomes a bore.

Fortunately, most of the millions with similar drives show
no such energy and ingenuity in their pursuit of boredom.
Why should they? Violence is readily available in television
and on the streetcorners. In the average magazine stand or
paperback bookstore about eighty percent of the wares are
murder stories, war stories, stories of crime and criminals,
gothic novels that turn on plots to murder, and so on. A
review of motion pictures and television programs would
probably yield about the same result. This is the standard,
often unrecognized, wish fulfillment even of the most respectable. I know a plush-lined Philadelphia suburb in which a
bishop and a banker, the pillars of local society, are avid

readers of murder stories and trade their new discoveries with each other. Has either committed a murder? Probably not. But they have had little temptation, much to lose, and steady, albeit imaginary, gratification of their anal-sadistic drives.

Such gratification—not to mention how-to-do-it demonstrations in motion pictures and on television—is more dangerous for the young who do not draw so sharply the line between imagination and reality and have less awareness of what crime could cost them. In the fifties there was a teenager in New York who loved to masquerade as Dracula. He headed a gang of "vampires," got himself a reputation as "the cape man," and finally murdered a couple of the boys of his neighborhood. There have probably been hundreds of thousands of such "crimes in character"—crimes committed, not just to be bad, but to be bad in accordance with some imagined pattern, some criminal character which the actor has chosen as his secret personality, and finally dares to live out. A study by the American Broadcasting Company is cited as indicating that twenty-two percent of the crimes committed by juveniles have been suggested by television programs (*New York Times,* April 25, 1978). Given the source of the study, the percentage may be thought a bit low. Yet television is far from the only source of suggestion. One thinks of such murderers in fancy dress as Hell's Angels, of Manson sending out his coven with the directions, "Do something witchy." Such crimes—like most accomplishments that demand a good deal of effort and preparation—are expressions of hope: the hope to be something, to achieve importance by identifying oneself as a member of a class, an example of a pattern. The pattern may have been derived from a single work, or formed by loose imitation and synthesis of the products of a whole school, but it must be there and it is, as St. Thomas would say, the formal cause.

How many such crimes are attempts to imitate such mental patterns, how many result simply from the desire "to be bad," how many have "normal, conscious" motives (theft, sexual aggression, personal hostility), there is no telling. But there is no denying the great increase in crime, especially in crimes of violence. Criminal bombings, for instance, increased by 12 percent in 1977. The increase in crimes by young offenders is particularly great. In 1975 the *New York Times* reported a 55 percent increase of crimes in city schools; an earlier report by the Subcommittee on Juvenile Delinquency of the Senate Judiciary Committee set the cost to the whole country of school vandalism at $500 million a year, and investigation of 757 school districts yielded more than 100 murders and over 70,-000 assaults on teachers annually. Of the 25,000 reported felonies per million of population expectable annually in a typical American city, about a third will result in arrests and about a third of those arrested will be juveniles. No doubt, being less experienced, they are more likely to be caught or framed, so it cannot be supposed that they are responsible for a third of the total, but the proportion is certainly high. Few of these crimes will be due to need for food, clothing, or shelter. The picture of "the poor, unfortunate, unemployed worker committing robbery to get the money for a little bread for his starving wife and children" is an anachronism dead as Dickens. "The poor, unfortunate, unemployed" mugger of today is unemployed because unemployable, unfortunate because hooked (on drugs), and poor because he used his welfare check to pay his pusher. As for wife and children—he never bothered to marry and doesn't really know whether or not he has any children.

VI

He is also commonly presented as an example of "the failure of the cultural tradition of western civilization to win the loyalty of the underprivileged masses of our people." In fairness it should be said that the cultural tradition of western civilization never had much chance. It was presented to him by the public schools, the motion pictures, radio, and television. But in school he was (legally) incorrigible ("Man, I never paid no heed to none o' that s---. If you don' do nothin' they can't do nothin' to you.") and although com-pulsorily promoted to the tenth grade (when, to everyone's relief, he dropped out) he can read only signs and simple sentences. As for the media—they permit selection of pro-grams and he consistently selects music and dance, crime and violence shows. From the traditional viewpoint of west-ern civilization he is a social failure, but from that of a cul-tural anthropologist he is "a representative figure of an im-portant North American subculture." As a mugger he is, indeed, an example of a relatively small group (numbered in the low millions), as a drug addict he belongs to a larger group (estimated at about twenty-eight millions), but as al-most illiterate he is typical of perhaps a sixth of our fellow citizens and legal equals. The National Assessment of Edu-cational Progress estimates the functional illiterates among seventeen-year-old high school students at 13 percent. At Ohio State University in 1978 tests given to freshmen re-vealed that 26 percent could not do high school arithmetic. The proposal to require that entering students in the *colleges* of the City University of New York show *eighth grade* levels of performance in reading, writing, and arithmetic was recently attacked on the ground (admittedly true) that it would re-duce the entering class by 30 percent. Defenders of open admission maintained that college education should be adapted to the native interests of the members of our na-tional subcultures and should not attempt to impose on them such alien cultural traits as literacy.

This argument extends to university education and to mi-nority problems the generally accepted principle of liberal schooling—that students should be encouraged to pursue whatever interests them and permitted to neglect whatever does not. This principle is pleasant to follow. It diminishes the problem of overcoming resistance and the need for per-suasive teaching. Accordingly it is no less attractive for lazy educators than dangerous for civilization. Most children are more interested by sensations than by ideas—the ability to be interested by ideas requires not only intelligence but considerable practice in argument and the building up of a *structure* of knowledge in relation to which the significance of the ideas can be appreciated. Consequently, encouraging children to follow their interests yields an oversupply of second-rate artists producing "gifte shoppe" bric-a-brac, hard rock music, hard-core pornography, and amateur theatricals—mostly amiable but mindless luxuries—and leaves us with one doctor for every thousand of the population and one physicist for every hundred thousand.

This general problem of education, however, must not now distract us from the difference between the traditional and the anthropological evaluations of our friend the mugger. Such differences in judgment illustrate another aspect of the current crisis of hope. We have already spoken of the discrediting of the traditions of Christianity, Judaism, and the major philosophical schools and political parties, and of the failure of actual systems in Russia, China, Britain, and the United States to produce satisfactory forms of government. But along with these particular failures, a tide of economic, sociological, and anthropological criticism has risen to attack, not only particular intellectual creeds, but the basic suppositions and value judgments of western civilization in general.

The attack has ancient roots in the denunciation of Israelite society by the prophets, the rejection of the standards of Greco-Roman society by the Cynics, the early Stoics, and many early Christians, and the rejection of medieval society by ascetic movements and heresies, and by the Jewish ghetto as an organized international counter culture. With Renaissance and Reformation came the spread of witchcraft and of enthusiastic and eschatological heresies, some essentially antisocial and almost all opposed to the existing social structure and standards. Such movements were often sporadic and consistently peripheral; although some had great influence in the long run, they rarely did much to change basically the characters of the societies they criticized. The French Revolution, for instance, was not in the main an outgrowth of the nonsense about noble savages that had been written during the eighteenth century; its major source was an effort by the bourgeoisie to secure reforms in the interest of their own (then economically prevalent) culture.

Marx, however, gave this anti-cultural attitude a basis in economic and political theory and a place, albeit ambiguous, in the program of the communist party. Thanks to his influence the ancient Greek insight, that the laws of a country commonly express the interests of the ruling class, was extended to discredit the ruling system of values. At the same time, Marx strangely took for granted that laws expressing the economic interests of the lower classes would be Good Things, deserving universal reverence and observance. Subsequent sociological and anthropological theory commonly accepted the insight, sometimes taking Marx's value judgment into the bargain, sometimes rejecting it in favor of complete relativism (each culture has its own set of values and should not be judged by that of any other), and sometimes adopting other standards of judgment.

In countries where communism has won control Marx's theory has had far-reaching consequences. They would have reached even farther had not bourgeois science been so important and bourgeois converts so valuable (as administrators) that neither the Russians nor the Chinese could get on without them. Hence we find that the Russians have preserved the imperial opera and the imperial ballet, continue to teach at least a selection of the literary masterpieces of the empire, have patronized many new works glorifying the Russian tradition, and have begun to take the Russian Orthodox Church back into favor. Marx himself foresaw these consequences; he said, "I have sowed dragon's teeth and harvested fleas."[8] The traditional culture of China was farther removed from western thought, both scientific and communist, so there the changes may be more sweeping. We shall see.

[8] He referred to the legend of Cadmus ((Apollodorus III.4; etc.) who sowed dragon's teeth from which arose a race of armed men, the ancestors of the aristocrats of Thebes. It is a pity that Marx had a classical education; so many of his comments are now unintelligible to his admirers.

Outside the communist world the attack on traditional western culture has been mainly by flanking movements. Instead of trying directly to get rid of the tradition as an expression of bourgeois values, the strategy has been to advocate cultural pluralism. Other cultures, too, have their peculiar values; those, too, must be protected. This line was particularly successful in protecting the buildup of native resistance to colonial governments in Asia and in Africa where Kenyatta, for instance, used his anthropological training (from the University of London) even to justify his followers' expression of their native religious tradition by forcibly and sometimes fatally circumcising British women. Similar arguments have been much used in attacking the cultural unity of the United States which many groups for many reasons would like to see disintegrate from a single American people into a congeries of mutually suspicious minorities. Besides the support for this policy by self-interested leaders of ethnic groups, and that provided sub rosa by hostile foreign powers, the academic support from departments of anthropology has been impressive and understandable: the more important ethnic groups become, the more anthropological studies of them will have to be financed. Sociologists and economists were of course quick to see the possible economic importance of ethnic studies for their own disciplines, so the concept of minority cultures has been extended to social and economic groups, which have now become "subcultures." If the members of these "subcultures" are generally deficient in matters of information, honesty, or good behavior, their deficiencies are no longer examples of "backwardness" or the like, but "group characteristics that contribute to our country's rich cultural diversity." Finally, the attack on the traditional standards of western civilization has produced a crop of cultural dropouts from the upper classes—beatniks and neoprimitives of various sorts—and a variety of centers and communities set up by different cliques with varying success.

Sometimes these have achieved publicity beyond their founders' expectations. Currently in the headlines are the

People's Temple, a Communist-Christian organization some thousand of whose members were persuaded to commit suicide and/or murder each other in the jungles of Guyana, and Synanon, notorious for alleged attempts at murder. A recent comparison of the two deserves quotation:[9]

> In both organizations, drug addicts were many of the first members; both organizations promised members a utopian community and employed communal living techniques, deemphasizing materialism and playing on . . . members' guilts; both used stern authoritarian leadership, hard labor, long meetings, and frequently frank and bitter criticism and ridicule of members to keep adherents loyal; both split families and stockpiled arms; both grew rapidly behind the enthusiastic support of political liberals; in both organizations rigid pursuit of nonviolence was replaced by increasing paranoia over outside criticism and defection; and both sought to intimidate the press. . . . They both had charismatic leaders—one called "the father," the other, "the founder"; both tried to operate in a sealed world away from everyone else—one in Guyana, the other in . . . northern California . . .; both believed the outside world was conspiring against them; both had specially trained security forces; both favored the use of corporal punishment . . .

Both, in short, were adult adaptations of the social structure of the adolescent gang, childhood's last and most intense effort to maintain its own subculture by exploiting the liberal generosity of the parental society while conspiring to circumvent it, and yet creating, as a substitute parent, its own father figure to provide the authority, and hence the security, that adult society now denies to adults. Many analogues, both modern (for instance, the Black Muslims) and from previous centuries (for instance, the Mormons in their early days in Nauvoo and Utah), will come to mind. It is clear that subcul-

---

[9] Robert Lindsey, "A Changed Synanon," *New York Times*, December 10, 1978, pp. 1 and 20. The excerpt given, from p. 20, is apparently based on, and partly quoted from, remarks by P. Morantz.

tures satisfy important needs of psychologically uprooted individuals and that the romantic admiration for them has
deeper sources than many of those who indulge it would care
to admit.

VII

Such utopian communities, however, have usually had little
success. Associations of the unattached proved understandably unstable. Few outside the founding group were willing
to entrust themselves to a group so founded. Hence there
have usually been many sympathizers, but few contributors
and fewer converts. (The great success of the Mormons has
been exceptional, and as they have succeeded they have lost
the characteristics of a subculture and have assimilated more
and more to the pattern of upper class American life.) Since
organized attempts to escape have thus proved unattractive,
most escapism is now private. However, even private attempts
to escape this dreadful culture are apt to confront the would-
be refugees with the more dreadful necessity of earning a
living. Accordingly it is better not to burn your bridges. Escape for a little while, then come back to your job, or at least
to the market for what may be sarcastically called "your
skills." The popularity of travel was easily understandable
before the devaluation of the dollar. No matter how democratic you may be, it's nice to go to a country where, by
comparison with the natives, you're rich. Now that our dollars
have begun to adjust to our policies, more of our dropouts
prefer to take their "trips" at home, by drugs. This may, in
the end, prove more expensive than travel; meanwhile it is
proving even more popular. The narcotics trade in the United
States reportedly grossed about twelve billion in 1975; an
informed estimate in 1977 put annual sales of marijuana
alone at about ten billion. That is probably more than any
religious group brings in. For comparison, the motion picture
industry has box office receipts of about two and a half billion
annually; annual sales of recorded music in 1977 barely

topped three billion. It seems that marijuana is now the opium of the people. Not that religious groups are out of the picture, nor astrologers, spiritualists, magicians, practitioners of various sorts of psychological self-abuse, and so on. We currently enjoy a revival of exorcism and speaking with tongues—the best way of speaking for those who have nothing to say. There are three times as many registered astrologers in Europe and the United States as there are chemists and physicists. America has always been famous for freaks, but the increase in their numbers and the numbers of their dupes during the past fifteen years may serve as further evidence for the current crisis of hope. Some of these poor people are actually deceived, but more go on because they "hope there's something in it." They hope for something to hope for.

As an opposite manifestation of this same hope we may notice the growth of philanthropy, the swarming of workers into social assistance programs, and of students into schools for the social service professions. The stated motive is commonly "to do something worthwhile," or "to help people." Beneath this lies the need to feel important, to tell yourself, "I'm doing something that really matters. They need me." Hence the most favored fields of effort are those in which the needs are most obvious—medicine, relief work, etc. But this need to be needed, and even more, this means of securing dependents, testify to a failure of hope. If a healthy, competent man has nothing better to do than tend the sick and incompetent, what are health and competence for? If, by some miracle of grace, all the sick, disabled, senile, insane, and criminal were restored overnight to perfect health, capability, and virtue, what would all their devoted caretakers do? Blake saw the problem two hundred years ago:

> Mercy could be no more
> If there was nobody poor,
> And Pity no more could be
> If all were as happy as we. . . .

And Miseries' increase
Is Mercy, Pity, Peace.[10]

The increase of the social services is to some extent a measure of the increase of persons who live on synthetic social virtue and pseudo-philanthropic goal substitutes, and never discover anything worth doing for its own sake, anything they can really hope for. Patching a person up, whether physically or morally, should not be an end in itself. It should be a means to an end, the end being the repaired person's functioning normally. But if the repaired person has no function worth performing, and at best can only look around for some other person in need of repair, on whom to fasten for self-justification, with the hope of producing yet another repaired philanthropist in pursuit of another object of philanthropy—we are caught in an infinite moral regression. No society can support itself forever by taking in its own psychiatric washing. The result in morality, as in economics, is starvation. The concentration on means and remedial measures rather than positive goals appears everywhere—in education, in public policy, in the hypertrophy of medical and psychiatric services, and so on and on. All these phenomena are undeniably the results of the complex interaction of many and various causes, but an important factor in all of them is the inability to conceive of more adequate objectives for hope. This is particularly clear in the materialistic social reform movements, whose upper class members often display extraordinary altruism and undergo great hardships for the sake of their admittedly hedonistic goals. Because they are dissatisfied with the life of material pleasures, they demand it for everyone, and willingly sacrifice their own enjoyments to secure for others the advantages they declare unimportant. Humanitarianism is the otherworldliness of our time, draws its strength from the rejection of the present, and will in turn be rejected if it prevails.

[10] The spelling "Miseries' " follows G. Keynes' edition (London, 1932), p. 88.

VIII

So much for our present predicament. Let us try to sum up what has been said and draw some conclusions.

The limitation of the earth's resources and the increase of its population indicate that we must soon make and enforce some plan for limiting population and conserving resources. Failure to do so may lead to the breakdown of civilization. Humanity is in danger of drowning in a flood of mankind.[11]

But we are in no condition to make such a plan, let alone enforce it. We have the greatest difficulty even in making domestic decisions. Part of the difficulty derives from our ability to carry out our plans, whence the frightening necessity of facing the consequences of our mistakes. But more of it results from uncertainty as to goals. We do not really know what we hope for. And we have the greatest difficulty in choosing between possible hopes because most traditional standards have ceased to command general acceptance. This is particularly true of the Biblical tradition and those of the major religious organizations and traditional schools of philosophy, but it holds also for political systems. "The American tradition," though justly celebrated, has failed to solve our domestic problems and offers no clear guidance to determine our hopes for the future; the political traditions represented by the other great powers have even less to recommend them.

This difficulty of formulating our hopes on the national scale is matched by the difficulties experienced by many people in trying to discover their own hopes, or in hoping for anything more than transient pleasures. There has been a vast

[11] Between 1965 and 1978, by expenditures of about $6.3 billion, the rate of population growth in less developed countries has been cut from 2.6 to 2.4 percent per annum. This, however, is cumulative; if the 2.4 rate is maintained the population of these countries will double in about 30 years. However, the generation now attaining sexual maturity is much larger than that now dying out; hence more rapid doubling is likely. *World Population; Silent Explosion*, U.S. Dept. of State Bulletin Reprint, 1978, pp. 4f., 10, 23, 25.

increase in the number of uprooted persons who live emotionally from hand to mouth. Part of this is due to rapid technological changes, consequent physical displacement, and the difficulty of planning ahead in a world of unpredictable developments. More is due to the change in the position of women, the breakup of the home ("the second womb for children") and the decline of family life as an ideal, with consequent changes in the general moral tone of our society. Another factor is the widespread attack on the general standards and tradition of our culture, often in the interests of cultural pluralism and subcultural groups. Our traditional ideals being thus discredited, there has been a great increase in the number of social dropouts, in drug addiction and other forms of irresponsible escape. By contrast to these, in morally responsible people, the same despair of finding something absolutely, in itself, worth hoping for, has led to the great growth of commitments to medical and social services, to care for the incompetent. Such care may be justified by obvious need, but is dangerous because it greatly increases the number of the incompetent, and is ultimately inadequate as an answer to the question, What can a competent man hope to do?

Presumably some answer to this question, or else the likelihood of its having no answer, should be indicated by the history of human hopes. That history has been almost completely neglected. Some of the reasons for the neglect will presently be mentioned, and some of them are excellent. Nevertheless, the problem is one which for many years I found again and again staring me in the face, both in research and in everyday life. Consequently I at last decided to try to sketch out what seemed to me the main lines of the evidence, both psychological and historical (for these are inextricably intertwined), and to find out in what direction they would seem to point. As to the direction I had no foreknowledge when I started to write. The writing has been an experiment, a sort of exploration in which the reader is now invited to take part. We shall not find the end of the rainbow, nor even the source of the Nile; the conclusion will be one like that of Johnson's *Rasselas*, "in which nothing is concluded." However, the analysis of the problem and the assembly and arrangement of the material have helped to clear my mind; I hope they may prove helpful to others. At least the discussion may do something to bring both the problem and the evidence to public attention, which both deserve.

II

Hope as a Factor in History

I

To suppose that by study of the past we can learn what to hope of the future will seem to many historians absurd. Many would think it so even if "hope" were taken in its secondary, limited sense, to mean "expect." All the more so, when it is given its proper sense and the attempt is admittedly to discover, from the course of human history, the goals towards which human effort should be directed. Most will simply dismiss the attempt as "hopeless"; some will go on to attack "psychologizing" in attempts to describe the past, or to insist on the uniqueness of each event and the consequent impossibility of making historical predictions, or to maintain that history should be strictly objective, a precise record of what has happened, and therefore should not be concerned with value judgments. I think these objections need not be answered in detail. In general it seems enough to say that all history is necessarily a structure of inferences. To limit ourselves to the observable data would limit our picture of the past to accounts of such data—bibliographies, museum catalogues, excavation reports without interpretation of the objects found. As soon as interpretation begins, one enters the world of conjecture. Conjecture almost necessarily involves notions of purpose and so of hope. Even to identify an object as a spoon or a knife is to conjecture the purpose for which it was made and to imply something of the hopes of the maker or the prospective user. The notion of purely objective history is an *ignis fatuus*.

Once the necessarily conjectural nature of history is recognized, the relevance of historical method for study of the future must follow. If this system of conjecture enables us to interpret data from the past correctly and to reconstruct the purposes and actions of those who produced them, it should do the same for present data and make possible forecasts of the future. The unwillingness of professional historians to accept this conclusion may or may not, practically, be wise timidity, but is intellectually unjustified. In fact, historical prediction of the future is a major factor in market research, insurance, banking, foreign policy, social and economic planning, and many similar fields where its utility and inaccuracy have alike been demonstrated.

Here, however, I do not propose to prophesy. In this chapter the problem is to try to describe hope as a factor in history, to indicate briefly the different sorts of hopes that motivate human actions, and their various roles. If even this modest proposal seems quixotic, let me say only, "Try it and see." Insofar as the present essay may succeed, it will answer the objections by example; should it fail, any arguments that might be presented here would be discredited by the failure. The reader has now been warned of the historical impropriety of the enterprise. "Road under construction, proceed at your own risk."

Nevertheless, it may be worthwhile to indicate one of the major difficulties in the way. This is simply human ignorance, an ignorance consequent less on lack of essential data than on the incapacity of the human mind to master such data as are available, an ignorance with which learning is in perpetual conflict. The problem of hope is ideal as an exemplification of this conflict, because both the conflict and the neglect of the problem result largely from the customary hope of historians.

Why is it that, although hope is one of the fundamental

factors that has constantly shaped history, it has almost never been the subject of direct historical investigation for its own sake? There are any number of particular investigations: the hopes ("motives") of Tom, Dick, and Harry are discussed interminably, monographs on major phenomena (the Crusades, the Gold Rush, etc.) are plentiful, but the history of human hopes is not attempted.[1]

Any historian will tell you that this is because the subject exceeds any historian's capacities. This historical despair is in part the consequence of the increase in documentation. The history of historiography in the nineteenth and twentieth centuries can be read as the story of the scholars' unwillingness to accept the necessity of ignorance, even after they had collected the documents to prove it. The tactics developed to resist recognition of ignorance are visible everywhere in modern historiography—specialization, increasing reliance on the sorts of data that can be handled mechanically, recourse to probability theory and development of techniques of sampling, team projects and institutes, conferences and conference volumes, the multiplication of bibliographies and abstracts and journals devoted to particular subjects . . . "You throw the sand against the wind, and the wind blows it back again." Blake's metaphor holds.

The fact to be recognized is that human knowledge in general is built on inadequate data. Listen to any conversation, or even to any "learned" discussion: Ninety percent of what passes for "knowledge" is at best plausible opinion. When plausible opinion is commonly accepted, it becomes "fact," when it leads to predictions that prove correct, it becomes "demonstrated fact." But in spite of this pretentious vocabulary, the problem of how we know is insoluble, even for the least sensations. Consciousness and the perception of "the external world" remain inexplicable. Yet we are well aware of

---

[1] J. Pieper, *Hope and History* (New York, 1969), a translation of his *Hoffnung und Geschichte* (Munich, 1967), is not an historical study, but a longish Roman Catholic tract; E. Bloch, *Die Prinzip Hoffnung* (Frankfurt a/M, 1959), 2 vols., is an enormously long Marxist tract, equally unhistorical.

what we cannot explain. Even if we are, as Wordsworth said, "moving about in worlds unrealized," we can move with precision to accurately predictable results. Complete knowledge of the data relevant to any detail is impossible, but complete skepticism as to the general structure of human knowledge is also impossible. The general structure of human knowledge is a colossal complex of successful ignorance. Consequently its nature and limits are defined by our notion of success, which in turn is a function of hope, i.e. of the proposed goals. Thus the knowledge of any society is shaped by its hopes and reflects them. A peaceable and self-contained society will "know" gunpowder as the material used in firecrackers, a belligerent and expansive one, given the same material, will arrive at other knowledge.

We must therefore begin this discussion of hope with the recognition that our own hopes (which are largely those of our society) will shape the results not only by influencing the choice and evaluation of evidence and the *Tendenz* of the argument (as the hopes of all authors inevitably do) but also, more profoundly, by shaping the criteria of "knowledge." This latent circularity of thought on the subject of hope seems to be inevitable. Our knowledge is likely to yield the results we hope for because the data's and the concepts' utility for yielding such results is what makes us think them "knowledge." The common, pragmatic definition of "truth" as opinions "that will work" (i.e., that yield predictable *and desired* results) similarly depends on hope, which defines our notion of what "works." Thus persons mainly concerned with physical and social objectives are apt to think of "truth" as, mainly, that body of opinions which leads to predictable, demonstrable, and desirable results in dealings with the surrounding world, and are therefore likely to be "rationalists," whereas persons mainly concerned with emotional states and subjective experiences will think of "truth" mainly as those opinions, and knowledge of those techniques for managing the psyche, which will produce the "feelings" and hallucinations they wish to experience or to make others experience.

II

With these notions of "knowledge" and "truth," what can we "know" about hope and its role in history? We may start with the primary definition given in the *Oxford English Dictionary:* "Hope . . . Expectation of something desired; desire combined with expectation." Our business here will be the psychological condition thus defined; secondary uses of the term, to indicate desire without expectation,[2] or expectation without desire,[3] are now mentioned only to be dismissed. Hope differs from desire not only by involving expectation but also by its exclusive concern with the future. The little girl with the lollypop no longer hopes for, but still desires, the object she is enjoying.[4] However, the more important difference, for our purpose, is the matter of expectation: As a New Yorker, I desire, but do not hope, to live in a clean city. This element of expectation makes any discussion of hope a discussion of what is thought to be possible. One who hopes for the impossible is a fool, that is to say, human, but because of his folly he thinks it to be possible, and he instinctively avoids consideration of facts that run counter to his wishes. Consequently, if you question the average American liberal about his hopes you will get a remarkable string of contradictions:

I hope food prices will go down.
I hope agricultural workers will be better paid.
I hope we shall feed the starving millions of India.
I hope we shall do something to prevent overpopulation.
I hope government interference in private life will diminish.

And so on. Such hopes, loaded with emotional charges, commonly exist in atomic isolation. When two suddenly collide

[2] E.g., "I hope we shall have a good spring next year."
[3] E.g., "If you go on drinking as you have been, you may reasonably hope to be dead before fifty."
[4] Apparent exceptions, e.g., "We hope for peace" (although we have it now), are not really exceptions, since the peace we hope for is not the present condition but a somewhat similar one in the future.

they are apt to produce an explosion releasing a good deal of heat. But if, when the shock wave has passed, rational discussion becomes possible, it usually begins with the platitudinous recognitions that "Hopes must be tailored to possibilities" and that, consequently, "We shall have to make some hard choices," i.e., we don't know what we shall do when forced to choose, but we are sure that we won't like it and are therefore determined to avoid, as long as possible, confrontation with the facts. Of these facts one of the most unpleasant is the fact that we do not know what we want. But we do not know what we want because one of the things we want is not to know what we want. In sum, since hope is the expectation of something desired, our problems are to know what we may expect and to admit what we do desire.

III

The problem of the subconscious mind is closely related to that of purpose in the lower animals and even in the vegetable and the inorganic world. One of the presuppositions that has most obscured and hindered western man's understanding of the world has been the sharp distinction, popularized especially by Descartes, between the conscious and the unconscious. Whatever consciousness may be, besides a mystery, it certainly is a matter of degrees, and the patterns of behavior that go with it, patterns customarily described in terms of hope, purpose, and choice, recur throughout all nature. Consider, for instance, a fire: It behaves for all the world like an animal. It seizes, devours, digests, and excretes; it grows, beginning as a tiny spark and becoming a conflagration; it moves about as if pasturing, and is guided by its food supply; if it finds enough food and grows very large it is apt to explode in an orgasm which sends out smaller fires in every direction. After such an explosion the parent fire will often be exhausted and die out, while the smaller fires take up their individual lives, repeating the same cycle—a cycle characteristic not only of fires but, with various modifications, of many forms of vegetable and animal life. The Neoplatonic notion of the world, that saw all creatures as impressions, more or less faithful, of the primary cause of existence and of life, at least recognized the common patterns that run through all and unite them in what once was called "the great chain of being."

At what link of the chain we should locate the appearance of hope and, with it, of purpose, is a difficult question we need not try to settle. Something of the sort seems present already in the care of most animals and even of many insects for their offspring, care that commonly involves self-denial and sometimes even self-sacrifice. It is easy to say, "Only those species survived of which the parents fed, sheltered, and fought to protect their offspring; therefore such behavior is now general." But why did any parents ever do so? None do so for their other excretions. Why were these particular droppings so much cherished? That the bitch licks the tasty uterine secretion off her puppy is readily understandable, but why doesn't she eat the puppy, too? Because she behaves like her mother, and if her mother had done so she wouldn't be there? But why didn't her mother do so? And so on back. Something like a hope—to preserve the young—seems ultimately unavoidable, and the consequence of this hope is the preservation of the breed. The animal surely cannot conceive of preserving the breed, but if we are to attribute specific hopes to the subconscious mind of man (as is now the custom in psychiatric practice), may we not speak of the subconscious mind of the animal, or of the hope of all living tissue to protect and propagate itself? But what is the meaning of the expression "the hope of the tissue?" Possibly, "behavior of the sort which, when it occurs in humans, we call purposeful." Again, it seems, we have to do with a chain of behavior patterns running throughout nature, and with a peculiar name given to that section of the chain which lies within our own experience.

Whatever its origin, we cannot ignore, in writing of human hopes, the deeply rooted and (in terms of pure individualism) irrational[5] hope to produce and preserve offspring: in Plato's terms, the hope for physical immortality, in those of the Old Testament, the first commandment, in those of biology, the instinctual basis for the survival of the race. It is particularly important now because it bids fair to cause the destruction of the race. It is the source of humanitarianism—the determination to protect the weaker, to favor the inferior—of which the most important form is care for children. So long as, with the best of care, infant mortality ran about 50 percent and the accidents of life and the constant pressure of poverty automatically weeded out the inferior types among the survivors, this care for the weaker and the inferior sufficed only to produce a slow expansion of the human population, mostly of the healthier and more capable sorts. But now, with modern medical methods, it has produced the population explosion, with the likelihood of gigantic famines that may lead to nuclear explosions, and with the certain increase of inferior types that may turn society into a gigantic welfare state, penal institution, and mental and physical hospital.[6] In the light of these consequences, man's animal nature seems the most dangerous threat to his survival, precisely because, without it, he cannot survive.

(Lest the combination of welfare state and penal institution be thought a rhetorical exaggeration, let me quote a report by D. Middleton (*New York Times,* October 3, 1976, p. 5):

East Germany has completed about two-thirds of an elaborate new barrier system that will run along the West Ger-

[5] *N.B.* "Pure individualism" is a high abstraction, far removed from actual experience.

[6] I have before me an appeal from Project Hope soliciting funds to support programs "teaching medicine, health care, sanitation, and good nutrition" in "the Caribbean, in Brazil, Colombia, and Peru, in Tunisia and Egypt" (!)—most of these being areas in which the major economic and social problems already result from overpopulation. In contrast to such sentimentalism, more responsible scientists concerned with "The Limits of Growth" (D. Meadows) are already urging us to "realize that what is good now may be bad for the future" and to practice *triage* as a means of limiting human survival to the more capable elements of the race (e.g., J. Forrester in his 1974 address to the Franklin Institute).

man frontier from the Baltic Sea in the north to Czecho-slovakia in the south. . . . It is designed to keep the East Germans in. . . . When completed [it] . . . will cover about 900 miles. . . . About 10 yards back from the border is a fence of wire mesh. . . . about nine feet above ground and three feet under ground. The concrete posts to which it is anchored are studded with antipersonnel mines, which can be exploded by trip wires. . . . Beyond the fence is an antivehicle ditch about 15 feet across and about five feet deep at the western side. This has been dug to prevent East German defectors from driving tractors or trucks through the barrier. . . . Next . . . is a plowed strip of soft earth on which footprints or tireprints would be visible to patrols of the East German Border Guards. Finally, two strips of con-crete slabs have been laid to parallel the fence. Along these pass motorcycle and jeep patrols . . . The cost of the barrier is estimated . . . at $415,000.00 per kilometer (roughly $682,000.00 per mile). . . . It is guarded not only by con-stant patrols but by watchtowers . . . with ports for machine guns.

It is, obviously, a prison wall. The hope of treating an entire subject people as a single forced labor camp—at once a penal institution and a "welfare" state—has been realized. Not that this is the first realization. The grisly examples of Czecho-slovakia, Hungary, and the Baltic republics are already being forgotten; earlier ones are matters of "history." Let us return to the question of subconscious hope.)

Another sort of evidence for such hope may be found in the reports of killing by witchcraft, a practice found in many prim-itive societies. Almost all reports agree that the deaths are not caused by sudden paroxysms of fear that might occasion heart attack or cerebral hemorrhage or the like. Instead, when con-vinced that the fatal spell has been cast and that nothing can be done to change it, the typical victim performs whatever ceremonies are customary in his society at the approach of death, and then takes to his bed, or goes off by himself to some unfrequented spot, and soon thereafter dies, less from lack of food or water—though these are often refused—than from "despondence," we should say, "from the destruction of his hope." But what is the physiological meaning of "despondence," and how does the destruction of hope affect the processes of the body? These questions bring us face to face with another ancient mystery, commonly called "the mind-body problem"—a bad name for it, because the name suggests what the people who made it up believed: that mind and body are separate, basically independent entities, geared to each other in some unknown way. Actually, research in neurosurgery and in the effects of drugs on "the mind" have all but demonstrated that "the mind" is a set of functions of the nervous system. The question is, therefore, "What physiological changes produced by seeing a gesture or hearing a few words (which may suffice to convince a man that he has been fatally bewitched) can cause the whole body to refuse food and water and presently cease to function?" If that question could be answered we should be close to a physiological definition of the term "hope."

The evidence from witchcraft, though widespread and uniform, is understandably suspect, but it can be seen as merely a set of extreme cases of the operation of a principle familiar already to the author of the Book of Proverbs (13:12):

> Hope deferred maketh the heart sick,
> But when desire cometh, it is a tree of life.

In medicine the importance of hope for recovery, and the danger of despondence are generally recognized. Dr. L. Thomas, President of the Memorial Sloan-Kettering Cancer Center, speaking at the Columbia University Seminar on the Nature of Man, has claimed for medical doctors the same deadly power that witch doctors possess.[7] There are, he said, a considerable number of patients who can be killed by telling

---

[7] L. Thomas, "The Unnatural Nature of Human Disease," *Minutes of the Columbia University Seminar on the Nature of Man*, March 28, 1976, p. 8.

them that they have a cancer likely to be fatal. The typical patient of this sort is a man in middle life, extrovert, often with a happy family and a considerable circle of friends, but hard-working and accustomed to success. You tell him that he has a cancer and will probably die of it, and he goes home, goes to bed, turns his face to the wall, loses his appetite, and is dead long before either his cancer or his refusal of food could do him any substantial harm. Here there is no question of coronary thrombosis, surreptitious use of poison, or anything of that sort. The death is clearly a consequence of the destruction of hope.

Should we say, "destruction of man's image of his future self," and compare the stories of magic in which a man is killed or enslaved by the destruction of his shadow? But "the man's image of his future self" is only a shadow, projected onto the silver screen of consciousness by the hidden motion picture machine of the nervous system, the fire in the depths of the Platonic cave. Since that was the source of the hope, what killed the man must have struck the machine, not the shadow, not the conscious image, but the biological organism that was the basis and cause of consciousness. The old principle, "Nothing in the mind if not first in the senses," must be revised to read, "Nothing in the mind if not first in the nervous system." As Skinner observes, we do not kick because we are angry; we both are angry and kick because of some physiological change.[8] Our conscious hopes are epiphenomena of such physiological changes; "unconscious hopes" may therefore refer to structures in the nervous system, and the system's consequent tendencies.

Closely related to this question is that of the effect of conscious hope on the body. E. Stotland, in *The Psychology of Hope*,[9] not only recognizes that destruction of hope can be lethal (p. 108) but also reports experiments in which the results of intelligence tests were improved by causing those tested to

[8] B. Skinner, *Beyond Freedom and Dignity* (New York, 1972), p. 72.
[9] San Francisco, 1969.

hope that they would do well (pp. 103 ff.). Thereafter he describes in detail the good results achieved by instilling hope in patients, especially mental patients, and especially by indirect means—treating them as if they were expected to behave normally, giving them tasks they could accomplish, etc. Beyond such controlled experiments lies the enormous but ill-documented domain of faith healing (and the adjacent one of acupuncture?) recently explored by D. Harrell.[10] From the mass of reports of various reliability, two things seem sure, that hope is often followed, and may be accompanied or preceded, by enormous changes in the functioning, and perhaps even in the structure, of the bodily organs, and that the mechanisms by which these changes, including conscious hope, are produced must involve some sort of neural condition or predisposition, the sort of thing described above as "unconscious hope".

Psychoanalysis has credited the sub- and unconscious elements of the individual with an amazing variety of complex and specific purposes, often presupposing considerable information the organism could never have acquired by its own experience. One recent book, for instance, tells me that I wanted "to flee the sex represented by the mother" because of my horror at her lack of a penis and my shock at "the toiletful of menstrual blood."[11] As an only child, I was in fourth grade before I learned how women differed from men. I well remember the occasion because I had an argument about the question with another boy, also an only child. We consulted a bigger boy who had a sister. He told us the facts. We had both been wrong. As for menstrual blood, I was in my late teens before I saw any. On these matters I think my ignorance was about normal for American boys of my time and circumstances. Consequently I read with skepticism attempts to explain the major elements of general subconscious motivation as results of the early experiences of each individ-

[10] D. Harrell, Jr., *All Things Are Possible* (Bloomington, Ind., 1976).
[11] E. Becker, *The Denial of Death* (New York, 1973), pp. 38–40.

ual. The complex patterns of animal and insect behavior, that by ordinary standards would be called purposeful, make it seem more plausible to follow Jung and such modern sociologists as Wilson and Dobzansky in conceiving of subconscious purpose as carried mainly by the cell tissue from generation to generation.

The detailed descriptions of motivation, its various elements, and the conflicts between them, that have been advanced by the various schools of psychoanalysis, remarkably resemble ancient mythology, not only by their mutual contradictions, but also by their common structure: the young gods chain the older out of sight, in the darkness of the underworld; the ego when developed represses the id in the darkness of the subconscious. Many psychoanalysts have noticed such resemblances, fewer have noticed the difference: most ancient mythology resulted from the attribution of consciousness and purpose to the powers of the external world; the mythology of psychoanalysis results from a similar personification of the elements of the psyche. In ancient Greece Aphrodite and Eros are exceptions in a pantheon of gods of the sky, the sea, and the underworld, rivers, the vine, and the earth, and so on. In the modern world it is a rare psychoanalyst who pays any attention to the psychology of "the lower forms of life," let alone to the patterns of physical or even biochemical processes. The amazing similarities of psychoanalytic theories to ancient myths—for instance, of Zeus' war against the earth-born giants, and the superego's war against impulses arising from the id—are explained wholly as due to the ancients' "projection" of their inner conflicts onto the surrounding world. But this is unfair to the ancients. Their mythology expressed their perception of the surrounding world, and that perception (as their art and literature prove) was often surprisingly sensitive and accurate. Consequently the similarities between their description of the outer world in terms of personalities and conflicts, and the psychoanalysts' descriptions of the inner world in the same mythological terms, should be seen as evidence that both are describing the same patterns of physical processes, patterns that appear in both the general structure of nature and also the animals, including men, which are parts of that structure. It is the intuition both of mythology and of psychoanalysis that these patterns are teleological—work toward goals. For studies of the role of hope in history, these goals will be the basic hopes of man, and the threats to their achievement will cause man's basic fears. In mythological terms, Hope and Fear are twins, but Hope is the elder, and her birth opened the way into the world for her brother, Fear.

IV

It is now commonly realized that subconscious hopes and fears have played a great role in shaping dreams and works of art and literature, as well as myths. In art and literature they appear disguised by the conventions of the media and the conscious, short-term purposes of the artist. In dreams they wear other disguises, commonly fantastic, Hallowe'en costumes put together from the ragbag of the individual's mnemonic associations. The brilliant success of psychoanalysis in recognizing the disguised hopes has distracted attention from the frequency with which dreams correctly predict, or even facilitate, their fulfillment. The subject has also been made unfashionable by other causes, especially the deserved disrepute of traditional techniques for interpreting dreams as signs of future events—a non-science that, from Babylonian times to the present, has produced innumerable manuals of nonsense. Nevertheless, the facts have to be recognized. They are as follows.

Dreams are closely related to imagination, and a most important function of imagination is to enable us to predict. We make mental models of situations that may arise, we imagine scenes in which we say this and she says that, and all of a sudden it occurs to us that we might do or say something useful (or harmful), or that she might do or say something that would help (or embarrass) us, and we alter our actions to produce (or prevent) the possibility imagined. Such model-making is carried on most freely in dreams. Dreaming seems to occur when, as it were, the brain is half awake, but the sense organs and motor command centers are still sound asleep. In this condition the brain's impulses are not checked by the influx of authoritative data from the senses, nor by the consequences of the movements they might otherwise produce. Hence, for most people the imagination has a freer rein in sleep and more fantastic models can be made. But in these models things still work for the most part in the usual ways —situations arise, actions and consequences can be foreseen, and suddenly we awake to find that in our dream we glimpsed a possibility that had escaped our waking thought. Such dreaming has often led to discoveries of historic importance: the American adaptation of Arkwright's thread-making machine, Otto Loewi's formula of acetylcholine, the theory of the double helix are famous examples. These and their likes illustrate the importance of freeing the mind from the compulsion of the commonplace. "Reality" as we commonly conceive it is very much the everyday set of objects, actions, and reactions. Though in philosophic discussion we should admit the possibility of unlikely alternatives, we suppress them in practice without thinking of them, because "one must be realistic." In dreams we are free from this compulsion. So dreaming enables the mind to explore a range of possible futures that waking thought will not consider. This exploration may be undertaken to gratify either immediate concerns or basic drives.

One of our most basic drives, one characteristic of human beings and absolutely necessary for human survival, is idle curiosity. Consequently much imagination—mental model building—both awake and asleep, is primarily gratification of curiosity. What would happen if . . .? By such gratification we are presented with a series of imaginary scenes, and among these hope often finds its objects. Does it find them, or create them? Which came first, the hen or the egg (a question on which Plutarch displayed much learning)? Hope shapes our imaginings, both asleep and awake, and imagination, both by dreams and by visions, shapes our hopes. Desires call forth appropriate images, but an image, like a spirit, once evoked is difficult to lay. It has a power and will of its own, and reshapes and redirects the desire that evoked it. Think, for example, how the images "liberty" and "equality" have reshaped the desires of the American people. Few of the slave-owning signers of the Declaration of Independence would not be horrified at the present social consequences of the powers that turned out to be latent in those symbols. Or think how history is now being shaped by elementary knowledge of geography and the notion that the whole of a geographic entity —say, Ireland or Africa—"belongs" to the native inhabitants of one part of it. Picasso, when asked the meaning of one of his paintings, is said to have replied with his inimitable cheek: "My work is to create these forms; to discover their meaning will be the work of subsequent generations." Every man, when asleep, is his own Picasso, but few are able to remember the forms, let alone copy them and sell the copies for hundreds of millions.

Among dreams, those repeated are commonly recognized to have special importance; so in history there are fancies (commonly called "ideals") that recur and recapture the hopes of generation after generation. "Liberty" and "equality" are examples of such ideals, but so are "the righteous king," "the holy city," and "the race of supermen" (Second Isaiah's "kings and priests," Plato's "guardians," and so on). To what extent they are anticipations by the organism of objectives towards which it is subconsciously directed is a question too complex for investigation here. For the moment we can only notice the existence of such recurrent dreams of western civilization and recognize that the historical importance of their individual occurrences may be far exceeded by that of their recurrence, by the significance they may possess as members of a class and therefore indicative of our deeper drives.

V

The dreamer awakes when he becomes clearly aware of his environment. We say, "of the real world," but "the real world" is itself a form he has created, his habitual way of organizing the data imposed on his consciousness by his sense organs, as his dream world is his habitual way of organizing the impulses and images provided by his central nervous system when disengaged from its sensible and motor controls. The gradual process by which a baby becomes aware of the world and the people around it, learns to distinguish "its own" body from things "outside," to recognize among those things various "objects" (regularly recurrent groups of sensations), and to act so as to affect them—all this is recapitulated almost instantly in an adult's awakening from sleep. Presumably no two babies organize their perceptions in exactly the same way, so each one's "real world" is slightly different from the other's. But their similar bodies and environments usually lead them to use a common set of signals—noises, language, gestures—with general "success," i.e., to produce the hoped for results. Again we come back to the use of "success" as a standard, and the consequent role of hope in shaping our notion of truth.

Conversely, hope is shaped by experience; there is a perpetual interplay between hope and reality, each molding the other. E.g., the conflict between the young and the old is essentially one between different types of hope resultant from different types of experience that produce different attitudes towards change. For the young, change is normally for the better. A boy has been changing rapidly as long as he can remember. Every day he gets bigger and stronger, his knowledge and understanding of the world around him increase, he rises in social position—at least, in the society of children, which is what matters. And the society of adults, who are not wholly unimportant, and his parents, who matter most of all, approve of change. "My, how he's grown! You're getting to be a real big boy, aren't you?" The bigger, the better—this is the tacit supposition of the Homeric poems and classical Athens (societies in which the ultimate power was in the hands of the young men, the spearmen and the oarsmen) and of the American frontier and the society it shaped (another young man's world). Of course, in the process of change, old things have constantly to be discarded. Every year, as long as he can remember, the boy has outgrown his old clothes. Consequently, for him, the rapid change in modern society poses no great problem. Indeed, if he thinks about it at all, it is comforting; it assures him that the changes he is undergoing are not abnormal: the world is changing, too; he is at one with it. And change, as he knows from experience, is generally a good thing.

Contrast the experience and consequent attitude of the old. The built-in optimism of youth may last through the thirties, but as the middle-aged man begins to lose the battle of the bulge, as daily experience begins to remind him of the decline of his physical powers and personal attractiveness, he finds himself caught in a net of changes that prove to be more and more often for the worse. And by this time he has built up lasting attachments to people and things in the world around, so their aging, breakdown, and replacement is, for him, a direct grief, as well as a reminder of his own predicament. What often hits him hardest is the aging and death of his parents, since all through his childhood and youth they had been the symbols of stability. However glad he may be, for various reasons, to see them go, their fate is nonetheless a reminder—*de te fabula,* the story is about you. If he is in the upper classes, the increase of his money, power, and social prestige may delay the alteration of his attitude towards change. Adolescent liberalism lasts longest in the rich; many wealthy women determinedly continue to wear it as a conspicuous claim to be young at heart, like a lifted face. Usually, however, it is merely a matter of adherence to certain political positions, and even these are often valued as justifications for complaints about "how things are going." Behind the façade there lies pure "future shock"—Toffler's book was a brilliant description of the world as seen by the old.[12] They find change is generally for the worse (as it is for biological organisms beginning to disintegrate) and they're against it.

Thus the young, in general, hope for change; the old, for stability. Societies dominated by the old—by the Roman Senate, the College of Cardinals, the mandarinate, the present gerontocracy of the USSR—are consequently organized for the maintenance of stability. The peculiar conflict in our society results from the fact that, although power is principally in the hands of the old (directors of corporations, senior politicians, bureaucrats), technological developments and, even more, international competition are forcing upon us an unprecedented rate of social change. The rulers hope for advantages that change can bring them, but they also hope for stability, for the preservation of themselves, their power, and the structures that make their power possible. From such conflict of hopes, the directive brain of a society may send to its organs contradictory messages; the results in China resembled those of functional psychosis in an organism.

Similar consequences follow from the changing relation of hope to time. The young have two classes of hopes—things they "really hope for," i.e., hope to achieve or attain relatively soon, and hopes "for the future," things they want to do or be "when we grow up," which means, in fact, beyond practically predictable time. The actual hopes of the young, being projections of their limited knowledge, are usually few and simple—a bicycle, a camping trip in the mountains, a passing grade in arithmetic—and can be realized, if at all, by relatively short and simple efforts. There is more than enough time both to achieve and to enjoy them, so time seems enormous —"*Ah! que le monde est grand à la clarté des lampes!*" Moreover, the changes time will bring are so vast and unpredictable that the future can hardly be conceived. Hence the constantly repeated riddle, to which one cannot know the answer, "What

[12] A. Toffler, *Future Shock* (New York, 1970).

do you want to be when you grow up?" is answered by almost random selection of some picturesque or publicized figure from the adult world—a fireman, a bank robber, and so on. One eminent scholar claims that when the question was put to him, at the age of five, by his uncle, a distinguished rabbi, he replied, "A sex maniac." Being practically unpredictable, the next ten years, when one is five, seem also interminable. Anyhow, one does not think about them, or not very much. One's mind is mainly taken up with the events of the day and the hopes for next day and next week.

As knowledge grows, hopes grow with it; and as knowledge of the steps necessary to realize these hopes increases, time begins to seem inadequate. Soon it becomes so short that hopes for the future must be cut down to fit it. So must the future—its shrinkage is far greater than its actual diminution in cosmic time. In cosmic time a man of sixty who will live to be seventy has as many years ahead of him as a boy of ten who will live to be twenty, but in time as a measure of hope, the difference is incommensurable. At sixty, seventy is almost tomorrow. Little change is expected, and less is hoped for. Childhood's vast, vague hopes for the future, about which nothing much had immediately to be done, have long since vanished, but so have most of the simple, readily realizable hopes of childhood. Now middle-sized hopes—to write a book, to perform or win a contract, to divorce or remarry— and all the predictable complications they entail, fill time to the last moment, so that one must also hope for a little leisure. The problem of adjusting hopes to time becomes one of the more difficult parts of the problem of happiness.

VI

With the consideration of such objectives we have gone over from hopes consequent on our general view of the world —hopes that are almost attitudes, and very close to the sub-conscious—to the everyday, short-term, apparently trivial hopes that make up most of our conscious lives. These two types of hope can be seen as the terminal forms of a range of variants of which the enormous number and intricate interrelations account for both the difficulty and the importance of the subject.

Commonly, hopes are classified by the things hoped for, and the different resultant groups are dealt with by the sciences that deal with those things. Thus subconscious hopes and deep-seated drives that shape the personality are the concern of psychology; the exploitation of these, the creation of symbolic satisfactions and short-term objectives is the business of advertising and propaganda; the estimation of an individual's hopes and their chances of realization is a matter for counseling; the hopes appropriate to each business and profession and those each is liable to occasion, should be (and sometimes are) dealt with by the several business and professional schools; the schools of the arts and sciences should discuss the objectives of the artist and scholar; the nature of happiness as the general goal of life is a recognized problem of philosophy; the political, social, and economic means to the good life are subjects for the corresponding social sciences; immortality and salvation belong to theology.

It is tempting to think of other possible classifications—for instance, by sources: One might distinguish between hopes generated directly by the body—for the continuance of its normal functions, the satisfaction of its needs and gratification of its impulses—and those suggested to the individual by the various social organisms of which he becomes a member —the family, the school, the gang, the church or synagogue, the state, the business, the group therapy circle, and so on. But such an attempt at classification would run immediately into the bramble tangle of mixed motives. It is often impossible, in the study of motivation, to draw a sharp line between the individual and the people around him, and even when it is indisputably clear that a particular hope has been derived from the surrounding society (as when the hope is centered on some artifact, heroin, for instance) one has to ask what precondition or need made this individual center his hopes on this artifact, when hundreds of other individuals, to whom it was equally available, did not do so.

When the forger of the Epistle to the Ephesians characterized the gentiles as "having no hope" (2:12) he doubtless meant primarily that they had no chance for salvation in the coming judgment, but he may also have had in mind what probably grieved him more, that they were neither won over by his offers of salvation, nor frightened by his threats of wrath to come. They lived for the most part, as most people do today, by an uninterrupted series of short-term hopes, at the longest plans for marriage, business or political ventures, their children's careers, their own retirement, but nothing that anticipated a fundamental change in their way of living, let alone the world. This pattern of hopes is correlative with the equally hand-to-mouth economic existence characteristic of well-adjusted people in the proletariat, but the pattern extends far beyond this class. Many people with the means and leisure for more extended planning lack the necessary imagination and use their millions to devote themselves to their family affairs.

In this field of relatively short-term, personal concerns, since we manage things ourselves, our hopes, though often foolish, are usually fairly consistent; serious inconsistencies will land us in the office of a psychiatrist. Next comes the social field. Here we know little of the facts, have less control of events, are usually passive spectators, and consequently are under no practical pressure to keep our hopes consistent. Hence inconsistencies are the rule. We hope for higher wages and less inflation, for less police surveillance and less crime, for democratic schools and better education, for national self-determination and international peace. Such inconsistencies are the business of the politician, who gets in power by nourishing as many hopes as possible, but then has the task of devising a policy partially practicable that will achieve most of his objectives and disillusion least of his supporters. Finally, both the inconsistencies of our hopes for society and the disappointments—or, often worse, the realizations—of our hopes for ourselves lead to a third type of hope, the utopian, for the Good Society, the Kingdom of God, the land of Cockaigne, or whatever—visions that have the consistency of dreams, and also the unpleasant tendency of dreams: to turn into nightmares.

These three classes of hopes—personal, social, utopian— may seem clear enough, but as soon as we get down to cases we find ourselves trying to grasp a subject like the Proteus of the *Odyssey*, that takes a different form at every moment. Our various objectives are so interrelated that any analysis must misrepresent what are really mere aspects of a single activity of a single individual who is at once animal and mind, separate entity and corpuscle of a social body that constantly conditions and is shaped by its components. Nevertheless let us attempt a clearer account. While we cannot justifiably draw sharp distinctions, we may succeed in identifying major centers of concern and the systems related to them.

VII

For all mammals, the beginning of life in the outside world is a painful extrusion; the first utterance of every human being is a cry of pain; the first desire in every human life is for relief. However, the little animal has not yet experienced relief and cannot know what it is crying for. The cry is an instinctive, unknowing appeal which the instinct of the mother, and of other members of the race, makes appealing. We are back to the question of apparent teleology in animal behavior. The same question is raised if we talk of a hope to perform or continue the normal bodily functions—a hope that scarcely enters our minds so long as it is fully and constantly satisfied, but becomes acutely conscious whenever its satisfaction is threatened, for instance, by heart attacks or choking spells. But does the hope exist when it is not thought of? This is a good example of the point already made—hopes exist as the biological processes which are undeniably directed to certain ends; when the attainment of these ends is delayed, or even threatened, conscious attention is directed to them, and the conscious correlatives of the bodily processes are recognized as hopes. In this sense we may talk of "health" (the normal performance of all bodily functions) as the common but unconscious "hope" of all animals.

Health, so defined, is perhaps the greatest of pleasures (as Epicurus, a sickly man, supposed), but it also opens the way to the others, and as pleasures are commonly the goals of hopes we can conveniently indicate the varieties of hope by describing the different sorts of pleasure.

Aristotle defined pleasure as the consequence of the unimpeded exercise of our natural capacities according to their nature (*Nicomachean Ethics*, VII,13). Since one of our natural capacities is to die, the definition is not entirely satisfactory, but neither is life. Those who pride themselves on living according to nature rarely say much about dying according to it, but the two processes are equally natural—*pace* Aristotelian arguments and Biblical myths. However, in this case Aristotle's definition is useful for our purpose. Accepting it *pro tem* we can classify conscious pleasures by the types of the organs exercised.

First will come the muscles, and first of all, the internal muscles and their functions—breathing, digestion, excretion, and so on. Some of these are almost always unconscious; others, often, fully conscious. Everyone has known the relief of a good breath of fresh air, and as for excretion, modern psychoanalytic idylls in which the Holy Grail turns out to be a chamber pot were anticipated by the Byronic parody of Rousseau:

> O what a joy it is, to be
> From social bonds at last set free!
> O natural, O perfect bliss,
> After so long restraint, to ----!

As the child develops, the exercise of the external muscles becomes more and more important as a source of pleasure, in handling (nursing, holding, touching, all pleasures of sheer manual dexterity, which is a contributing factor in everything from boxing to playing the piano), in walking, running, dancing, and so on, and in pleasures derived from the whole bodily system (swimming, gymnastics, sex, and other athletic activities).

It is clear even from this sketchy list that pleasures derived from the exercise of muscles often have important psychological aspects. Yet more important are the mainly psychological pleasures they suggest. The baby's muscular pleasure in controlling things—pushing them over, picking them up, squeezing them into new shapes, tearing them apart, and throwing them away—is one root of that later, psychological love of power which finds similar satisfaction in similar treatment of people. Another sort of muscular pleasure with important psychological ramifications is that of relaxing the muscles, letting go, falling asleep. This plays a great part in the notion of leisure as pleasure—a notion that often leads to disillusionment. Beyond the hope for leisure lie the practice of asceticism and the hope for death (conceived as total relaxation). Asceticism is commonly a way of dabbling with death, taking a teaspoonful every day and pretending it's medicine. For such subtly suicidal self-denial innumerable philosophic and theological excuses have been found; they are discredited no less by their variety and self-contradictions than by the fact that ascetic practices are often found without any such rationales, often, it would seem, as direct outgrowths of the pleasure of muscular relaxation, of giving up, submitting, being handled and held (perhaps even before birth—is massage a partial return to the womb?). Quite apart from its psychological affinities, the pleasure of relaxation, if sufficiently indulged, may entail asceticism as its economic and social consequence. For people of average appearance, *dolce far niente* does not pay. Anybody can become a hippie, but to remain one requires an extraordinary talent for asceticism (or stupidity).

All pleasures, from whatever organs they seem to be "derived," are of course functions of the nervous system, but this is most obvious in those derived from the special sense organs and therefore commonly called "the pleasures of the senses."[13] These are familiar, though the common notion of them is too sharply limited. As with the basic bodily functions, we do not realize our pleasure in their normal operation until it is threatened or interrupted. The delight in clear vision after a change of glasses, that in the music of ordinary speech after a temporary loss of hearing, the perfect pleasure of a glass of cool water when one is hot and thirsty, are all examples tacitly correcting those discussions of aesthetics that limit their attention to works of art, gourmet cooking, and the like. The Epicurean definition of happiness as the normal, undisturbed functioning of the body has a great deal to be said for it. It was such joys that Epicurus had in mind in his famous invitation: "I call you to [a life of] *continuous* pleasures, and not to virtues of which the hopes are empty, vain, and troublesome."[14]

One of the minor ironies of history is the common use of "Epicurean" to describe elaborately contrived pleasures and the sort of man who pursues them. Such pursued pleasures are commonly those "of the senses" (in the narrow sense) and of sexuality. They are pursued because they are fleeting. As the author of Ecclesiastes observed, "The eye is not satisfied with seeing, nor the ear filled with hearing" (1:8). Sensual pleasure does not satisfy, it palls. The first experience is a revelation, the thirty-first, a routine.

In general, the pleasures derived from exercise of the muscles and the peripheral nervous system are the ones that come to mind when "pleasure" is spoken of. A good many people —and, in particular, a good many "educators"—do not seem to have realized that the exercise of the central nervous system, and especially of the brain, can also be a source of pleas-

---

[13] Aristotle's "according to nature" in the definition cited above is probably in anticipation of the objection that we exercise our senses no less in perceiving disagreeable objects than in perceiving agreeable ones—into this controversy we need not enter.

[14] *Letter to Anaxarchus* (=Usener, Fragment 116).

ure. It is. The delight of clever children in learning is nothing short of a passion. Their spontaneous imitation is probably instinctive; it begins already in the higher primates: "Monkey see, monkey do" is a truism the psychologists hired by television networks have not been able wholly to discredit. But the learning of children goes beyond spontaneous imitation (and equally spontaneous memorization) to the attempt to *understand.* The child's constant question, "Why . . . ?" expresses the most characteristically human hope, and the one which, if mankind is fortunate, will be most important. Animal hopes can serve only to perpetuate us as they do the other animals, and all animals are destined to death in the coming destruction of this planet. But the hope expressed by "Why?"—the hope to understand—may possibly enable mankind to escape.

In praising this hope, however, we have run ahead of our subject, which here is not the utility, but the pleasure derived from exercise of the brain. Even in ordinary affairs the utility is often so great that the pleasure is disregarded, but it can be seen clearly in the love of useless puzzles, riddles, problem games like chess, and so on, to say nothing of the voluntary mastery of complex bodies of useless information, e.g., the names and batting averages of baseball players. Equally notable is the pleasure in repeating the knowledge acquired, but this is often a matter of display rather than pure intellectual exercise, and so again takes us over to the consideration of utility.

The notion of utility itself is profoundly shaped by the brain's pleasure in recognizing and producing patterns, which is the fundamental element in "understanding." Think of the efforts of individuals to realize in their own lives the patterns admired in their societies—the monk, the priest, the "parfit gentle knight," the philosopher (of whatever school), the rabbi, the revolutionary, and so on—and then compound this by men's efforts to realize in the societies around them some pattern they think desirable—the Spartan, Christian, Jewish, Japanese, or whatever "way of life," the socialist state, etc.—and you will only have begun to sketch the ways in which the brain's pleasure in conceiving and producing *patterns* (orders of one sort or another) has shaped not only the hopes of mankind, but also our notions of what is useful or harmful, our whole view of the world. Its influence extends even to our perceptions: we customarily arrange our sensations in the orders to which we are accustomed, and see not what is there, but what we think ought to be there. Hence the difficulty of catching typographical errors; hence, too, the innumerable devices for producing optical illusions, figures that seem to be square when their sides are actually curved or vice versa, patterns that protrude from the paper at one moment, recede into it the next. The entasis of Greek columns is a familiar application of this principle and all *trompe l'oeil* art depends on it.

Our perceptions of such matters are at once the results and guides of action, for it was action—reaching, handling, etc.—that taught us to interpret some sensations as indicating nearer things, others farther, and the like. Children delight in coordinating sensations with actions to produce innumerable patterns of action that correspond to particular situations—the pattern of going down stairs, for instance, which had to be learned slowly and laboriously, then becomes a matter of pride, a display of mastery, and at last a mere matter of fact, a reaction handled by the subconscious. The same sequence appears in adolescence—in learning to drive an automobile, or adjustment to sexual relations—and even recurs in adult life, for instance in acquiring new languages.

In all such matters the brain's delight in order, in pattern-making, is both directed and limited by the facts, physical and social, with which it has to deal. Physical facts are usually as regular as the brain could wish them—this may, indeed, be the cause of the brain's delight in regularity. But even the physical world is sometimes deceptive, witness Aesop's fable of the child who was collecting locusts and came on a scorpion. (The widespread phenomena of natural mimicry seem evidence of something like perceptions of order even in the vegetable and insect worlds.) In the social world exceptions are everywhere. The most common verbs are irregular; so are the most common people. The brain's delight in order here becomes a cause of error (produces, for instance, the regular conjugation "I says, you says, he says," etc.), but the disappointments consequent on error lead to more complex concepts of order—expressed, for example, by works on grammar or psychology, with the apparent exceptions catalogued and "explained"—and the mastery of these more complex orders becomes a new goal.

This process is important in the formation of moral standards. The desire "to be good" is in large part the desire to comprehend and conform to an approved order. This is true whether the order is a set of unarticulated rules learned as forms of behavior (as by infants) or a written code of law, or "the works of the spirit," whether "the spirit" be conceived as "the sense of the meeting" or "the voice of conscience" or, as Paul supposed, an actual *daimon*. The "spirit directed" man is a psychological type recognizable in most societies, and in each he is recognizable because he conforms at least in essentials to the sort of pattern for such men that is customary in that society. Whatever the standard, whether behavior pattern, explicit law, or spiritual guidance, the aspirant to goodness commonly adopts it as his own and follows it, largely because of his delight in order, even when he is alone. Often he will try to impose it on others and may even make it a cosmic principle "as it was in the beginning, is now, and ever shall be, world without end. Amen."

This love of order appears not only in men's sacrifices to realize their self-images, but also in their unwillingness to change patterns they have developed. It is an important factor in habits, and does much to explain why "You can't teach an old dog new tricks," a principle conspicuously exemplified in the lives of many "successful" men. Theoretically, acquisition should destroy avarice; the man who has made his millions should realize that he has more than he can spend and should have to face the question: *"Now* what do you want to do?" But actually acquisition often becomes a way of life, a pattern the brain perpetuates whether or not it is needed. Along with satisfaction and the ease of following a familiar pattern, it offers a sense of achievement and form of reassurance that its addicts cannot forgo. Most therefore continue to the ends of their lives the routines they developed to secure a freedom which, because they had to secure it, they cannot enjoy. Only a few of the children of the very rich have grown up with the knowledge that they would always have the means to do as they chose, and that, if they did not choose, they need not do anything. Careful study of such individuals might be of considerable value for the history of hope, as evidence of the relative importance of social suggestion and practical needs for the formation of hopes and consequently for the organization of the personality. There should be lots of material in their psychiatrists' files.

Not only do men create patterns in their own lives, they also delight to impose them on others. This is the basis of much education, and also of the deep disappointment of many parents. Children assimilate patterns and standards not only from their parents but also from playmates, teachers, and the models provided by the media. Thus cultivated parents are often forced to watch their children being vulgarized and brutalized by an environment from which they cannot legally withdraw them. Such seduction of children by society may be compared to the rape of a wife in her husband's presence— an episode popular in contemporary motion pictures. The rape scenes concentrate the action and by their violence and dramatization of the conflict arouse more violent reactions; but the involuntary and brief humiliation of an adult is not nearly so serious nor, in its consequences, so painful as the corruption of a child. Again the question is one of establishing patterns.

Such patterns are basic not only to moral but also to artistic, scientific, and political judgments. Aldous Huxley, in his reconsideration of *Brave New World*, [15] brilliantly described these consequences of what he called the "Will to Order" (though

[15] *Brave New World Revisited* (New York, 1958), pp. 21 ff.

he did not recognize in it the role of the pleasure of exercising the brain). After describing science as "the reduction of multiplicity to unity" and observing that, "In the same spirit the artist takes the innumerable diversities and uniquenesses of the outer world and his own imagination and gives them meaning within an orderly system of plastic, literary, or musical patterns," he went on to comment: "Within the realms of science, art and philosophy the workings of what I may call this 'Will to Order' are mainly beneficent" (in spite of "many premature syntheses"). But, "it is in the social sphere, in the realm of politics and economics, that the Will to Order becomes really dangerous. . . . In politics the equivalent of a fully developed scientific theory or philosophical system is a totalitarian dictatorship. In economics, the equivalent of a beautifully composed work of art is the smoothly running factory in which the workers are perfectly adjusted to the machines." He might have added that a particular peril of plans for society is that they often appeal most deeply not to the conscious self-interest of those who advocate them, but to the mind, because they "seem reasonable." Men want a society they can understand; they deeply resent one (like the present) where complexity baffles comprehension. In this respect the hope to understand can be a stultifying force, as a cause of destructive simplification. The hope of ordering all things according to a plan was among the motives that brought about the liquidation of the kulaks, Stalin's slaughter of perhaps five million people.

Like the pleasure in muscular exercise, that derived from intellectual exercise is greatly increased by the sense of power it produces. The power is felt first in dealing with the subject matter, in the ability to recall, understand, and arrange it; hence we speak of "mastering" a subject. But understanding commonly results in effective action, and science in technology. Every *techne* (art, craft, skill, technique), as Aristotle said, presupposes the notion of an end or goal to which it is a means, and Paul agreed—the ploughman plows with the hope of getting a crop. In this sense hopes are fundamental to the development of the arts and crafts, and even of the sciences, if we consider an organized, coherent, and consistent body of knowledge as a goal that the techniques of research and reasoning are used to attain. If we do, we touch again the realm of pure intellectual pleasure—the pleasure of exercising the brain—of which the most curious monuments are the great structures of useless learning. "Here's to number theory," said a great mathematician, "it never has been of any use to anyone; may it never be useful!" But such pure, conscious intellectualism requires extraordinary training and is therefore comparatively rare. It should not be confused with studies of questions now discredited. The libraries of literature on phlogiston, the Trinity, the Sephirot, and suchlike, are impressive examples of the scientific study of nonexistent objects, but were believed by the people who produced them to be of the greatest practical value.

Delight in understanding and in the sense of power that understanding gives does not stop with the mastery of subjects and the organization of the arts and sciences; it goes on to the general understanding of practical affairs and the consequent power to manage those. The love of such power—the love Swedenborg thought characteristic of the devils of the lowest hells—is characteristic of many political rulers and thus has greatly affected the course of history. Probably few rulers are much concerned about increasing their own wealth; reputation may concern more, but often seems secondary, at best; some few are genuinely committed to one or another plan of political, social, or economic action; but the majority have probably become rulers because they wanted to rule. (Here lies the greatest weakness of Marxian thought—its too narrow notion of human motivation, a notion consequent on its preoccupation with the needs of the poor. Of course air, water, food, shelter, and clothing rank first among human needs and therefore among human hopes—for those who are short of them. But once these are assured, the actions of human animals are directed by other hopes: for physical pleasures, affection, prestige, patternmaking, understanding, power. The higher up the social and intellectual ladder one goes, the more important the latter terms of this list become. To try to explain from economic motives the behavior of a man like Marx would be a stupidity of which only a Marxist might be capable.)

Understanding is commonly considered a halfway house in relation to the hope for "wisdom," conceived as correct understanding of the present, correct anticipation of the future, and the ability to adjust satisfactorily to both. This conception of wisdom must be extended, however, to allow for the nonutilitarian functions of the brain and the pleasures we derive from these. The brain is a filing system able, like other filing systems, to receive data, store them, and, on demand, either reproduce them, with more or less delay, or lose them forever. But the brain also recombines data to form pictures of events and objects not experienced. This recombination is an important and pleasant part of its activity. When it corresponds with the order of the objective world we call it "imagination"; it is our means of solving problems and anticipating future events, in short, the guide of life. When consciously released from the considerations of probability that harness it to practical questions, and left to play freely in its own flowery field of images, it is called "fancy" (the distinction was made famous by Coleridge) and produces literature like the *Arabian Nights,* the medieval romances, and their modern equivalents, the works of "science fiction." In private life these are daydreams, and easily and often pass over into sleep, in which the combinatory power of the brain is yet more freely exercised. The possibility of anticipating the future and solving problems in dreams has already been mentioned; their greater importance, of course, is the pleasure they give, their role as substitutes in fulfilling wishes we could never fulfill. This gives them extraordinary power and has made them much sought after. Elaborate techniques for securing dreams, and also for inducing "visions" (hallucinations experienced while awake) and "possession" or "ecstasy" (discontinuous alteration of the personality) formed an important part of ancient mystical and magical practice, while simpler but probably more effective pursuit of similar hopes supports the modern drug trade.

VIII

All these human objectives thus far reviewed—basic health and the pleasures consequent on the exercise or relaxation of our muscles, our senses, and our brains—are at least theoretically accessible to an isolated individual. But practically speaking there are no isolated individuals. Perhaps the first thing of which an average child becomes aware as something other-than-himself is another person, and while formation of the concept "another person" may be relatively slow, the adjustments that anticipate and contribute to it begin very early. From then on the child finds itself constantly dependent for its needs and pleasures on a circle of other persons, its "family." As time goes on, the makeup and structure of the circle changes, and other circles are added—playmates, fellow students or workers, colleagues, fellow citizens or believers, "Men, brother men"—as the individual comes to live in more worlds than one. The different circles are known in different ways, and each presents different opportunities and dangers, the occasions of different hopes and fears. Moreover, as the circles change, the individual changes, not only vis-à-vis society, but even in his notion of himself; he conceives himself successively as child of his parents, brother or sister of siblings, member of a team, parent of children, worker, employer, customer, colleague, etc., and each new role produces a new *persona*. The Latin word means both "mask" worn by an actor, and "person"; the equivalence is psychologically true.

Knowledge of the family is at first principally a matter of the sense of touch and muscular adjustments—the other people are those who pick you up, hold and handle you, nurse you, and so on. All this can be summed up in the one word, "care." The futile, pathetic hope for "perpetual care" persists through life and goes with us to the grave; it is illustrated by innumerable grave inscriptions, from the tombs of Egyptian kings to the *Spoon River Anthology,* and it is basic in the constitution of the personality. As a consequence of infantile experience, all our subsequent relations with others, even with enemies, are probably conceived subconsciously as claims for care. Such claims make up the tesserae of our mosaic picture of ourselves, the individual items in our private account of our own importance. The moment of truth, the moment of death, came for Auden's Miss Gee when she asked herself:

> "Does anyone care
> That I live in Clevedon Terrace
> On one hundred pounds a year?"

Stripped of others' care, she was left to herself, and left to herself, she died.

To this basic concern for care, each new circle of society adds a new concern, a new goal for hope. With the circle of playmates comes the question of status—leader or follower, attractive or avoided? With the circle of schoolmates comes the question of success in meeting the standards set by an impersonal, objective program of assignments. With emergence into adult society the questions of social role, privileges, powers, and obligations become acute; money as a means of power or pleasure acquires an importance that often obscures its mere utility; and so on. Each social structure—the political system, the Church, the bar, the stage—presents itself to the agile adult as a monkey cage to a small boy, a contraption designed for climbing. But other adults see the same structures as tools by which to change the rest of their environment. And others see them as expressions of ideals, as forms in which their own lives can be cast so as to give them recognizable identity and significance as parts of something larger than themselves.

This function of social groups has become more important in our own time because of the decline of belief in a personal afterlife. Long-term hopes seem to be possible only for composite bodies—religious communities, regional and ethnic groups, nations, social classes, mankind. Hence the willingness of many individuals to identify themselves with such bodies and even to sacrifice their individual interest for the group's well-being. But such comparatively rational considerations are far from accounting for the immense attraction exercised by such groups and the intense loyalties they generate. Here we have again to do with age-old biological conditioning, of the sort that in the insect world sends bees to commit suicide in defense of their hive.

The biological basis of such social attachments is probably indicated by the importance of uniformity in expectations of the hereafter. A major element in eschatological expectation was the hope of being with your own kind. The Israelite world to come was a spiritual ghetto to which "all Israel," and, in the main, only Israelites would be admitted. "Israelites" came to include converts to Israel, and, from Second Isaiah on, there were some who held that at least some gentiles would be kept on as servants; but the basic hope was not just for a good community, it was for a good *ethnic* community, and part of the goodness was being among your own people. Elijah Muhammad's exclusion of whites from salvation reflected the same mentality. In classic Christianity and Islam the tribal and racial requirements have been *de facto* transcended (though Christianity still claims to be "the Israel of God"), but a basic likeness is still required: all the saved will hold the same beliefs. "There is no salvation outside the Church," said St. Cyprian. The hope of heaven is the hope for a community whose members, if no longer of like ancestry, or like physical characteristics, will be at least like minded.

The root of this hope is partly fear. A group of children, left to itself, will immediately pick out and penalize any one of its members who, in any way, differs from all the rest, unless the difference is a closer approximation to some goal they all have in common—a bigger or stronger boy or, among small children, girl is not penalized, but admired, because they all want to grow bigger and stronger. But as soon as the girls

begin to reach their normal size, a girl who threatens to out-
grow it will immediately begin to be the butt of malicious
jokes about her size, will become unfashionable and be left
out of things until she mates or until the mating period is
over. When she thus moves out of the competitive area her
fellow females will relent and take her back to their company,
but only then. Is there some sort of memory of primitive
experience which warns children that exclusion from the
group means death? Primitive groups, of course, behave in
the same way—hence their absolute uniformity in everything
from physical appearance to mentality. A little Greek boy
from a mountain village once served as my guide to a remote
monastery. He had wretched teeth—as did everyone in his
village—covered with green slime (perhaps there was something wrong with the village spring). Anyhow, I happened to
have in my bag a spare toothbrush, brand new, still in its
unopened box. I showed him how to use a toothbrush, and
tried to give him the new one. He wouldn't take it. I urged
him, took out a mirror and made him look at his teeth and
compare them with mine, reminded him that all the men of
my age, in his village, had lost their teeth completely, and
asked him if he wanted to lose his. He didn't; he began to cry;
but still he refused. "Nobody in our village has such a brush.
If I had one and used it they would laugh at me." That settled
it. Laughter can be a very serious thing. In it, society shows
its slimy teeth. It is the warning that an individual has over-
stepped a bound, has momentarily become different. It also
has fear in it, for the different is not only hated—it is feared.
Hence the sorcerer is often, in primitive societies, someone
who has left the society and survived, has anticipated the
ultimate penalty of exclusion and has overcome it and lives
and returns to the society, still a member of it, but armed with
the awful power of the outside. In more complex cultures,
where expulsion is no longer possible, he will die and rise
from the dead, or go down alive to the underworld and return.

But why should children, and primitives generally, react in

this way to the different? Most of the differences penalized are minor and obviously harmless. Can the root be biological, the desire to maintain a group that will breed true? Most mutations are malformative, many lethal. The safest thing, accordingly, for the survival of the group, of the precious, viable pattern, is to reject immediately any deviant, any member that seems likely to produce variant progeny. Once again, the beehive is the goal.

IX

For human beings, however, the beehive is still far off. They doubtless begin their lives as creatures of society, but they rapidly develop individualism, and only slowly are won back to social concerns. Moreover, this transition is not inevitable. Many who find social problems hopeless turn deliberately to private life. The great example is the history of Greek philosophy. One of Socrates' major achievements was to turn rational criticism to the subject of social standards. So many other problems, at that time, were being solved by reason, it was inevitable that the new tool should be tried on society, as a boy with a new pocketknife or new colored marker must try it on everything in sight. Socrates did it. And he taught his pupils to do it. When his attempt at Athens ended in disaster, his disciple Plato tried again at the court of the tyrant of Syracuse. When he, too, failed, and was forced to live out his life in retirement, Aristotle took refuge in the role of an objective observer (which was all his position in Athens, as a resident alien, would permit) and other aliens (Diogenes and Zeno) and even natives (Epicurus) turned to private life with the hope that, by rational management of it, they could attain independence of the unmanageable, irrational world around them. This is why Greek philosophy produced Utopias. The "Republics" of Plato, Zeno, and the later Stoics, are only superficially expressions of hope. More deeply they express despair. The authors must dream of Utopia because they are sure that the good society, as they define it, cannot be realized in any actual state. Their practical thinking, therefore, is directed to private life and especially to the task of making it independent of the vicissitudes of the surrounding political and economic worlds. That this can be done by rationality is their greatest hope.

This is one of the reasons why Greek philosophy lost out to Christianity. Christianity had no more to offer, but promised more. "Faith," as the author of the Epistle to the Hebrews observed, "is the evidence of things hoped for" (11.1). Christian faith turned to the eschatological tradition and confidently foretold a complete reorganization of the world— of course, to the Christians' advantage. Humility and industry are Christian virtues only *pro tem,* in the present, evil world. Come the revolution, all will be changed. On this, Paul is explicit (I Cor. 4): That he has to work with his hands is, he thinks, one of the signs of his humiliation, like being dishonored, hungry, thirsty, ill-clad, beaten, and homeless. It is not the proper condition of a Christian. Christians are destined to king it, to be rulers, not workers. The Jewish tradition summed it all up in one sentence: "The blessed will sit with crowns on their heads and enjoy the glory of the presence of God" (*Berakot* 17a).

It was the genius or good fortune of Christianity to combine these eschatological hopes with practical policies for dealing with the present and so to produce a great organization that ultimately gained control of society and proved an immensely powerful instrument for fulfillment of the hopes of the worldly. In Christianity, therefore, eschatological and practical hopes lived side by side, like the family cat and the family dog, in comparative reconciliation. Other groups that decisively lost the battle for this world—the heretics, the Jews, the Manichaeans, the surviving cults of paganism, and so on— formed little *cénacles* of their own, self-isolated communities for the preservation of their peculiar practices and ideas. Within Christianity, too, the mushroom growth of monasteries showed the psychological need for such "imaginary heavens" (to use Swedenborg's term for what Castaneda would call "bases for alternative realities"). Even more impressive is the modern history of the Jews—released from their tiny ghettos they have, with enormous energy and heroic self-sacrifice, brought into being the State of Israel.

Self-sacrifice is characteristic of many such imaginary heavens, particularly of those that survived. Relatively few libertine communities were founded, and these rapidly broke up: their capable members found they could have more fun in the outside world. In the ascetic communities the sacrifice is not only of intelligence, though that is often the most conspicuous victim. The personality is the ultimate quarry, and it is plausible to see in most such social structures disguised expressions of the desire for death. Sometimes this issues in complete prohibition of procreation: every monastery dies out in every generation and is renewed only by recruitment from the outside world. More often sexual life is more subtly discouraged. In this respect the history of Sparta, anciently the most famous and influential of all such communities, is typical: although celibacy of older men was penalized, boys were trained in homosexuality and younger men had lovers until they were thirty (Plutarch, *Lycurgus* XXV); when marriage was arranged the partners at first continued to live as if single, for years their meetings were surreptitious, family life was reduced to a minimum and children were educated mainly in public establishments. With these measures the number of adult male Spartans declined from perhaps eight or ten thousand in 500 B.C. to about 700 in 240 B.C. and the most conspicuous ancient attempt to create a national prison camp dwindled into an historical curiosity.

X

But the men of the western world, in general, have not taken refuge either in private asceticism or in communal daydreams. The greatness of occidental civilization and its present dominance throughout the world are due to the fact that, instead of accepting nature as his ruler (as did Confucius and

Hinduism) or rejecting it and trying to escape it (as did Buddha), western man has taken it as raw material to be reshaped according to his hopes. Accordingly, hope is consistently represented in classical literature not only as man's unfailing consolation, which "springs eternal in the human breast," as Pope said, and alone remains in Pandora's box when all the evils she brought have taken wing through the world (so Hesiod), but also as the root of civilization, the source of agriculture and of the arts of the hunter and fisher: "Hope nourishes the farmers; it is hope that advances on credit, to the ploughed furrows, the seed that the field will pay back with high interest; hope takes birds with snares and fish with hooks," and so on (Tibullus, II, vi, 19 ff.). There was even a school of Greek philosophy called the elpistic (from *elpis*, "hope"), which declared that hope was what held life together because life would be unbearable without it. I suppose the question, "What did they hope for?" is the one most important for the historical understanding of any time, including our own. If we can get at people's hopes we can understand their actions—not always, of course, nor easily. Some acts are petulant, many are ignorant, more than we commonly suppose are self-destructive. But we have seen that there is also a hope for self-destruction, a desire to relax, let go, submit, no longer try to assert our will or maintain our identity, but be carried along, as a child, by whatever power is stronger. "It is not a good hope," said Hesiod, "that lies with the lazy man in the shade, when he has not yet laid up enough food [to carry him through the winter]" (*Works and Days*, 500 f.). In the western world such hope has been the minor tradition. The major tradition has been reported, not only by funerary inscriptions, but by fables, proverbs, and popular songs—King Alfred and the spider, "If at first you don't succeed, try, try again," "As He died to make men holy, let us die to make men free."

Since hope in western civilization has been thus extrovert and active, it should be a central theme of historical studies. But just because it is a universal and ever-present factor, historians have tended to take it as something like gravity which, because it has consistently shaped all historical actions, is not a proper subject for historical investigation. As gravity belongs to the physical sciences, so hope has often been thought to belong to psychology, not to history. But hope, although ever present, is neither constant nor uniform, it not only has shaped, but also has been shaped, by historical events. Striking examples of this are the great epidemics, both of hope and of despair, which have had historical consequences comparable to those of the greatest physical epidemics but have never, to my knowledge, been studied as a class. Even the studies I have seen of individual outbreaks have invariably begun with the historical circumstances and have treated the hopes as consequences of these. This method is proper; hopes are indeed formed by the course of history. But history is also formed by them and may arise from the psychological (often psychopathological) adventures of individuals and groups of individuals whose cases have personal or even biological explanations quite independent of the major "history" of their times. The whole subject of contagious psychological diseases has been too much neglected by historians; conspicuous epidemics have been treated in isolation—so the Crusades, the witchcraft trials, the acceptance of Nazi doctrines in Germany—without attention to their parallels in mob psychology or in results achieved by advertising and propaganda. Yet such epidemics are recurrent phenomena of western history. Thucydides described that which swept Athens before the Sicilian expedition, as he did the physical plague which ravaged the city fifteen years earlier. His description of the physical plague has received far more attention, but the psychological one probably did more to cause Athens' downfall. The remains of another such psychological epidemic appear in the crop of eschatological prophecies that sprang up all over the Mediterranean world in the first centuries B.C. and A.D. More serious outbreaks accompanied the expansions of Christianity and Islam. In modern times the South Sea Bubble, the French Revolution, the Gold Rush, the

Shabbetai Zvi risings, the Ghost Dance movement, "the Great Awakening," the sudden growths of Communism, Nazism, Zionism, and any number of similar phenomena, stand out like volcanoes on the psychosocial landscape, as evidence of the unstable psychological structures on which the apparently calm countryside is built, and of the power of obscure shifts in these structures to generate intense heat, set off vast explosions, devastate the world for miles and decades around them, and leave deposits fertile for centuries to come. How do these huge bubbles of hope build up and burst? More comparative studies, like those made of the cargo cults, are needed. Another closely related and equally important topic for study is that of conflicts between different types and levels of hope, which have often caused social crises. A good example is the present problem of overpopulation, which is so difficult because it involves three types of hope—the fundamental animal drive for maximum multiplication, the conscious hopes of individuals for children (as signs of social and sexual success, as objects for love, as cheap labor, and as means of vicarious survival), and the conscious hope of the ruling classes for social and cultural survival, which overpopulation threatens.

It would be a mistake, however, to concentrate on the crises and volcanic outcroppings when studying the role of hope in history. As volcanoes can be understood only from a knowledge of the strata basic to the stable landscape, so the epidemics and conflicts of hopes must be seen as byproducts of larger structures. An attempt, however, to demonstrate the hope-structure of any major period, or even of a single great country in a major period, would require an assemblage and discussion of evidence far exceeding the limits of this essay. Here I hope only to indicate the need for the study and some of the lines it may follow.

III

History as a Factor in Hope

I

Now that we have sketched the varieties of hope, from physio-logical imperatives to the projects of the pure mathematician, we can ask how these forms have been developed in the past and, accordingly, how they may change in the future. As history displays and explains the varieties of hope, so the study of hope reveals the significant changes of history; it distinguishes different ages and states not by the accidents of dates and rulers, but by the different activities that could be carried on in them, the different lives and achievements that those who lived in them could hope for.[1]

It is clear that as far as particular hopes are concerned, there has been a perpetual interrelationship between hopes and historical events (taking the word "events" in its largest sense, so as to include, e.g., the availability of artifacts, and other cultural characteristics). Hopes have constantly led to historical events, events in turn have occasioned new hopes; the hen-egg-hen sequence makes discussion of priority pointless.

Often this process is in part subconscious, as when, threatened by an accident in driving, we do "without thinking" the things that should be done (or vice versa, if we are subconsciously self-destructive). When Jack and Jim were in camp Jim was troubled by sleepwalking: he walked, several

---

[1] For example, see the last two chapters of E. Bickerman and M. Smith, *The Ancient History of Western Civilization* (New York, 1975).

times, into Jack's bedroom. He was genuinely asleep at the time. Such evidence is familiar, as is the conclusion drawn from it: that hopes can be driven by social pressure and private censorship into the subconscious mind from which they can still control our actions. Moreover, it is plausibly argued that such suppression has been practiced in our society from time immemorial on some major aggressive drives, which are now buried so early, so deep, and so generally that most people are unaware of having them. Most of the taboos on incest with closer kin are of this sort; many men go through their lives without feeling any conscious sexual desire for their mothers and sisters. Similarly, Bertrand Russell remarked that "Law, where it has long been firmly established, causes a partial atrophy of impulses to violence. Civilized men do not so readily use physical force in arguments with each other. . . . A civilized man differs from an uncivilized man not only in education and knowledge, but in habits and impulses."[2]

Such repression of desires into the unconscious appears in many other bans as well. The attempt to be "natural" is one few men would wish themselves to carry through—let alone recommend to their sons. Since "human nature" has been thus abridged by training in the course of its historical and prehistoric development, it must be accessible to discipline; further alterations may be made. In fact, some have been made by "brainwashing," "programming," "deprogramming," and so on, which have shown the possibility of producing considerable changes even by brief but intensive training of selected individuals. Long-term training, especially if begun in childhood, has even greater possibilities, as the Jesuits early realized. St. Ignatius' *Spiritual Exercises* is a handbook of demonstrated efficiency. The results achieved by this treatment of the brain are sometimes no less striking than those formerly attained in China by binding the feet.

[2] *New Hopes for a Changing World* (London, 1951), p. 83.

II

Important as is the social repression of hopes into the subconscious (the housebreaking of humanity) the development of conscious hopes by historical change has been perhaps equally important and certainly more spectacular.

At the beginning of the process must have been the gradual transformation of man from an ordinary animal (moved mainly by reactions to immediate stimuli) to a unique creature motivated mainly by hopes for objects or events not immediately present and by purposes—plans of action to achieve these hopes. This transformation, presumably a consequence of environmental and biological factors now forever forgotten, resulted in a radical change of man's relation to time. Time became short, a precious resource to be husbanded for various purposes. Men now had, during most of their waking hours, "something to do." To have something to do is an exciting experience. A purpose is a challenge and calls forth the capacities of the individual—attention is focused, perception is sharper, thought clearer, action more vigorous—and all these exercises of our capacities give us pleasure, as Aristotle said they would. At the same time, a purpose is a counterirritant. The focus of attention is primarily on the goal, and the goal is some future state of affairs, conceived as satisfactory; therefore the unsatisfactory elements of the present can be put up with more patiently. "Don't cry, darling, Mother will give you some when we get home," is normally followed by a short interlude of sniffling and then by, "Mama, let's go home"—an expression of purpose. If going home can be started at once, the social reformer may become so much involved in it as to keep quiet for the next ten minutes. Since purpose is thus both stimulant and sedative, most capable men become purpose addicts. For them, to lapse into leisure is at best a brief relaxation. Deprived of their customary purpose they become irritable and must be kept quiet with some sedative (usually liquor), pseudo purpose (games, boating, fishing), or physical pleasure (food, sex, sunbathing). But even these palliatives soon become unsatisfactory. As the twin brother of sleep is death, the twin of leisure is boredom; but leisure and boredom are almost Siamese twins. "Teach us to care and not to care" is a petition fulfilled by the ordinary game, but "Teach us to sit still" requires for its fulfillment either advance to nirvana or regression to animality. Hence the difficulty of describing heaven, conceived as man's ultimate goal. The characteristic of an ultimate goal is, by definition, that once it is attained you want nothing more. Those who have achieved perfect beatitude are left without any further purpose, in eternal bliss. Or eternal boredom? For better or worse, most men have never had, and never wanted, to confront eternal salvation as a practical problem. We return to the history of their lesser hopes.

Most practical skills make possible two hopes—the hope to succeed, rather than fail, and the hope to succeed with distinction, so as to heighten the prestige attendant on success. The false notion of equality in achievements is a luxury few primitive societies could afford, even if it occurred to them (which, being false, it rarely did). When Hesiod began his great poem in praise of justice, labor, and the farmer's life he sang in defense of that "better rivalry, which stirs up even a lazy man to work when he sees what is being done by another" (*Works and Days,* 19 ff.) and his song expressed the wisdom of a poor society that needed every man's work. Contrast the ignorance of contemporary "educators" who try, in the name of "equality," to obliterate the difference between degrees of success, or even that between success and failure, and therefore teach by implication the unimportance of what they are teaching. Their essential lesson is, "It makes no difference whether you do this well, or not." Such teaching is the shortest way to destroy in their pupils not only hope but even self-respect. It implies that the pupils are unimportant: they can do nothing better than these trivial tasks in which the quality of the performance does not matter.

With the development of artifacts, skill acquired enduring

monuments. A well-cut ax or a well-made bowl was different
from discovery of a school of fish, or a well-laid snare for a
bird: the artifact endured, it remained observable and, therefore, if beautiful, was a continuous source of pleasure. Every
artist who makes a beautiful object increases the hopes possible to humanity; from then on men may hope to see his work.
(Conspicuously bad artists do so too—men may hope not to
see theirs.) Hopes for success and distinction were thus augmented by hopes for beauty and for a change in the quality
of daily life—perhaps also for survival. Was the ax buried with
the man so that he might live with it, or because he did live
in it? We do not know, but we may suppose that even primitive men sensed the importance of work as a form of self-
realization. The artist lives in his work and his work lives in
him. He is shaped first by the experience of making, and then
by the form he has made. Kafka seems to have become almost
as loathsome as his stories.

The domestication of animals was probably at first an expression of man's affection for them; they would not have
become domesticated had they immediately been eaten. Indeed, the eating of domesticated animals was felt as a sin at
Athens down to classical times; myths were invented to explain and excuse it. We may therefore postulate that hope for
animal companionship as well as for animal products was the
basis of shepherding and a factor in farming, which developed
about the same time (roughly 8000 B.C.) perhaps in part to
feed the animals. Of course these new objectives and the new
skills to achieve them, like all other objectives and skills, provided new fields for hope.

With flocks, herds, and grain came wealth, a new distinction
between man and man and therefore something new to hope
for. Job, who is pictured as a bedouin magnate, "had seven
thousand sheep, three thousand camels, five hundred yoke of
oxen, and five hundred she-asses, and very many servants; so
that this man was greatest of all the people of the east" (1:3).
The domestication of animals and accumulation of foodstuffs
must rapidly have been followed by the domestication of men

who, like other animals, will attach themselves to you if you feed them and thus, particularly if you get them young, can be trained to obey orders, sit, stand, and perform as directed. (The pronouncements of Cicero, Seneca, and Jefferson on man's natural and necessary liberty were written by slaveowners who were thinking, when they wrote, of themselves, not their chattels.) The picture of Job shows the patriarch as head of a single, apparently self-sufficient "family" (including domestics), but from early times there had also been more complex groupings of families in tribes, and with these had appeared a new type of rivalry and field of hope, that for social position and influence outside the family group.

With development of fixed and more populous centers of settlement—cities—the problem of regulating the relations between families or tribes became acute and at the same time the leadership of the whole community became a position of considerable importance. Hence two new hopes, one for good relations among members of the city—a general hope gradually defined in terms of friendship, loyalty, justice, charity, laws and their observance—the other for political power, whether for its own sake or for the sake of shaping and organizing the community's structure and activities, tasks which again might be hoped for either because of the pleasure of grappling with the problems or the desire of the results to be attained. The making of a society, like that of a pot, is a work of art in which the artist not only expresses, but also makes, himself.

The development of social distinctions brought to light a bipolarity of hope. We have seen that some lower animals and insects will sacrifice their immediate interests, sometimes even their lives, to care for their young, protect their herd, anthill, beehive, or the like. They are thought to act without conscious purpose or hope, but the actions so much resemble those sometimes inspired by human hope that it and they may have a common biological basis. In primitive societies now observable, and presumably in primitive man, the sacrifices made by adults for their children and for the family as a group seem on the border between such instinctive reactions and the conscious altruism found in more highly developed cultures. Many primitives seem to think of their families as personalities of which they are parts, "members" in the literal sense of the word, so that anyone who wounds or benefits any member of the family is felt by each as a personal assailant or assistant. Even in the family, it is true, as soon as differences of role or function become conscious, the members begin to have "their own" hopes as distinct from those of the rest of the group; as Ruth Nanda Anshen argued in *The Reality of the Devil,* [3] individuation is a form of alienation from the individual's society and environment. Nevertheless, it seems that in primitive families the consciousness of membership is more important than individual interests. The tribe, as an extension of the family, extends this sense of membership, but also weakens it. Group loyalty diminishes as social and political units become larger, until, in the superstates of the present, most members have little loyalty, and some are even hostile, to the organizations to which they legally "belong."

While the growth of societies thus attenuated the concern their members felt for them, it made possible new hopes for those who controlled them, and in these new hopes, to some degree, the members shared. As the cities' manpower was organized, expeditions for trade could be fielded on a scale and through an area larger than before. Agricultural operations involving great expenditures of labor, notably for irrigation, became feasible. These increased the food supply and so the stability of the social order. The surplus of food made possible more extensive efforts to control those aspects of the environment that could not be managed by ordinary means —the weather, floods and droughts, fertility of animals and crops, blights and plagues, wars, and life after death. All these were recognizedly in the hands of the gods and demons with whom primitive imagination had peopled the world. The members of this supernatural population had now to be pla-

[3] New York, 1972.

cated—men had made themselves a race of immortal masters —and it was hoped that this could be done by building them magnificent houses (temples), providing them with plentiful servants (priests) and with food, drink, clothing, and so on, to their hearts' desires. These desires it was the priests' function to discover, communicate, and, so far as possible, carry out.

With priesthood and kingship, therefore, came monumental architecture, new applications of the arts, development of ceremonies, of hymns, prayers, myths, etc., all primarily to secure the order of the state and the benevolence of the gods, but also ends in themselves and objects of hope for the artisans/artists engaged in their production, the people of the city who enjoyed the products, and the kings and priests who planned these projects and oversaw their execution. In rulers, the primitive, biological identification of personal hope and hope for the society could persist. (It still can. Persons in such positions have often felt social and religious programs, military campaigns, building projects, and the like as hopes of their own; not a few have sacrificed their lives for the success of such projects or killed themselves because of the failure. But the more complex the project, the less the ordinary citizens of the state are apt to understand and care about it; if they hope for its success at all they usually distinguish between such hope and their "real" hopes for their personal and family affairs. In contemporary terms, the complexity of the society is the source of the "alienation" of those members employed in subordinate positions, able neither to understand the large plans, nor to appreciate the need of the measures required, nor to play significant roles in their realization. They revenge themselves for inferiority by indifference.) Thus social distinction produced a distinction in hopes, the masses came to be motivated mainly by personal hopes, usually for relatively short-term objectives, at most extending to the times of their children, while some, at least, of the kings and priests were primarily concerned about their states or temples and about measures that sometimes required generations to develop and centuries to bear fruit.

This cleavage between the many living for the present and the few for the future was soon extended by inclusion in the latter class of architects, artists, and authors. The new state projects opened to architects a new hope, that of being individually remembered, like the kings and high priests with whose names their own might be perpetuated on their monumental buildings. Artists, too, could put their names on their works and did. A statue of King Djoser of Egypt, who died about 2600 B.C., carries, besides the royal inscription, a brief note commemorating "the seal-bearer of the King of Lower Egypt . . . ruler of the great house . . . the high priest of Heliopolis, Imhotep, the chief of the sculptors, of the masons, and of the producers of stone vessels."[4] Imhotep was also famous as a physician and architect, and as author of a book of precepts. The increasing complexity of society and the need of teaching its complicated system of writing provided a market for copybooks full of good advice, and these books commonly carried the names of their authors. They are the earliest expressions of the hope for literary immortality. Imhotep achieved it; indeed, he ultimately came to be worshipped as a god. He is perhaps the first named private individual of whose personality something is still known.

Imhotep's immortality depended on the survival of a class of learned men who could read his works; for these men his works made possible experiences, objects of hope, that the ignorant could not share. Thus the growth of learned literature and of complex or otherwise inaccessible forms of the other arts creates new hopes that are shared by the artists and by limited, privileged audiences, but not by the masses whose labor supports the artists, the literati, and their admirers. It may or may not be to the masses' advantage to be directed by a cultivated ruling class, but the question of advantage is not here at issue. The point here is that, for good or ill, with the development of a "higher" culture, there develops a difference between the hopes of most people and the hopes of the

---

[4] D. Wildung, *Egyptian Saints* (New York, 1977), p. 32.

few involved in the higher culture. Both groups are alienated from important aspects of their society. The workers are not concerned about the interests of the cultivated or the projects of the rulers; the "I dunno, I jus' work here" attitude develops. The cultivated take the indifference of the masses as evidence of stupidity, insensitivity, or selfishness, despise them accordingly, and are thus alienated from the majority of the people among whom they live.

How long it was before the rulers became aware of this growing discrepancy of hopes, recognized it as a danger, and decided to do something about it, we cannot tell. When they did, an obvious remedy was to involve the state in activities that would require the cooperation and engage the hopes of all classes. One of the most important of such activities, moreover, was one in which the state had long been involved for simpler and more obvious reasons—war, i.e., armed robbery by a sovereign power. This was a profitable way of putting to use the city's newly organized manpower, but it led to further social complications. Successful robbers soon realized that, if their victims were not destroyed but were left alive with enough property to sustain themselves, they could accumulate more property and be robbed again. Presently robbery was commuted to annual payment for "protection" and the robber city became the capital of an "empire." The increase of its wealth enabled it to hire more soldiers and rob further afield. Expertise and manpower made it more difficult to resist, so by about 2300 B.C. Sargon of Agade was able to claim that he ruled "from the upper sea to the lower sea" (probably from the Mediterranean to the Persian Gulf). His victories made him the archetype of "the conqueror"—a new ideal figure that shaped the hopes of innumerable later rulers. His successors took the first step toward a related figure, "the world ruler," by adding to their titles the epithet "King of the Four Quarters" (i.e., of the earth). Thus the hope of a single world government (predictably, a despotism) was born. Of course it began with those who also hoped to be the governors; they are still among its most vigorous advocates.

Once conceived, the hope for a single, universal world state had its own rationale. From the peasants' point of view it was more economical to have one set of robbers than many; from the merchants', a unified government could provide protection everywhere. Such considerations were backed up by the prestige of bigness. At the same time, however, compulsory extension of civic order generated the antithetical hope of a return to anarchy, now romantically conceived as the state of nature without its natural disadvantages—the golden age of the individuals' infancy projected into the history of society. Understandably, the hope of extended empire had most appeal for the rulers; the hope of anarchy and simplicity, for the ruled. However, neither hope was limited to one class. The man in the ancient city street usually hoped that his city would triumph and be great; romantic rulers dreamed of golden ages in which they would enjoy the good things of life without the trouble of ruling. Vergil's prophecies of a return to primitive culture were popular with the Roman aristocracy; visitors to Versailles can still see the "cottage" in which the Queen of France played at being a milkmaid.

With emergence of the hope for a world government, shortly after the Sargonid period, the historical development of human hopes seems to have come to a temporary standstill. The major societies of the Bronze Age in Mesopotamia and Egypt had reached their mature forms. For another thousand years and more they would continue to present their peoples the same set of possible hopes, modified in one way or another to accord with particular circumstances, but not essentially changed. Perhaps an exception should be made for Egypt where in the late Empire, around 1300 B.C., a great change seems to have taken place in the notion of the afterlife, which had always played a major role in the hopes of Egyptians. From a world of simple, sensuous pleasures waiting for those who had pleased the gods (those who had not were tossed to a crocodile waiting for them) it suddenly becomes a mysterious realm full of monsters to be dealt with by magic. The evidence for this change comes from the walls of the tombs, where pictures of dinners and dancing girls are replaced by enormously long serpents and longer magical screeds. This change may have had considerable importance for the later history of hope: the stories of the soul's journey and adventures in the underworld may have contributed to Christian and especially to gnostic pictures of the afterlife, and the presumable increase in the importance of magic (for which Egypt was to remain famous until modern times) may have resulted in its influence on Jesus. He was said to have learned magic in Egypt and the report is corroborated by many parallels between Gospel stories and Egyptian magical practices. But while the connection is not impossible, the details are lost and even the precise nature of the change in the picture of the afterlife remains obscure.

III

Only with the rise of Greek civilization do we meet a new set of hopes, correlative to the new forms of life that the Greeks devised. Greek originality was largely a consequence of peculiar geographical circumstances. The northern tribes who overran the southern end of the Balkan Peninsula in the late second and early first millennium B.C. conquered a country insufficient to support them, but ringed by the wine-dark, intoxicating sea and by islands beyond islands that led the voyager ever farther on. In the following centuries they conquered the islands and thence the adjacent coasts of Thrace, Turkey, Italy, and Libya. Thus they became a scattered people, a "diaspora," held together by the constant travel of many members, and in touch on many sides with many cultures. This gave them more knowledge of the world, both physical and social, than most of their neighbors; it also trained them to take a somewhat skeptical view of local taboos and traditions that had no obvious justification. "The Persians say [this] . . . the Phoenicians say [that]." By the mid-fifth century Herodotus was willing to go on, "But I shall neither vouch for nor contradict either of these opinions but shall begin with what I myself know for fact" (I:1–5). He hopes to find out the truth for himself, and calls his great work *Investigations*, though thanks to him the word he used has come to mean *Histories*. Historical writing, defined as "recording reported events", is far older than Herodotus, but his is the earliest preserved work known to have resulted from historical *research*, the implementation of the hope to find out what really did happen.

The diaspora in its later stage had grown chiefly by colonization. Colonization involves planning, a colony is a planned society. From planning for an actual colony to planning an ideal society is a short step. It was taken in the mid-fifth century by Hippodamus of Miletus (who also planned an Athenian colony to which Herodotus went in his later years). Hippodamus unknowingly created not only a particular state and pattern for states, but a pattern for hopes, a way in which men might pinpoint their discontents with the present world, define their hopes for a better one, and calculate practically what would have to be done to meet their objections and satisfy their wishes. By such specification and calculation they might see to what extent their proposals were contradictory or otherwise unfeasible, and so might approach the problems of actual states with a clearer understanding of what they hoped for. From Hippodamus the tradition of utopias rose rapidly to the peaks of Plato's *Republic* and *Laws*, less than a century later.

This speculative development was complemented by the greater achievements of the Greeks in actual politics. The basis of these achievements is commonly supposed to have been a new military technique, the use of a solid line of heavily armored infantry (spearmen) as a decisive factor in battles. Since the men had to contribute their own armor and weapons (which were costly) and since the ability to use heavy armor and weapons and to maneuver simultaneously required good physical condition and constant training (for which the average worker had no time), the development of this technique shifted control of the cities from the former kings to elite corps of wealthy citizens and their adult sons. (A man was liable for military service from eighteen to fifty, so fathers and sons sometimes fought side by side.) When differences arose among these citizens, each appealed for support to his own followers in the citizen body, roughly speaking, the rest of the army and the men too old to fight. In assemblies of the citizens it became customary to settle disputes by majority vote, the settlements being made acceptable by tacit understanding that the victorious side would not press its advantage too far—there were some things the winners could not do, things prohibited by what was in effect an uncodified set of constitutional laws. Prominent among the disputes settled in this way were those for tenure of the chief offices (including the chief priesthoods) which thus gradually became elective, while minor disputes between individuals were settled by smaller groups with powers delegated by the assembly, in effect juries. Thus public election of officials, a constitution limiting their authorities, decision of important public questions by majority vote of the citizens, and trial by a jury of one's fellow citizens, in sum, the foundations of what we call "democratic government," were all developed (most of them for the first time in human history) in Greece between the years 800 and 500 B.C., not as a result of hope for the system they came to constitute, but by many *ad hoc,* practical settlements of individual disputes about one question or another. Once the system had been constituted, it was recognized as a coherent whole, a peculiar way of political life. Its perpetuation was a center of Greek hopes for seven hundred years and has for the past two centuries been one of the greatest hopes of the western world.

One of the causes of this constitutional development was the individualism of the Greeks, which again was connected with their geographic distribution. In the loose and expanding Greek diaspora with its constant travel among a thousand little cities, most of them self-governing and many in need of manpower, a man did not have to stay where he had been born. He could go where he chose, win acceptance for what he could do, and be proud of himself, not his ancestors. In an alien city he would probably never acquire the rights of a citizen, but he might acquire enough wealth to be important and respected. Many were. Others, fortunate enough to have creditable ancestors and good positions in their native towns, were proud of these. As the elite corps pushed out the former kings, the rivalries of their members for the leading places in the cities became intense. This spirit of competition was communicated to all members of the society, the more so because cities were generally poor and competition was cutthroat. Hence "one potter is the rival of another," said Hesiod, in the the sequel to the verses quoted above, "and one builder of another, and beggar envies beggar, and poet, poet." We have archeological evidence that such rivalry was more intense in Greece than it had been in previous civilizations: signatures on artifacts, especially on pottery, extremely rare in the Bronze Age, now became common. This was not merely a consequence of the introduction of the alphabet, a more convenient form of writing, which made literacy generally accessible. The Phoenicians had the alphabet, too, indeed, they taught it to the Greeks, and they, too, were a people who lived largely by manufacturing for trade, but almost none of their artifacts are signed. The Greek craftsman had more pride in himself and in his work, he hoped to be known by it and remembered for it. The same held, *a fortiori*, for artists of more important works, especially sculptors, painters, and architects. In the Bronze Age Imhotep and the few like him had been isolated exceptions, but now "the great artist" becomes a familiar social type, a new objective for the hopes of the gifted boy. The same thing happens, too, in literature. "Wisdom literature" continues to offer the hope of immortality; the form is recast and individualized by Hesiod and Theognis, but the old aspiration is retained. Moreover, it now finds expression in other forms. There had always been some lyric poetry. "Love songs appear in every age," said Heine, "as violets in every Spring." The same could be said of drinking songs, songs of workmen, religious lyrics, and so on. But a body of lyric poems on various subjects, known as "the poems of" a single person and written as expressions of that person's skill, thoughts, and moods—no such thing has come down to us from any earlier culture.

After the upper class council and the citizen assembly, the most important social center for expression of this new individualism was the gymnasium, another creation of Greek genius. Its importance arose from the necessity of physical training for the new military technique, but the Greeks made it also a tool for education and a means of gratifying their love of contests, of leisure, of talk, and of beauty. On the physical side, the importance attributed to athletic contests not only made victory in them the greatest hope of thousands of young Greeks (not to mention their fathers, uncles, friends, etc.) but also led to the development of a new profession, the training of athletes, which was closely connected with the rise of rational medicine. Basic was a new hope—that by observing the consequences of various diets, regimens, and courses of exercise, one could learn to select those best suited for a particular purpose.

It was individualism and pride in their bodies that led the Dorians first to exercise naked. It was love of beauty that persuaded the rest of the Greeks to follow their example, gave the gymnasium its name (from *gymnos,* "naked"), made it the afternoon club of the well-to-do, the center of leisurely discussion, and consequently an instrument for intellectual as well as physical education of the boys and young men who there were brought into conversation with their elders. Among these elders were the artists; the gymnasium contributed greatly to the Greeks' development of a new art, above all a new plastic art formed by a new hope—to communicate the four-dimensional reality of the body, to present it not as a flat picture, but as a solid and moving object. This hope, although occasionally obscured, remained the most pervasive element in western plastic art until World War II. Even now, it lives on; the human body has some strange appeal for human beings.

The Greeks who frequented the gymnasia were not insensitive to this appeal; the conversations begun there rapidly developed into homosexual love affairs of which Greek cities were remarkably tolerant. (Many of the lovers came from the elite corps of the army and the army was necessary for the city's survival.) The cities' tolerance made possible a new freedom in expression of the diverse forms of human sexual life, and many Greeks came to believe that both men and women have two sides to their characters, passive and dominant, and that both of these may properly prevail in turn—a boy if loved by a man may properly return his love, as would a girl; a woman may properly make love to, and be loved by a girl, as might a man. This notion reflected the hopes of millions of persons throughout antiquity, as it does today, but the Greek expressions of it were socially unique and became classical. In consequence of them, intimate friendship with a man became a recognized part of a Greek boy's education, and with the new acceptance of this extension of sexual activity the hopes of individuals changed accordingly, each interpreting the newly possible relationship according to his own temperament, some as an opportunity for sensual pleasure, others, for ambition or affection or instruction or influence, Plato, as an image of man's desire for disembodied beauty.

The notion that an individual might have more than one role had been fostered from time immemorial by storytelling and its gratification of the (often subconscious) hopes of the audience. As soon as the storyteller says, "Once upon a time there was a prince," the little boys in his audience subconsciously say, "That's me," and look forward to killing the big old ogre. Now the Greeks found a way of making storytelling more vivid—the theater. The stories were not only told but acted out, with the characters represented by persons dressed to suit their parts. Staging was rudimentary, but even this primitive illusionism enabled many citizens to identify themselves with the characters, gratify their hopes for other lives than their own, and live out in imagination the consequences of other, hidden hopes that they would not have acknowledged even to themselves.

Both theatrical performances and homosexual attachments had an incidental advantage—they did something to educate the adult men: they forced them to face the profound philosophic questions that great dramatists and adolescents persistently ask, and they gave them more oportunities to indulge their Greek passion for argument. The passion now had a practical side: given the development of trial by jury, ability to argue might be a matter of life and death. Teachers of argument ("sophists") were thriving. Nothing seemed safe from question. Out of this crisis came Socratic philosophy—the expression of a hope for clarity, for clear definition, precise discussion, a habit of mind that carefully scrutinizes suppositions and ruthlessly insists on exposing their implications.

Gymnasium, theater, and philosophy were alike manifestations of a new hope characteristic of Greek culture, the hope of taking leisure seriously. The leisure of earlier societies, if recorded at all, is shown as devoted to eating, drinking, and merrymaking; dances and an occasional tug-of-war, footrace, or the like appear on Egyptian tomb paintings; hunting is common—but is it for business, or pleasure? Both. But apart from it there is little constructive use of leisure, the sort of things that made the gymnasium so important. This constructive use of leisure also appears in the odes of Pindar celebrating the victors of the great "games"—the Panhellenic athletic contests which were among the chief Greek festivals. Pindar's purpose is *at once* "to delight and to instruct," as Dr. Johnson said, not so much to impart information as to shape the characters of his hearers by the simultaneous impact of the majesty of his thought and the beauty of his expression. The same notion again dominates classic drama—even Aristophanes' ribald comedies have serious didactic purpose. Much Greek art has the same inspiration, and the new architecture—in the service of the citizens, as architecture never was before—creates not only assembly places, law courts, and porticoes for the transaction of business, but theaters, music halls, stadia (all of these being architectural forms hitherto unknown) as expressions of the belief that leisure is a proper concern of the state, and of the hope that it may be a means, not only of relaxation, but of recreation, a form of adult education that teaches by pleasure. Huxley put his finger on the point in *Brave New World:* one basic requirement in his hedonistic nightmare was that leisure should be used exclusively for infantile pleasures. Before Greece, there is little evidence that it was used for anything else. The hope for a *whole* life, a life not split into irrelevant segments of work and play connected only by their occurence in the same body, but bound together by the constant exercise of will and intelligence, like a work of Greek art, as a single, harmonious *whole*—this hope is first suggested by the sculpture, painting, and literature of Greece. Pericles is said to have held it and to have claimed that in Athens it was realized (Thucydides II, 34–46).

Wo viel Licht ist, ist viel Schatten. The creation of an implicitly constitutional government based on the consent of the citizens made possible the hope of overriding it. The tyrant appears as a new social type (though with an old name: *tyrannos* originally referred to any absolute ruler). The stories told of many tyrants suggest that they were motivated by sadistic hopes, not only by ordinary avarice and ambition. Every civilization, by the mere fact of existing as a manifest achievement of order, must provide a target for the sadistic, those who find pleasure in destroying others' achievements because they hate their own failures. A beautiful statue or building in a public place will be defaced by those who hate beauty because of their own ugliness. All who delight in destroying others' works are parasitic on the workers who provide them with opportunities for satisfaction. Thus each advance in civilization, each development of a new form of production or realization of a new aspect of beauty, offers new opportunities for vandalism, new hopes for the sadistic. It is therefore not surprising that sadists (including vandals) have become more common in western society, but they have particularly increased in recent years as we have taken more care to assure the survival of those for whom it would have been better not to have survived.

Fortunately civilization makes possible not only rejection, but also further development. Specifically, the appearance of government with consent produced the tyrant on one side, on the other the statesman who had the skill, without violating the freedom of his fellow citizens, to persuade them to act in the ways he perceived to be best for the interest of the state. Thucydides, who created political history and so gave mankind a new hope (of understanding its own political life), also created the statesman as an ideal, by his portrait of Pericles. The importance of this portrait as an object of hope can scarcely be overestimated; it shaped generations of politicians, perhaps even more in the modern than in the ancient world. The British Empire was so well governed because the upper class boys believed what they were taught in Dr. Arnold's school, and tried to realize the ideal in their own lives. There were great British statesmen because British politicians had been taught what great statesmen were, and hoped to be like them. By contrast, one of the chief dangers to our own society arises from the failure of contemporary education to provide socially useful ideals. It's always easier to debunk, and it sells better; but when education and entertainment are devoted to debunking, children are left with no notions of what they might want to be—except, of course, heroic debunkers —and no society can be run by debunking.

Even Pericles was far from perfect; the politicians who succeeded him did more to deserve censure and therefore resented it more. The conflict between critical thought and practical politics came to a head in 399 B.C. when Socrates was condemned and executed for "corrupting young men," i.e., for teaching them to question accepted opinions and cross-question influential politicians. Warned by Socrates' fate, his pupil Plato carried on his philosophic teaching behind the façade of a private religious society dedicated to the worship of the Muses. By leaving his estate for the support of this society he created the world's earliest endowed institution for philosophic research,[5] an object for practical, worldly loyalties and hopes. His philosophy is instinct with the hope of a unified, consistent explanation of the objective world, both physical and intellectual, and of man as part of the world. This is a great extension of the hope of most earlier Greek "philosophers," who aspired only to arrive at a consistent explanation of the physical world, but it also goes beyond the hope of Socrates, who abandoned "natural philosophy" (as the physical sciences would later be called) and devoted himself to ethical questions. While the goals of Plato and Socrates are still beyond our reach, the hopes of the natural philosophers have been largely realized and their realization has made modern civilization possible.

These earlier philosophers are known to us mainly through the works of Plato and his followers (including Aristotle), so we have only glimpses of other important hopes they may have launched—notably the Pythagorean dream of a semi-secret religious society of which the more advanced members would live lives partly cut off from the world and devoted to occult studies, while the junior members, under their influence, would be active in politics. Pythagoreanism had some attraction for Plato. Socrates had already set an example by rejecting the behavioral standards of his society, neglecting his own economic interests, and consequently living as a poor eccentric. But he was by no means withdrawn from the world. His involvement cost him his life and so led to Plato's withdrawal. The Pythagoreans may have provided the model, but Plato could take seriously neither their peculiar rules nor most of their speculations. He dropped the rules, retained the speculations (when at all) mainly for their poetic value as images, and justified his own withdrawal by his picture of the soul's escape from concern with material images and ascent towards reality by contemplation of true forms (ideas). Enjoyment of this contemplative life (variously interpreted)

[5] As distinct from temple schools, which were to perpetuate traditional practices.

becomes from his time on the hope of many students of philosophy.

Other varieties of the philosophic hope were developed both by Plato's students and by his opponents. Aristotle laid the foundations of systematic and universal scientific knowledge by substituting, for Plato's shadowy world of ideas, detailed studies of one field of knowledge after another. He thus effectively transformed the philosophic life into the life of scholarship. Diogenes on the contrary dropped intellectual concerns, identified the goal of philosophy as the greatest possible independence from the requirements both of society and of nature, and equated the practice of philosophy with the ascetic discipline by which he thought this independence could be attained. What the philosopher was to do, after attaining it (other than demonstrate it by shocking and insulting his neighbors) he never made clear, but by his example and popular success—thanks to his brilliant wit— he won a recognized place in society for antisocial types who appealed to him as their teacher. Epicurus and Zeno took the same tack, but with more concern for intellectual justification and less emphasis on conspicuous practices, whether ascetic or merely impolite. Nevertheless, all three have independence as their ultimate goal, differ basically in their opinions as to how and how far it can be acquired, and agree in being concerned about cosmology, if at all, only as a means to independence, and in equating mere, independent human life with happiness. This basic optimism as to human nature, the notion that if a man were free of outside distractions he would then find himself happy and at peace, has some appeal to the psychologically healthy, and more to the sick but superficial who want to blame their condition on anything but themselves. Consequently Cynicism (from Diogenes), Stoicism (from Zeno), and Epicureanism are perennial forms of human hope, though often as attitudes instinctively adopted by persons ignorant of their classic expressions and implications.

Those classic expressions, however, did more than merely

defend the tacit assumptions and work out the consequences of the attitudes represented. Like the philosophies
of Plato, Aristotle, Pythagoras, and some other Greek thinkers, they provided directions for peculiar ways of life, objects of hope which, if realized, would make the philosopher
a man apart from the society around him, primarily a member of a small sect or class of fellow believers, those who
also knew the truth and lived according to it. Such hope for
acute alienation from society was not a new thing. From
time immemorial "medicine men" of various sorts—priests,
shamans, and so on—had gone outside the society, into the
wilds or the temples, for initiations, and had returned to live
peculiar lives, either alone or in groups, as representatives
of alien powers. Later on a series of historical accidents
would make an entire people, the Jews, self-isolated representatives of one such peculiar discipline. Antiquity knew of
several other such peoples or tribes of "philosophers", as
they were called—the Brahmins, the Magi, and so on. Many
were yet to arise. But the peculiarity of the Greek philosophical schools was that the knowledge setting their members
apart was to a large extent rational. It therefore could lead
to rational criticism and remodeling of the structures of the
surrounding society. In this respect the philosophic schools
presented extreme cases of the peculiar form of alienation
produced by the development of scientific knowledge. The
scientist's hope for knowledge and devotion to research
alienate him from most of his contemporaries, and their lack
of these alienates them from him. As the increased knowledge of philosophers and other scientists enables them to
plan social changes and entire new societies designed to realize their own intellectual goals, the more ancient gap between rulers and subjects is complicated by a new fission,
between rulers and intelligentsia. This is potentially far
more serious than the earlier alienation of the artists and
literati; but only with the scientific revolution of the past two
centuries and the consequent emergence of scientists as key
figures in society did the potential become clear.

Finally to this review of the new forms of hope created by the Greeks, we should add the revival, by Alexander the Great, of the old form of world conqueror. There had been no previous "world conqueror" in Greek history or myth. Zeus' defeat of his opponents was told as a battle for the citadel of the gods on Mt. Olympus; it resulted in his rule of the world, but there was no early legend of extensive conquests. Greeks may have known the legendary figure of the world conqueror through their contacts with Persia, but they rejected the Persians as barbaric and were contemptuous of them, as defeated. Now, suddenly, Alexander made the world conqueror a living figure in Greek thought, a hope he had almost realized and a hope that would continue to tempt great political leaders from his time to the present, often to their own destruction: Crassus, Mark Antony, Julian the Apostate, Napoleon, Hitler.

If we now look back over this section to summarize what the Greeks did by way of extending the range of human hopes, we must allow for three facts: (1) extension need not be a matter of absolute novelty; e.g., although a few Bronze Age artists signed their works in hope of immortality, the general practice that appears in Greek society indicates a great extension of hope; (2) when research reveals in earlier cultures long lost traces of traits later famous as Greek innovations, we must remember that the Greek achievement, not the lost anticipation, became the model for the western world; (3) the preceding account is an outline, specifying only the most conspicuous matters; additions could easily be found.

These facts premised, the changes in hope effected by the Greeks can be summarized as follows: First, the range of pleasures that the ordinary citizen might hope for was enormously increased. Not to mention the newly permissive political practices and sexual mores, there was a great extension of entertainment for spectators—gymnasia, games, theaters, orations, displays by sophists, discussions by philosophers, the constant spectacle of the masterpieces of the new art and architecture. All these were accessible to the average man, accordingly extended the hopes of everyday life, and by their intellectual content and educational function were of such importance to that life as to make it potentially a harmonious whole. Second, the class of persons who might hope for things beyond the common pleasures of daily life was greatly increased. Not only could artists working in minor forms now hope for fame, but ordinary citizens could hope for distinction in government, athletes, in games, performers, in dramas; ordinary lovers of all sorts could clothe their affairs with the passions of the poets; the common grouch could hope to realize true Stoicism, or Cynic freedom. In the third place, the variety of goals that might be hoped for was also increased. All new techniques offered new hopes of excellence and consequent distinction. Especially important, besides the civic offices, were the professions; now, for the first time, one could hope to be a famous trainer of athletes, sophist, orator, statesman, city planner, philosopher, historian, scientist. The outline of the intellectual world was now discovered (as that of the physical world was to be discovered by Columbus and his successors), its many areas were open for exploration, and the explorers were led not only by the hope of fame but also by the hopes of learning, understanding, and using their understanding for new creations. This multiplication of goals yet further increased the number of persons who hoped to attain one or another. Finally, a good number of these goals were not merely particular objectives, but involved more or less new types of life, e.g., that of the traveling professional—trainer, doctor, sophist, poet, philosopher. Particularly important was the formation of new social groups to make new sorts of life possible: The Pythagoreans, the Platonic Academy, the Aristotelian Lyceum, the Epicureans. These show the beginnings of a sharp divergence of the hopes of intellectuals from those of their societies. Some also foster the hope of a coherent, *rational,* explanation of the world as a whole.

IV

Hopes dependent on achievement are encouraged mainly by those able to achieve—lawyers and doctors interest the young in their professions, scholars in scholarship, craftsmen in the various crafts, and so on. All such teachers depend on support by their societies, which provide the stable conditions necessary for teaching and the respect and other rewards for achievement that incline the young to learn. Even our devoted teachers of criminal practices could never have achieved their present stupendous success without their loyal supporting staff of corrupt police, lawyers, judges, and wardens, idealistic sociologists, and mercenary writers, actors, and motion picture and television producers, who have cooperated in assuring the young that a criminal's life is enjoyable, adventurous, gallant, even heroic, relatively safe, and enormously lucrative.

It was the diminution of such social support that led to the great change in the hopes of many Greeks during the centuries following Alexander's death. The cities could no longer provide the security and importance that had previously rewarded civic achievements. The new hellenistic kingdoms, far greater organizations than even the Athenian "empire", dwarfed to insignificance the average citizen's possible achievements. Even if he lived in a free city, his fate might depend on the actions of these kingdoms. Within them men were governed arbitrarily by rulers they had no part in choosing and no hope to control. At the same time, these kingdoms spread a veneer of Greek language and manners over many near easterners who had little acquaintance with traditional Greek culture and less hope of distinguishing themselves in the new society of Macedonian monarchs and Greek bureaucrats. Of course most people went on, as best they could, doing as they were accustomed. Hopes are mainly for day-to-day matters determined by the opportunities—people, property, jobs, markets—that happen to be available; the young want more of what they can see, the old fear change. These facts are the foundation of human society. But the relatively few men and women for whom day-to-day concerns were not enough began in the course of hellenistic and Roman times to turn more often to hopes that did not depend on achievement, but were said to be available to all adherents of one god or another, often gods from some near eastern country—Isis of Egypt and her son Harpocrates, Yahweh of Judea and his son Jesus, Cybele of Phrygia and her consort Attis, and so on.

The variety of hopes offered by such gods was enormous (it ranged from cures for gonorrhea to eternal beatitude) and the change from hope for achievement to hope for salvation was slow: almost six hundred and fifty years elapsed between the death of Alexander in 323 B.C. and the effectual triumph of Christianity with Constantine's defeat of Licinius in A.D. 324. But, looking at the period as a whole, one can see the gradual rise to importance of three types of hope which in the ages before Alexander had been relatively insignificant.

The first of these types was that called "eschatological"—hopes for the end (Greek, *to eschaton*) of the present world order, or of the world itself, and the beginning of a new age or world in which things would be more to the tastes of the hopeful. The roots of this went back to the Bronze Age, when Sargon's conquests first created the image of the world conqueror and the hope of a single kingdom to rule the whole earth, while experience with imperial administration created the hope of a new golden age when administration would be no more, a return to the imagined infancy of society. At some time and place unknown to us these antithetical hopes were combined in the dream of a righteous world ruler whose reign would see not only the universal administration of justice, but also radical changes in the course and condition of human life, usually the flowering of virtue (so that the universal administration of justice would be bearable, and irresistible government would be complemented by free obedience). This combination is adumbrated in texts attributed to Jeremiah (active about 626–586 B.C.) and in "Second Isaiah" (Isa. 40–

55, written about 540 B.C.); it appears fully developed in Jewish apocalyptic works of the late Persian and hellenistic periods. Second Isaiah anticipated not only conquest of the world by Cyrus of Persia (whom he thought Yahweh's Messiah), but also conversion of all peoples to the worship of Yahweh. These two forms of hope for universal dominion, religious and political, remained closely connected till the end of World War II. "Jesus shall reign where'er the sun never sets on the British Empire." He was all but metrically equivalent with Queen Victoria. When in the French Revolution the advocates of "liberty, equality, fraternity," took over the ideal they also took over, from both Christian and political tradition, the hope of its compulsory realization. The "natives" of Europe were to be converted, whether they liked it or not, and the spread of the French gospel was presently effected by French armies and followed by the establishment of the French empire. Communism, too, appropriated the notions of world rule and compulsory conversion. From these the Russian and Chinese empires have emerged, each having its own version of the Marxist gospel to which all mankind is to be converted. Let us hope they end by trying to convert each other.

As to the dates and details of mankind's destined bliss, innumerable variations have been proposed. Both Jesus and Marx hoped for it within the lifetime of their contemporaries. Prophets less sanguine adopted another device to secure its benefits—it might not come in their time, but when it did come, they and all the righteous would be raised bodily from the dead to enjoy it. (The sadistic had the wicked raised, too, for eternal punishment.) Proposed physical changes vary from minute revisions of the present natural order to complete destruction of this galaxy and creation of a new one. Constitutional details are equally various. Sometimes the righteous ruler is replaced by, or equated with, God Himself. The Marxists promise an equal miracle—all government will wither away. These fancies do not affect the essential character of the hope, which is less for a new order than for the cessation of the present one. Pictures of actual life in the future age are extremely rare. Most prophecies concentrate on destruction of the present world and especially of its rulers; the glory of the new age is foreseen, and with its beginning the vision prudently ends. Evidently discontent with the present is a more important factor in this sort of hope than is desire for the future.

The second type of hope that greatly increased in importance during the centuries between Alexander and Constantine was that for life after death. Again this hope did not begin with Alexander's time—indeed, it long antedates history, if the prehistoric practice of burying men with the equipment needed for life can be taken as evidence of the hope that they will somehow revive or continue to live. Egyptian culture, particularly, seems to have been dominated by the hope of a future life (though the evidence may be somewhat misleading because most of it is funerary and most of the burials are upper class). The ancient Etruscans, too, and some of the other peoples peripheral to the sphere of Greco-Roman civilization seem to have been animated by vivid hopes of life after death; in India such hope became one of the presuppositions on which the whole structure of the civilization was built. But in ancient Greece and Israel either good fortune or good sense pushed such expectations into the background. The authors of the Old Testament say almost nothing about the dead, and what little they do say is mostly contemptuous and hostile. (Incidentally, this attitude does not seem to have destroyed either their hopes or their morality, though some Catholic writers assure us that these are impossible without belief in personal survival.) In Greece there were various ceremonies, both public and private, that were said to guarantee the recipient a happy life hereafter. Most famous were the Eleusinian mysteries which were part of the established religion of Athens. However, the lower classes, who believed in the efficacy of such rites, were relieved by them from fear of the future, while the upper classes, who were skeptical about the rites' efficacy, were even more skeptical about survival after death, so the subject was of relatively small importance in classical Greek culture (in spite of Plato's emotional plea for immortality of the soul). As Greek civilization gradually prevailed in the lands around the Mediterranean, men's hopes were centered more and more on life in the present world, this not only because of Greek skepticism about the future life, but also because Greek culture, being richer and more various than those it replaced, gave men more to hope for here and now. Lucretius' passionate attack on fear of postmortal punishment stands out as an exception, unjustified by most data from its time and probably to be explained from the author's personal abnormality. Epicurus, of whom he was the professed disciple, was more concerned about prudent management of the present life than about the fear of death; when he does treat of the latter his purpose most often is to dispel the fear of *dying,* not the fear of what may happen after it.

It is impossible here even to sketch the multiple steps by which the predominantly this-worldly attitude characteristic of hellenistic times and republican Rome was gradually replaced by that of the later Roman empire which saw in this life, as one rabbi said, "only the vestibule of the world to come." The change was not solely due to the triumph of Christianity. If anything, the triumph of Christianity owed more to the change, which created an attitude that Christianity could appeal to better than could most other cults. Moreover, Christianity itself changed with the times; the orientation of Paul and the Gospels, especially their earlier elements, is far more this-worldly than is that of many "fathers of the Church" in the fourth and fifth centuries. And Judaism, paganism, and philosophy underwent similar changes. For such a general change of the focus of men's hopes, and consequently of the theories by which they sought to justify them, we must look for some general cause, and the most likely is the social and economic history of the Mediteranean world.

When Augustus put an end to the civil wars of the late Roman republic and established an apparently unshakable order throughout the whole, now-Roman "world," his adherents were able to represent his achievement as the fulfillment of the eschatological prophecies that had before been circulated, and of the hopes they had aroused. Consequently such expectations declined. The worst thing for hope is fulfillment. Those who found the new order unsatisfactory but probably permanent turned for consolation to hope of some future life. The security of the social order encouraged the development of such hope, for it made one's future in this world foreseeable. Hope depends on an element of uncertainty in the future, as well as on social stability sufficient to encourage planned action. At the one extreme, complete chaos makes planning impossible and hope difficult. At the other, when the established order is so secure that there is no chance of its being overturned save by divine intervention, and when expectations of divine intervention are conspicuously disappointed, as they were in the great Jewish revolts of A.D. 66–70 and 132–34, then hope, like Astraea, takes flight for the heavens, and death begins to be seen not as the end of life, but as the door to the soul's heavenly home. In a world orderly and predictable, death is the first event of unforeseeable consequences, and therefore the first opportunity for significant hope. Again, as in the case of eschatology, the hope was primarily for a change from the present order, not for some specific future state. Pictures of heaven were even rarer and sketchier than descriptions of "the world to come." The life after death, like "the Messianic age," was not *something that* men hoped for, so much as it was *not this*. The *not this* was the real object of their hopes. They wanted out.

By contrast with these two types of hope for escape from this world, the third hope that rose to prominence in the centuries between Alexander and Constantine was for mastery of this world by supernatural powers. Here again the roots were ancient. Men supposed to enjoy such powers— magicians of various sorts—are found in most primitive societies and had been known in the Greek and Israelite traditions from remote antiquity. In Greek they came to be called "divine men"; the Israelite term most nearly equivalent was "prophet," which meant a man able not only to foretell the future and declare the wishes of his god, but also to do miracles: cause drought, bring rain, send plagues, heal sickness, even raise the dead. Different societies or different groups within a single society often have different theories as to how such supernatural powers are attained. Some speak of the miracles as individual favors done by the gods; others say the man has been given "the spirit," or has in one way or another got control of a spirit; others say he has changed his own nature, or realized the powers latent in his nature, so as to become himself a god. All these (and other) terminologies refer to a single set of facts—that some men have extraordinary powers over others, can command their obedience, use them as agents, cause them to see visions, cure or kill them by mere words. Such power often goes with remarkable prescience and extraordinary knowledge of what is in others' minds.

These abilities, if thought to be gifts of the gods, offered a way of escape from the established order, a way available to men whose other achievements were not sufficient to get them what they wanted. But here matters become complicated. As philosophy began to develop in Greece, several persons gifted with such powers became philosophers. Such were probably Pythagoras and certainly Empedocles, whose poems, claiming miraculous powers, demanding worship, and declaring, "I am present among you, no longer as a man, but as a god," have been preserved. Socrates, too, seems to have had something of such power—extraordinary control of other persons, ability to read their thoughts and to foresee what should be avoided (as Plato admits) and what should be done (as Xenophon claims).[6] It is said that he sometimes heard voices or saw forms (Greek *eide*, "ideas") and stood as one possessed, indifferent to the surrounding world. His devotion to this abnormal power was the basis for one of the

---

[6] Plato, *Apology* 21 B; 31 C–D; 33 C. Contrast Xenophon, *Memorabilia* I.1.3–4.

charges on which he was convicted, "He recognizes not the gods recognized by the city, but other new divinities."[7] The example of Socrates set the pattern for subsequent philosophers. Cynics, Epicureans, and Stoics successively used the language appropriate to the "divine man" to praise the freedom from the world and consequent bliss that they promised to those who would follow their teachings. Epicurus, indeed, provided in his will for the establishment of his own cult as a hero, and was revered by some of his followers (including Lucretius) as a god. All this was in obvious contradiction of their philosophic principles. Therefore it is probably to be explained, not only by the influence of the legend of Socrates, but also by the hope to appeal to a side of Mediterranean popular opinion that looked for "divine men" to reverence. Similar appeals were made by politicians who organized the worship of the Greek kings, by military men (beginning with Alexander and including Hannibal and Scipio Africanus) who encouraged belief in their divinity or supernatural powers, by mythographers who remodeled the legends of old heroes such as Hercules and Asclepius along these lines, and by popular magicians and prophets, some of whom became leaders of important political and/or religious movements, among them Christianity.[8]

The philosophers' takeover of these claims to supernatural powers made salvation, conceived as freedom from the world, something allegedly available at once. Jesus reportedly made similar promises to his disciples. They were to remain in him as he was in the Father; they would know the truth and the truth would make them free (Jn. 8:32; 15:4; 17:21). Accordingly, as imperial order closed down on the Roman world, men hoping for power to become independent of this order

---

[7] Plato, *loc. cit.* That this refers to his *daimonion* is proved by Xenophon, *Memorabilia* I.1.2. For the seizure and vision, see the story in the *Symposium,* where Plato tries, as usual, to explain away the supernatural side of Socrates.

[8] See M. Smith, "On the History of the 'Divine Man'," in *Paganisme, Judaïsme, Christianisme (Mélanges . . . Simon)* (Paris, 1978), pp. 335 ff., and *Jesus the Magician* (New York, 1978).

turned to philosophy and to Christianity. In the letters of Paul (our earliest Christian documents, a generation prior to the Gospels) we already find the three forms of Christian hope side by side and even in competition. Paul not only hopes for the coming end of this world and the beginning of the Messianic age, he is also torn between the hope to die and be at once with Christ (Phil. 1:23), and that to continue his ministry, which is the triumphant manifestation of the life of Jesus in, and in spite of, his mortal body (II Cor. 3:5 ff.). Moreover, it is clear from what Paul writes of his opponents and from the care he takes to insist that he has not yet attained full salvation, that there were other members of the early Christian movement who went far beyond him in claiming immediate salvation and the present enjoyment of supernatural powers. Both they and he promised their followers such powers and at least a foretaste of salvation—"the downpayment of the spirit" which God gives in advance as evidence and guarantee of what is yet to come. Even more spectacular claims were made by philosophers and magicians. Apollonius of Tyana, a contemporary of Paul, claimed to be a god on earth. Two "Chaldean" magicians who were fashionable in the court of Marcus Aurelius practiced a set of ceremonies believed to confer divinity here and now. The obscure poems in which they set forth their theories, the so-called *Chaldean Oracles*, became in effect the Bible of Neoplatonism, the most influential form of philosophy in the later Roman Empire. Some philosophers and magicians were among the most savage enemies of Christianity; when the Christians finally attained power the practice of theosophic rites was made a capital crime.

Thus there was literally cutthroat competition between the peddlers of immediate salvation, as between those of future worlds and various happy hereafters. In this competition Christianity won out for a variety of reasons, but mainly because it was best able to appeal to the practical, short-term hopes of ordinary people of the middle and lower classes, whose necessarily down-to-earth lives limited the importance

of their occasional dreams of divinity. What they most hoped
for were interest-free loans, some sort of health insurance
that would guarantee support and care during sickness, assurance of care in old age or in event of major disability, education for their children, funds to pay for their own funerals
(then as now important occasions of conspicuous waste), care
for their widows and orphans, cheap and just arbitration of
their disputes with each other, and, above all, simply "care,"
membership in a family-for-adults that would replace the family they had relied on in childhood, a circle whose members
could be trusted to help and protect one another, keep each
other's secrets, give each other their business, and use to each
other's advantage whatever influence they had. Christianity
partly took over from Judaism, partly developed for itself, a
type of community organization that offered all these services.
As a network of such communities, essentially a society of
mutual-benefit societies, it spread through the Roman world.
Among the philosophers and magicians, only Epicureanism
had any considerable development of this sort, but its appeal
was mainly to the upper classes and the wealthy, who could
rely on their own means and were therefore less attracted by
such services. Of the competing religious cults which offered
similar spiritual blessings here and hereafter, none developed
so early a comparable social organization.[9] The reasons for
their failure would take us too far afield; the important thing
was Christianity's success. Its unique offering of fulfillment
for everyday, practical hopes together with the hopes of present regeneration and future salvation enabled it, in spite of
being legally prohibited, to plant colony after colony
throughout the empire and eventually to win toleration from
the rulers, then official acceptance, then the prohibition and
destruction of most of its rivals.

Perhaps in this development the criminality of Christianity
was an advantage. Among the strongest bonds of children's

[9]Mithraism and Manichaeanism may later have done so, but by the time they did,
Christianity had taken over most of the market.

gangs is the sense of participation in defying the parents. This continues—parents replaced by civil authorities—in juvenile gangs and organizations of adult criminals where the camaraderie is further strengthened by awareness of common danger, of the dependence of all on the secrecy, the faithfulness, the "brotherhood" of each. Consequently it is not surprising that the most publicized of contemporary criminal movements is organized in "families." Indeed, the failure of criminal organizations to achieve (thus far) a recognized social position comparable to that attained by ancient Christianity is probably due less to the public's loyalty to legality than to the inability of the criminal leaders to cooperate, and their lack of any significant hopes (other than gang membership, adventure, neighborhood prestige, and financial profit) to offer their followers. Most of those commonly said to be leaders, like those of the labor unions with whom they are often in cahoots, seem to be men risen from the ranks, with little education and consequently little interest in matters outside their proper business, which is merely making money. What they will do with the money is a question each answers according to his private hopes, usually for personal pleasures, occasionally for respectability, but never, it seems, for any goal that could engage the hopes of his followers. Behind the superficial mystique of membership in a criminal organization there lies only a business. You might as well work for ITT or IBM. Christianity, by contrast, held together and was eventually able to take over and transform the state because it was a mutual-benefit organization that claimed to secure for its members not only short-term personal advantages, but also supernatural powers in this world, life after death, and enjoyment of the world to come. To support these claims it had to reorganize society, so it did.

In the process of reorganization the latent differences between the three major Christian hopes emerged. The eschatological hope, for a new world or world order, was clearly expressed in the books of the New Testament and was popular so long as the Church and the civil government were at odds. Once they became allies it began to fall into disfavor. To encourage ardent expectations of the coming end of the world, or even of the present social order, was potentially subversive; to teach that the end was already beginning and to advocate practical measures by which it could be hastened was open subversion. Such Christianity the civil authorities were not prepared to tolerate; the authorities of the Church commonly justified intolerance by declaring the eschatologists heretical. On the other hand they were not willing to expunge the New Testament passages and the clauses in the creeds that were the bases for such hopes. From these roots, therefore, as from a buried tangle of witchgrass, millennarian movements sprouted up in generation after generation, wherever conditions of one sort or another—usually famine, plague, war, or misgovernment—inspired men to hope for radical social or cosmic change. Hence in generation after generation the Church and the civil government reacted to the revived hope with one or another combination of repressive measures, modified by attempts to turn the popular enthusiasm to some practical advantage (e.g., in crusades, pogroms, penitential practices).

An even colder reception was reserved for those who claimed too optimistically that they had realized the Christian hope of present salvation. From the viewpoint of an average Church official, the only good saint is a dead saint. A live saint at large in the neighborhood is a threat to the authority of an official who can rarely himself pretend to sanctity let alone to the miraculous gifts supposed to accompany it. The potential for conflict between saints and clergy was already becoming apparent by the end of the first century, when tracts written by bishops and their defenders began to view with skepticism the claims of wandering prophets, while writers favorable to the prophets (for instance, the author of the Johannine epistles) replied with polemic against individual bishops. With the coming of the persecutions the situation got worse. Persons who had been imprisoned and/or tortured as Christians, but had escaped death, were known as "confessors" and because of their demonstration of faith were credited with extraordinary spiritual powers, including the power to forgive sins. When a confessor forgave someone a bishop wanted to discipline, a local crisis ensued. Usually the bishop won. He controlled the local church's funds and services, and these controlled the membership. But difficulties kept recurring until the triumph of the Church as a whole cut off the supply of confessors.

By that time a new form of Christian holy man had become prominent, the "anchorite." The word meant "runaway" and had often been used of peasants who abandoned their properties and took to the wilds to avoid paying their taxes. Hence it was extended to others who reneged on their social obligations, resorting to the beatnik solution of the problems of life. This practice had been made popular in the early empire by philosophers of the Cynic school, some of whom had claimed extraordinary spiritual powers. Christian anchorites exaggerated such claims. Many wandered about the empire as self-appointed saints, living on what they could pick up by demonstrating their indifference to hardship—a generally recognized proof of sanctity—and by putting their supposed power at the service of anyone who wanted a blessing or a curse, a prayer or a prophecy, forgiveness of sins, or simply the good luck that kindness to a holy man might bring. Thus they became competitors of the regular church officials both as sources of blessing, forgiveness, and the like, and as recipients of Christian charity. The reaction of the officials was predictable (i.e., not "Christian"). Eventually the competition was relieved somewhat by the development of monasticism, an efficient worldly organization to finance and regulate rejection of the world. Most Cynic types now went into monasteries; many who did so stayed there and were thus removed from contact with the secular clergy. The anchorite became the monk—a new social figure, a new form for hope, and a major element in the history of the Middle Ages.

Christianity had augmented the Cynic hope by promising immediate spiritual powers far greater than Cynics had ordinarily claimed, and adding a promise of material rewards hereafter. There is no telling how far these changes altered the psychological drives that produced both Cynics and anchorites, but the similarity of the resultant social types is clear. However, as a result of the Christian changes the hope for freedom no longer stood alone. Freedom was equated with Christian holiness, but holiness had other aspects as well. The emphasis shifted to these and so made possible the organization, subordination, and discipline of monasticism. Cynicism had long emphasized self-discipline which often led to some notion of progress; in monasticism this became discipline by the superiors of the community, the need for progress was emphasized and the hope for present salvation, for immediate enjoyment of supernatural powers, was pushed far into the future. But it lived on as a hope, particularly in eastern monasticism, a hope expressed by innumerable stories of the holy fathers of the desert and their miracles. Thus throughout the history of monasticism there runs a tension between the organization man and the individualist. On the one side is the monastery, the brotherhood, the regular life, a visible, tangible ideal to be loved and worked for, and of which the enrichment and perpetuation is the general hope; but on the other side there are the stories of holy hermits who went off by themselves to live in caves, fight with devils, talk with angels, and do wonders—and there are always a few enthusiasts who try to put these stories into practice.

In spite of this latter strain, monasticism did much to solve the problem posed for church officials by Paul's emphasis on present gifts of grace, and the traditional Christian hope of immediate salvation. There was now a "way of perfection" into which potentially troublesome characters could be safely directed and which, if they followed it, would quarantine them in appropriate institutions, leaving everybody else to follow in peace the more comfortable way of the world. The system was not infallible. Monks had a way of getting out of their monasteries and preaching repentance, social and moral reform, and suchlike troublesome things. Also, cases of sanctity and abnormal spiritual powers kept occurring here and there among persons who were not in monasteries and showed no inclination to enter them—Joan of Arc, for instance. Such characters gave the church officials some of their most difficult hours; not a few had to be burned as heretics. But until Luther, the heresies remained minor by relation to the Church as a whole. In spite of some severe local crises (especially in southern France, Bohemia, and England), it must be said that Christianity met very well the challenge posed by sanctity to established religion. What has been lost by discrediting its solution can be seen from the hordes of modern children, rebels without a cause, Cynics without philosophical knowledge, and anchorites without religion, who recently wandered the streets looking for a way of perfection they could hope to believe. Observation of these consequences should not be taken to recommend the discredited Christian solution, but to imply that rejection of common social standards, often accompanied by claims to holiness and sometimes by the desire of it, is a recurrent phenomenon of human life, especially among adolescents, and that a society which can justify such impulses, prevent the saints from becoming nuisances, and use them for some good purpose, is in these respects preferable to a society that leaves them uneasy and unsatisfied, likely to damage themselves and their surroundings.

When both eschatological hope and the hope of immediate salvation were thus pushed to one side by triumphant Christianity, the hope of salvation after death was left as the chief officially recognized motive of the religion ("officially recognized" as distinct from considerations of self-interest, conformity to the prevailing social system, etc., which were the major but unacknowledged elements of the structure). When Dante sat for his theological examination in heaven and was asked by St. James, "What is Christian hope?" he replied, as he said, "promptly and gladly," like a boy who had done his lesson—with the accepted doctrine out of Peter Lombard *via* Albertus Magnus, "Hope is the confident expectation of future glory" (*Paradiso,* XXV, 64 ff.). When prodded, he went on to add a reference to the ultimate resurrection of the dead, but this clearly had not been uppermost in his mind. Nevertheless, he passed; the saints shared his opinion. In heaven they were already in glory and bliss, enjoying the vision of God which was their hope. To that vision Dante's poem leads and with that it concludes. The resurrection of the body is foretold because it stands in the creed, but is at best a faint and far-off refraction of the immediate heavenly glory.

For fifteen hundred years, at least, from A.D. 300 to 1800, this hope was predominant, and even since 1800 salvation after death has perhaps remained the major hope that the religion admittedly offers its believers. The same has also probably been true of Judaism, though messianic (eschatological) movements have been more important there in proportion to the total number of members, and so have hopes of immediate salvation by various forms of cabalism. During these centuries, notions of salvation after death have varied considerably, but less than one might expect, because they have not often been sharply defined. Detailed descriptions, such as Swedenborg's *Heaven, Hell, and the World of Spirits, from Things Heard and Seen There,* have been exceptional and have not gained general acceptance, while such descriptions as have been generally accepted, notably the visions in the canonical *Apocalypse of St. John,* have been resolutely but vaguely allegorized. In general, it was taken for granted that God would be able to satisfy man. This would be, indeed, the greatest evidence of his omnipotence. "Our heart is restless," said Augustine, "till it find rest in Thee" (*Confessions,* I,1). With that magnificent gesture the problem of hope is dismissed. Man is unable to discover what he hopes; let God do it.

Nevertheless, the images chosen to describe the indescribable have changed with the changing environment. The Apocalypse is interesting in this respect. Its earlier chapters are modeled on the proceedings of the imperial court. But in later chapters, where the author is drawing on earlier traditions, he sees "the *city* of God, the new Jerusalem, coming down from God out of heaven" with walls of gold and gates of pearl, but no public water system. Instead, "a river of the water of life" flows "in the middle of its [central] square" (22:1 f.). By Roman times respectable cities had aqueducts leading to reservoirs from which water was piped to street corner fountains and private houses (Pausanias, X, 4:1). The cultural lag of the new Jerusalem is evidence not only of the author's dependence on an earlier source, but also of his lack of interest in the details reported. He is concerned with them as symbols, not as literal descriptions. Mohammed took things more literally. For him and his followers from the desert, heaven was not a city, but a garden. Again, however, the details remained indefinite. Though the Muslim philosopher al-Ghazzali wrote a treatise on hope, his only defined hope was "to get into the garden." What he would do when he got into the garden was something he never considered. (In this respect he was less perspicacious than my dog.) Another conception of heaven, in the pre-Christian *Book of Enoch,* envisioned it as a palace or a series of palaces, one within another. But here again we are already dealing with allegory; the palaces are built of fire and rivers of fire rise within them.

These four motifs—kingdom, city, garden, palace—can be followed down through the Middle Ages, variously combined by various authors. Another ancient motif was that of ascension into the physical heavens. Of this the most magnificent expression is now in Dante—vision after vision of wheeling balls of light, combined with medieval romantic imagery: heaven is a vast white rose spread open to God, the sun, and visited by the angels, like golden bees. Magnificent poetry, but not actual hope. The actual hope of most people was probably a reflection of the literary tradition as known to them from hymns, paintings, and stained glass windows, while behind the literary tradition lay actual experiences and hopes of the (relatively few) real mystics, their visions of lights, jewels, flower patterns, structures of fantastic architecture, and beings of extraordinary brilliance, beauty, and majesty.[10] Already in the seventeenth century the more cultivated clerics, for instance Baxter in *The Saints Everlasting Rest,* were at work to psychologize the literary tradition. By the beginning of the present century one of the few things about which almost all educated Christians were agreed was that biblical descriptions of heaven did not mean what they said.

Much more specific than the hope of attaining heaven was the hope of escaping hell. Vivid pictures of the postmortal torments of a few distinguished sinners seem to have begun early in Greek storytelling; they are among the additions that now stand in the *Odyssey*'s account of the underworld. Complete guided tours of the torture chambers become common in the preserved material from the second century A.D. and thereafter. The imagined tortures developed with the development of techniques of torture by imperial officials; accounts of methods used in religious persecutions during the later empire and descriptions of hell produced at that same time show significant parallels. By Dante's day, a thousand years of medieval ingenuity and imagination had produced the raw material for that unrivaled chamber of horrors, his acknowledged masterpiece. Significantly, ecclesiastical writers were much less willing to allegorize hell than heaven. Sensible images of bliss were in danger of verging on the sensual, but there was no objection to threatening the wicked with sensible punishments—the only kind that, being wicked, they would really find disagreeable. Nonetheless, the change of fashion ultimately made itself felt. "In the nineteenth century," said somebody (Leacock?), "hell was discovered to be a state of spiritual torment; that finished hell." In other words, it almost

10 See the review and analysis of the evidence by A. Huxley, *Heaven and Hell* (New York, 1955). Huxley's argument that, because these accounts are consistent, they must (even when produced by drugs!) be based on experiences of "outer reality" is not persuasive. More likely the visions of lights and colors result from stimulation of those areas of the brain that produce such sensations; the patterns result from the patterns of the structures of the nervous system; and the jewels, flowers, buildings and beings result from subjective interpretations of these sensations. It is probably significant that the buildings and beings—the most developed of these subjective interpretations—are the elements that vary most from mystic to mystic.

finished the fear of it and so the hope of escaping it, for fear and hope in this case were related as fire and light—when the fire was quenched, both went out.

However, the decline of hell resulted from other causes, too, and perhaps less from rationalism than from competition. From the Renaissance on there has been a steady growth of secular horror stories to rival the supernatural. From vigorous but jejune beginnings—tragedies, accounts of plagues, reports of murders and executions, then the "Gothic" novels —artificial nightmares have steadily increased, to become our most popular form of entertainment: murder stories, crime comics, violent movies and television programs, accounts of wars, concentration camps, mental hospitals, prisons, slums. Moreover, much of this material, especially during the past forty years, has justified itself as accounts of facts. Its avid readers have been able to use the excuse of historical or sociological study to conceal, even from themselves, its attraction for them. On the one hand, the claim to be factual gave it an extra kick, but on the other, accounts of hell, like all other visions, lose something of their appeal when fulfillment brings them down to earth. All this material testifies to the need for scenes of torture, violence, and misery as one of the major, permanent factors in the fulfillment of human hopes. From the gladiatorial games through Dante's *Inferno* to the televised prizefight and the holocaust industry, the tradition is uninterrupted and unequivocal. But I do not know any "serious social planner" who has condescended to recognize the existence of this need, much less to provide in his planned society for its satisfaction.

V

The preceding account of Christian hope should not be understood as suggesting that the hopes described (for spiritual powers, resurrection in the messianic age, salvation after death, and eternal torture of the damned) were the only ones held by Christians. They were, however, the ones that characterized the Middle Ages. After the triumph of the Church a vast amount of property and labor was devoted to its support and therefore, implicitly, to the realization of its declared hopes. The maintenance of the huge ecclesiastical personnel (patriarchs, metropolitans, archbishops, bishops, priests, deacons, subdeacons, acolytes, exorcists, lectors, doorkeepers, abbots and abbesses, monks and nuns), their labor, the materials, land, and labor necessary for the erection and operation of innumerable churches and monasteries, for vestments and other liturgical equipment, for books, scriptoria, libraries, etc.—all this added up to a sizable share of the wealth of what was, by our standards, a wretchedly poor society, and to all this must be added the time, labor, and incidental expenses incurred by private believers in order to attend church services and to carry on their own devotions. We do not begin to have the data necessary to determine the direct cost of Christianity to the later empire and the dark ages, but an estimate on the order of twenty percent of gross annual production would not be prima facie implausible. As for the indirect costs—e.g., for religious conflicts, church councils, civil administrative time devoted to church disputes, police and military actions to suppress heretics or support the orthodox, vandalism by both sides, destruction of opponents' property and the property of pagans and Jews, flights of productive workers from their lands or even from the empire, military losses consequent on heretical, pagan, or Jewish support for the government's enemies, etc.—these are simply incalculable. The achievement of the stated aims of early Christianity was one of the major charges on the Christian state.

In spite of all this private hopes continued as usual. Saints remained exceptional; the hopes of most men were primarily for themselves, their families, and their property. Rulers hoped to defeat, deflect, or buy off the barbarians. In the courts and cities of the empire the customary hopes of civilized life continued to animate citizens and courtiers. Yet within the sphere of worldly hopes there were also changes.

As the society changed it made possible new careers and brought into prominence new social types, each of which presented a new possibility for hope. A man could now hope to be a monk or an anchorite; a woman could hope to be a nun, a new career for women in a women's community of which the superior might be a person of considerable importance in the outside world. The hope to become a Christian priest led to consequences far different from those that had followed on pagan priesthood. Bishop, patriarch, and heresiarch were figures for whom earlier antiquity had only remote parallels. Literary and artistic aspirations changed profoundly. The hopes that shaped the stupendous dome of Santa Sophia or the austere and magnificent mosaics of Christ Pantocrator were immeasurably removed from those that had produced the elegant Parthenon and its circle of aristocratic deities, comfortably *chez eux* while receiving the services of the citizens. In the West, where the flood of barbarian invaders swept away the political and much of the social structure of the empire, changes were even more profound. The types that eventually emerged had behind them complex histories. Chaucer's "verray parfit gentil knight" was the product of a long campaign by teachers, confessors, poets, noblewomen (who set the style of behavior in their courts and castles), and legislators both lay and clerical, all of whom applied themselves for centuries to the domestication of the barbarian warrior. "The knight" would be replaced in the Renaissance by "the courtier," and "the courtier" in the eighteenth century by "the gentleman," as the increase of bourgeois wealth and power made it possible for men of lower hereditary position to hope for acceptance in "good society" and as the ideal figures of "good society" changed in recognition of the new facts of economic and political life. With the shift of political and purchasing power to yet lower classes in our own time, "the gentleman" has been replaced by "the wonderful human being" (American for *Mensch*). The next step will perhaps be "fellow animal". While each lowering of the standard produces a more easily achievable ideal, and so increases the number of those who can hope to succeed, it also lowers the quality of the hope and the importance of the success. A perfect democracy, in which all men were created equal and compelled to remain so, would be a society in which nobody could have any social or moral hope.

While the forms taken by private hopes were thus changing, the course of the "official" (political, institutional, and military) history of the western Middle Ages was directed by quite different aspirations—for restoration and reorganization of the Roman Empire, reform of the clergy and unification of the Church under papal authority, consolidation of the various ethnic kingdoms, preservation of the traditional rights and independence of the nobles, conversion of the surrounding barbarians to "orthodox" Christianity, extirpation of heresy, and reconquest from the Moslems of the Holy Land and of Spain, creation of leagues of traders with independent cities as their bases, extension of monastic and related orders, revival of learning and of the arts, development of universities, and creation of intellectual, architectural, and aesthetic structures expressive of the vision of the new world that was emerging from the ruins of the old. All these great enterprises, the conflicts they engendered and the monuments they left behind them, lie somewhat outside the scope of our present inquiry. Although they created a new world, they can be seen as developments of hopes already exemplified in antiquity. Historically, no doubt, every event is peculiar, but typologically, the keyboard of human potentialities and ambitions had already been so far explored that the new compositions exploited rather than extended it. Empires, kingdoms, and wars, trading networks and religious orders we have seen before, and the religious and intellectual developments of the Middle Ages show rather extensions than new beginnings. The Papal Roman Catholic Church is—as it claims to be—*essentially* not different from the Catholic Church of antiquity. Even the idea of the university is latent in Aristotle and in the Museum of Alexandria. The hope of harmonizing the Bible with Greek philosophy in a single intellectual system, one that

would explain both the world and its relation to God, had
begun with Philo of Alexandria. If Gothic architecture expresses a new hope, it is a hope inseparable from the architectural perfection in which it was realized.

VI

In the Renaissance the formation of new hopes began with
loss of the old. While the Church in this world and heaven in
the next had been created as refuges from the impersonal
order of the Roman Empire, their triumph had been shortly
followed by the Empire's breakdown. In the chaos of barbarian invasions that followed they had lived on and had increased their importance as centers of hope for escape from
the miseries of the disintegrating society. But when order
began to be reestablished it was far from the *rigor mortis* of the
later Roman Empire. The effort to revive the Empire was
fortunately a failure, while that to defend the powers of the
nobles was long successful. Consequently from the dark ages
there emerged a medieval world of infinite variety with innumerable tiny centers of power sufficient to accumulate a little
wealth and make a few luxuries—among them, civilization—
possible. These little principalities were fiercely independent
and consequently irreducible to any fixed "international"
order. Like the innumerable cities and colonies of the Greek
diaspora, they constituted a world ideal for adventure and
hence for the development of worldly hopes. The Church and
heaven were not at first rejected, but neglected. However,
rejection soon followed. Already in the thirteenth century,
when Aucassin was warned that his love for Nicolette could
cost him his hope of heaven, he replied, "What would I do in
paradise? I don't want to go there. I want to have Nicolette,
the girl I love. Nobody goes to paradise but the types I can
tell you—this old priest, that old cripple, the other old monk,
who spend all day and night coughing in front of their altars
in their empty crypts; those who wear old, worn out capes and
ragged habits, go barefoot, are covered with chilblains, and

die of hunger and thirst and cold and discomfort. These go to paradise, and I want nothing to do with them. I want to go to hell, for to hell go the beautiful clerk and the gallant cavalier who dies in the tournament or in war, and the good squire and the freeman. And I want to go with them. There go the beautiful and gracious ladies, either with their husbands or with their lovers. And there go the gold and the silver and the fine fabrics, the harpers and the jugglers and the rulers of this world. And I want to go with them, provided I have Nicolette, my girl, with me."

The mere shifting of the focus of hope back to this world did not suffice, by itself, to create new hopes. Aucassin is new only in his explicit rejection of paradise; his hope for Nicolette is old as Adam. The appearance of new hopes could only follow the glimpse of new possibilities, new powers which were to be given men by the development of the physical sciences and the new understanding of the world that their development made possible. But here, as often, the first glimpses were given by dreams and visions that foreshadowed the actual achievement. In this case they were the waking dreams of the alchemists and utopians.

Alchemy seems to have begun in the hellenistic world as the forgers' science, the study of techniques for making imitation gold and silver, fake precious stones, etc. Soon came the notion of making the real things and magic was called on to help. Magic was also involved in the ancient search for immediate salvation; a whole class of rites were intended to secure supernatural powers for the magician or even to deify him. Under the influence of these rites alchemical experiments were allegorized as attempts to transform the nature of the alchemist, but the hope to transmute metals and other materials was not abandoned. Different practitioners, according to their temperaments, emphasized one or the other aspect of "the great work." The metallurgic aspect led to the accumulation of much knowledge ultimately organized as chemistry, the search for salvation found expression in a fantastic literature and iconography of which the psychological significance was pointed out by Jung. Essential was the notion that man's nature can be transformed by experimental study of the physical world, so that by learning to master and transform nature he can also master and transform himself. In this respect alchemy was the dream of which biochemistry seems to promise the fulfillment, but with a difference (as fulfillments always differ from dreams). In alchemy since the experiments never achieved their goals, it was never necessary to define precisely the character desired—that was simply a projection of the virtues admired by the society or the powers sought by the magus. In biochemistry, since the changes that can probably be produced are both great and predictable, the biochemist is faced with the problem of deciding what sort of person he wants. Again an artist's vision, *Frankenstein,* proves to be a prophecy and a warning. What should the biochemist hope to make? If Jung was right, the alchemists' imaginations may conceal the answer to this question—their symbolism may contain the clue to the psychological structure of the harmonious character. If they do, however, we shall probably not recognize the clue until the structure has been discovered by other means.

Utopian thought had a history even longer and more complex than that of alchemy. One source we have seen—the Greek experience in planning colonies, and hence Hippodamus' plan of an ideal state, conceived as an architectural, political, and legal structure. The notion that defining the good state is a matter of laws and politics resulted not only from the Greeks' experience with colonies, but also from their temperament and from the importance given politics by the necessities of life in the tiny, poor, but self-governing Greek cities. A Babylonian or Egyptian asked to describe the best possible society would have thought of different things. The Greeks' thought of political structure shaped that of the western world.

An older tradition, exemplified in the *Odyssey,* derived from the storyteller's practice of describing an imaginary country for the mere pleasure of imagining it. Often these imaginary countries have praeternatural inhabitants, fauna, flora, etc.—all the people are one-eyed giants, or live on narcotics, or whatnot. The two traditions were soon combined and continue in combination to the present, e.g., in much "science fiction." Their combination often makes it difficult to decide how far the author of a "utopia" is making serious recommendations, how far he is indulging in the pleasures of imagination (which are not incompatible with acute observations on actual society). At one end of the map of utopias lie the countries of *Gulliver's Travels,* equally remote from the ideal and the possible, at the other, the dismal but allegedly ideal communities of the nineteenth- and twentieth-century social reformers, for which every provision was written in deadly earnest. Even more dismal, albeit imaginary, are the pessimistic utopias that have toadstooled since the successes of *Brave New World* and *1984.* These modern equivalents of medieval descriptions of hell are no doubt sprung from the same subconscious motives as their precedents. Presumably few designers of such societies *consciously* hoped to find themselves either in or in charge of one. Why, then, design them? Purportedly to warn the readers of the dangers revealed. But can the claim be trusted? Huxley's rejection of the sexual promiscuity of his brave new world was certainly overdrawn, not only to make the book salable to British readers in 1931, but also to achieve the intended psychological effect. How far was Orwell "of the devil's party without knowing it"? Similar problems are presented in reverse by those who thought their pictures ideal. Imagine Marx's explosion of anger had he ever been incarcerated in his own equalitarian society, with no excuse for hating or bossing anybody, and nothing to denounce. The old tyrant would have found it intolerable, and how he would have roared!

Nevertheless, when allowance is made for such ambiguities the development of modern utopian literature leads gradually to a new form of hope. As the alchemical tradition concealed within itself the hope that human nature could be changed by the experimental study and eventual mastery of the physical world, so the utopian tradition contained the hope that human nature could be changed by the study and control of man's social environment. This hope, *in nuce,* is implicit in the notion of any school, i.e., a special environment in and by which the characters of the students are to be changed. Extension of this notion to that of a limited society, conceived as a school for its members, was probably implicit in the thought of Pythagoras and certainly far developed in monasticism, an important root of utopian speculations. From monasticism, for instance, Rabelais took the idea of his Abbey of Thelema, organized for enjoyment of body and mind, where the sole rule of the order was, "Do as you like." Similarly neo-Pythagoreans, alchemists, and monks, as well as the Knights Templar and the learned societies of Athens and Alexandria, all contributed to the organization of "Salomon's House" in Bacon's *New Atlantis.* But here, too, the organization pictured is a carefully limited group, actually a company of magicians; its members shape the surrounding society, not *vice versa.* The recognition of the extent to which human character is a social structure, and the consequent change of the conception of utopia from a static creation to a creative environment, developed only slowly through the past century.

Hence the earlier literature of utopianism yields less than might be expected for the history of hope. Most programmatic utopias were written to advocate one or another combination of social and economic gimmicks intended usually to take care of the poor. The authors commonly begin with the common assumption of liberalism, that men are basically good, and go on to the common conclusions, that men quarrel only because of competition in meeting their physical needs, and that all problems of humanity can be solved by giving everybody adequate food, shelter, clothing, medical care, etc. Therefore they sketch some economic, social, and governmental system which, they hope, will do this. Like God in the second chapter of Genesis, they plant their earthly paradise, locate their creatures in it, tell them to work for a living, and themselves go back to rest, their own work finished. They should have gone on to Genesis 3 which tries to account for original sin by the serpent's malevolence. The account is a myth, but at least it recognizes the existence of the problem: when all men's physical wants are supplied the result is not beatitude, but more leisure to make trouble. By that recognition, Genesis is one up on Marx whose vision of the ultimate future is a mere fairy tale: when Adam and Eve enter the classless Eden they just "live happy ever after." What, if anything, men could reasonably *hope to do* once the physical needs of the race were attended to, is a question that has rarely been considered.

This neglect by the earlier modern authors is explicable not only by liberalism and stupidity (which are not identical), but also by the fact that the mere achievement of a system that could and would provide the basic needs of all mankind seemed a task almost beyond hope of realization. Renaissance discoveries and the explorations of subsequent centuries had made Europeans aware of the miseries of millions in Africa, Asia, the Indies, Australia, and the Americas. Even in England itself the swarming slums that grew with the growth of industrialism presented problems many thought insoluble. This is why so many utopias were admittedly utopian, while more were plans for small, ideally self-supporting communities. Their designers hoped that, once an earthly paradise was planted and operating, it would become a model for others, and these for others, and so, at last, society would be saved. Many such utopian communities were in fact founded—and the histories of most of them followed the outline given in Genesis: the people of paradise proceeded to get wise and fight with each other. Sexual aberrations, or struggles for power, or both, developed and the community disintegrated.[11] The history of such groups would make an amusing

[11] Notice the difference between these economic and social utopias and the small religious communities founded in the seventeenth to nineteenth centuries, many with some utopian traits, but most, primarily, to make possible some religious way of life. These more often survived.

chronique scandaleuse, but besides original sin there was a less entertaining, although equally practical, reason for their failure.

All these plans had as their more or less conscious model the historic example of Christianity which in fact did spread, as a network of communities, to capture the Roman Empire. But Christianity had the good fortune to spread through a society first stagnant, later decaying. The society's failure made Christian social services and hopes for the hereafter of great importance to their beneficiaries. By contrast, the utopias of the past two centuries were founded in a society of which the productivity and power increased at a rate beyond even the hopes of most of its members. Consequently the outside world had more to offer than did the utopias, especially those planned to achieve stability by careful economy and self-sufficient farming. (Whatever may be said in its favor, self-sufficient farming as a way of life is a bore.) When the wicked world outproduced the Garden of Eden, Adam and Eve either left the garden without waiting to be expelled, or incorporated Eden (read Oneida) as a profit-making element of the more profitable society around it.

In fact, the goals of earlier utopianism were in large part realized by the general progress of western European and American society during the past two centuries. This can be seen from Bacon's list of objectives for his ideal order of "natural" magicians.[12] They were:

The prolongation of life.
The restitution of youth in some degree.
The retardation of age.
The curing of diseases counted incurable.
The mitigation of paine.
More easie and lesse loathsome purgings.
The encreasing of strength and activity.

---

[12] *Magnalia naturae praecipue quoad usus humanos,* appended to the *New Atlantis* in the 1631 London edition of the latter, together with the *Silva Silvarum.*

The encreasing of ability to suffer torture or paine.

The altering of complexions: and fatnesse and leannesse.

The altering of statures.

The altering of features.

The encreasing and exalting of the intellectual parts.

Versions of bodies into other bodies.

Making of new species.

Transplanting of one species into another.

Instruments of destruction, as of warre and poyson.

Exhilaration of the Spirits, and putting them in good disposition.

Force of imagination, either upon another body or upon
the body it selfe.[13]

Acceleration of time in maturations.[14]

Acceleration of time in clarifications.[15]

Acceleration of putrefaction.

Acceleration of decoction.

Acceleration of germination.

Making rich composts for the earth.

Impressions of the aire, and raising of tempests.

Great alteration; as in induration, emollition, etc.

Turning crude and watry substances into oyly and unctious
substances.

Drawing of new foods out of substances not now in use.

Making new threds for apparell, and new stuffes, such as are
paper, glasse, etc.

Naturall divinations.

Deceptions of the senses.

Greater pleasures of the senses.

Artificiall minerals and cements.

Practically all of these, except control of the weather and
transplantation (of members?) from one *species* to another, are

---

[13] In modern terms, hypnosis and autohypnosis.

[14] E.g., forcing plants.

[15] I.e., of fluids in chemical processes. This and the following nine all refer to
chemical and physical operations.

now to some extent within our power[16] and many are every-day procedures basic to our economy.

The means to the achievement of Bacon's goals—the scientific and technological discoveries necessary for these feats—have also resulted in the realization of many of the goals of utopians concerned for social benefits. As Bertrand Russell recognized, "The Western world has achieved, not completely, but to a considerable extent, a way of life that has certain merits that are new in human history. . . . It has cut down illness and death to a degree that a hundred years ago would have seemed fantastic. It has spread education throughout the population, and it has achieved a quite new degree of harmony between freedom and order." And again, "In certain important Western countries extreme poverty has almost disappeared, famine is unknown, large scale pestilences have yielded to medical science, and a low birth-rate has made it possible to preserve a high level of prosperity when it has been reached. All this is new in human history."[17] Moreover even some fantastic hopes of ancient utopians—flight, interplanetary travel, mechanical servants, transplantation of organs—have now been realized. As Oscar Wilde said, "Progress is the realization of utopias."[18] He should have added, "It is therefore a series of disappointments."

VII

Both the failures of socialistic utopias and the disappointments entailed by realization of utopian goals have combined to discredit a third aspect of utopian thought—the notion of making over society as a whole—which was long fashionable as a means of satisfying the most important hope inculcated

[16] Greater pleasures of the senses are made possible by the use of drugs, most commonly tobacco, caffeine, and alcohol. "Natural divinations" are practised by the National Weather Service.

[17] B. Russell, *New Hopes for a Changing World* (London, 1951), pp. 12 and 154.

[18] "The Soul of Man under Socialism," in *Complete Works*, ed. R. Ross (New York, n.d.), Vol. IV, p. 299.

in childhood: to be good. As increasing scientific knowledge disposed of the medieval hopes for an end of this world, resurrection of the dead, and life after death, pious persons unable to believe the traditional teachings of their religions turned to the improvement of society as a Worthy Cause that would give them the moral purpose they needed for self-righteousness, and enable them to be justified by works, if not by faith. This *ersatz* religion was adumbrated in Germany two centuries ago by Lessing's representation of human benevolence as a substitute for religious orthodoxy (*Nathan der Weise,* 1779). Half a century later, Leigh Hunt summarized it in his story of Abou Ben Adhem. Blessed by a vision of an angel writing "the names of those who love the Lord," Ben Adhem dared to ask if his were among them. On learning it was not, he answered,

> "Then
> Write me as one that loves his fellow-men."
> The angel wrote, and vanished. The next night
> It came again, with a great wakening light,
> And show'd the names whom love of God had bless'd,
> And lo! Ben Adhem's name led all the rest.

From this attempt to substitute charity for faith came the theological developments culminating in "the social gospel," the ecclesiastical equivalent of the utopian movements and, like them, an attempt to find salvation in this world (hope of any other having been tacitly abandoned). The emotional importance of this attempt accounts for the uneasy fanaticism, not to say desperation, with which believers in the social gospel cling to their faith in spite of conclusive evidence that their gospel is not sufficient for satisfaction, let alone salvation. The mere proposal of a just society should lead to the reflection that few things would make more people less happy than to get what they deserve and have everybody know they deserved what they got. As for the notion that economic security will produce good behavior, let alone good will, it can be refuted out of hand by the history of the upper classes. Nevertheless, even today reluctant converts to common sense are still coming forward to testify. Thus Robert Heilbroner, in a recent issue of *The New York Times* (October 10, 1977, p. 29, col. 1), announced among his new discoveries, "1. *We cannot expect social contentment from economic growth.*" (His italics.) "This strikes me as one of the few important lessons we can learn from the last half century." (It is also one of the many important lessons he could have learned from Genesis.) "There was a time, not so long ago, when statesmen and scholars alike believed that economic growth brought social well-being in its train—that the cure for social and political disaffection, for riots and radicalism, was simply more income. I no longer think we can indulge in that lulling belief." Two cheers for Rip van Winkle! Better late than never.

Through the latter half of the nineteenth and the whole of the twentieth century both the social gospel and the most formidable forms of utopianiam—socialism and communism —gained steadily in strength. One factor in these gains was the growth of historical thought and the extension of the circle acquainted with it.

The habit of thinking historically directed men's thoughts beyond the present. Greater understanding of the past led to more attempts to predict and shape the future. The extension of information (by news broadcasts, even to the illiterate) has spread the habit of thinking about historical objectives, and even some concern for them, to an extent unprecedented. Along with this has gone persistent propaganda, by advocates of various social causes, all of them anxious for converts and therefore insistent that a happy private life is "not enough"; the good citizen must be involved in some cause of historical significance, must have some hope for a far-off future that transcends mere personal concerns.

Such missionary preaching in more or less historical disguise has made many converts. Most people, of course, are still happily self-centered. But many, even of this majority, have been so disturbed that they now feel some malaise about their lack of social interests and are apt to pretend to have them, or to apologize for not having them. Talk about social and historical questions is *de rigueur* in many circles whose members are grossly ignorant of them, but know they are expected to be concerned about them and, by dint of expressing much concern, come to feel a little. Accordingly they are uneasy when the political and social horizons are clouded, as at present, and their uneasiness is apt to find expression in adhesion to some cause or organization, usually one advocating some form of social gospel or utopian scheme. When prospects clear up, these converts relapse and may even turn to criticism of the plans they formerly advocated.

Striking examples of such relapse appeared in England during this century in two periods when optimism was possible, one just before the rise of Nazism, the other just after its collapse, from 1945 to 1950. During these brief intervals it was commonly believed that the enormous powers made available by science were at the disposition of basically reasonable and benevolent governments capable of acting together for the common good of mankind. Was it by accident that, just at these moments, appeared the most influential English attacks on the utopian tradition—Huxley's *Brave New World* in 1931 and Orwell's *1984* in 1948?

Huxley's book is the more profound, though Orwell's may be better known because of its use as political propaganda, its motion picture success, and its sado-masochistic appeal (to which we shall return). It is admittedly a brilliant narrative. But philosophically considered its critique of utopianism was based on one "accident" (the history of Hitler) and made to depend on another (the malevolence of "big brother"). There is no necessity of a dictator's being malevolent. One might, theoretically, be a man of the highest moral principles, honestly convinced that his policies were the best ways to achieve the greatest good for the greatest number, and selflessly devoted to the pursuit of this goal. Churchill's comment on Cripps, "There, but for the grace of God, goes God," sums up the frightening possibility, and Allende may have come near making it a frightful reality. Consequently, as an attack on utopianism *1984* is merely a horrifying example of what *might* happen if the system fell into the wrong hands. But *Brave New World* is a study of what *must* happen, under the best conditions, to make such a system work. The benevolence, intelligence, humanity of Mustapha Mond, his secret love of Shakespeare, his understanding of what he cannot permit, highlight the latent conflict between utopian hopes and hope itself. For the essential horror of the brave new world is that the people in it have nothing to hope for—nothing beyond a little more of the same. They have bought security and comfort at the price of stability, and part of the price of stability is the elimination of hopes for things the stable order cannot steadily supply. Food, shelter, clothing, exercise, employment, religious rituals, sexual gratification, and entertainment by bumblepuppy and the feelies—these can be steadily supplied and suffice to keep most people happy. Of course the happy are not realizing their highest potentialities. But if they tried to realize their highest potentialities they would probably fail, make themselves miserable, and destroy the social stability on which the happiness of all others depends. Would that be worthwhile? Is it not better that most people should (as they do) resign themselves to filling adequately some modest social position, devote themselves to ordinary pleasures, and hope for nothing more than the continuance of this routine?

Such considerations are commonly attacked by the rhetorical question, "Which would you rather be, a pig satisfied, or Socrates unsatisfied?" Neither choice, however, is possible. The total lack of imagination necessary for porcine content is a rare gift of the gods (except to pigs), while as yet there has been only one Socrates (and he claimed to be satisfied, *Apology* 41d). To restate the question so as to present the choices correctly is difficult. The alternative is commonly used to recommend intellectual interests as opposed to sensual pleasures. But the opposition is false. Plato reports that Socrates was intensely sensitive to some sensual pleasures (especially to the beauty of young men). Nor is it true that intellectual activity and dissatisfaction go together. Everyone knows the

brainless, whining person who is never satisfied with anything; on the other hand, men of outstanding intelligence are
reported to have lived unusually happy and contented lives.
The true antithesis seems to be that between a disposition to
make the most of what is available and one constantly striving
for something out of reach, whether it be understanding or
political power or wealth or physical pleasure.

Such "dispositions" are probably determined by social suggestion as well as physical makeup and private psychological
history. E.g., that so many American Jewish children are compulsive achievers is very likely due to domestic training. The
"identity crisis" is also a socially determined phenomenon. In
a homogeneous culture, where children normally follow the
callings of their parents, identity crises and inordinate ambition are rare. The wider the range of hopes made available,
the more difficult the choice between them, the more adolescent crises, resultant maladjustments, and discontent. This is
particularly so when the choices are offered in such a way that
most aspirants are certain to fail, as in a great lottery or
democracy. Supposing about two million boys attain maturity
in the United States each year, and the average tenure of the
Presidency is six years, to teach that "Every American boy has
a chance to be President," is to prepare 11,999,999 of every
twelve million for disappointment. Our democracy works so
well as it does because most children quickly learn not to take
its promises seriously. From such considerations it is tempting to conclude that the happiest societies are those of which
most members are prepared from childhood for the positions
they will ultimately occupy, prepared not only by vocational
training, but also by emotional training, by proper direction
of their hopes. Unfortunately, matters are not so simple. We
have also to remember the despondency apt to result when
life is too easily predictable.

The problem is not purely theoretical. As little as fifty years
ago most "underdeveloped" countries were peaceful and
pleasant places because the common people there "had nothing to hope for." Consequently most did not hope for things

they could not achieve. They resigned themselves to menial jobs, did their work well, lived peaceably with each other, and were pleasant to visitors. Living economically in their native fashions, to which they were accustomed and attached, they not only maintained themselves, but produced a vast surplus of the materials that supported western civilization and made possible its extraordinary scientific and cultural achievements. Then they were encouraged to hope for greater things. They and their countries were to "develop." The first thing that developed was discontent, then rivalry, hatred, vandalism, civil war, dictatorships. Now most of these countries are full of ruins and malevolence, most of the earnings of their peoples are spent on armies and police to protect their native tyrants, and tyrants and people alike would soon be reduced to starvation if we and the Russians stopped supporting them. *"Und das hat, mit peinem Singen, der Liberalismus getan."*[19] Were their new hopes worth what they cost?

· *Brave New World* imaginatively explored this problem, not as exemplified by the underdeveloped countries, but as it might occur in an imaginary history of England itself. From this exploration Huxley came out on the side of hope—the side he had chosen from the beginning. Most of his readers followed him, not only because he represented his choice as the condition of all traditional moral values, but even more because he portrayed most of the supporters of stability as frightfully vulgar, down-to-earth, and bureaucratic—three unforgivable sins in British intellectual society. Also he conveniently stopped with a caustic picture of what would be wrong with a totally planned society. He left his readers to face the problem the picture raises: Given the general development, everywhere apparent, that is forcing large societies towards greater regularity and organization, and given the fact that hope seems to depend on some degree of uncer-

---

[19] A paraphrase of the last line of Heine's so-called *Lorelei*, (actually *Buch der Leider, Die Heimkehr*, II), which tells of the wreck of a ship whose pilot neglected the rocks in order to watch a river nymph and listen to her song.

tainty, what means are there, if any, by which the possibility of hope can be preserved in the progressively more mechanized and predetermined world?

Awareness of this problem had been growing during the nineteenth and twentieth centuries. Writers of the early eighteen hundreds had described their imaginary states as forever changeless, but even the most determined organizers at the end of that century looked for a future in which governmental constraints would diminish. Marx and Engels, as is well known, at least claimed to hope that "public power will lose its political character" and government will be replaced by "an association in which the free development of each is the condition for the free development of all."[20] This claim may have been occasioned by the increasing chorus of protests not only from conservatives, but also from moderate socialists and anarchists who foresaw the possibility of tyranny by an omnicompetent state. Along with such protests went increasing recognition by economists of the importance of individual

[20] "Communist Manifesto," in K. Marx, F. Engels, *Collected Works* (London: 1976), Vol. VI, p. 505 f. cf. Engels, "Socialism: Utopian and Scientific," *ibid.*, Vol. II, pp. 150 ff. This hope has proved a considerable embarrassment to their followers. Already in 1917 Lenin found it necessary to explain that, "Until the 'higher' phase of communism arrives, the socialists demand the *strictest* control by society *and by the state* of the amount of labor and the amount of consumption. . . . As soon as equality is obtained for all members of society *in relation* to ownership of the means of production . . . humanity will inevitably be confronted with the question of going beyond formal equality to real equality. . . . By what stages . . . humanity will proceed to this supreme aim we do not and cannot know." (His italics.) In the meanwhile he advocated subjection of all the rest of society to a "factory discipline" to be imposed by "the proletariat," i.e., its self-appointed representative, the Communist Party—"State and Revolution," in *Selected Works* (New York, n.d.), Vol VII, pp. 89 ff. Later Che Guevara had to recognize that this "dictatorship of the proletariat" over the other classes of society was not sufficient; it had to be exercised over the proletariat, too, by a "vanguard" of which he, of course, was a member. "The vanguard group is ideologically more advanced than the mass. . . . The latter see only by halves and must be subjected to incentives and pressures of some intensity . . . [This] is the dictatorship of the proletariat being exercised not only upon the defeated class but also individually upon the victorious class." (*Socialism and Man* [Cuba, 1968], p. 11). On towards the liberty, equality, and fraternity of a steadily shrinking elite! Compare the comic claim of Brezhnev at the presentation of the latest USSR Constitution to be rubber-stamped by the Supreme Soviet on October 4, 1977: *"The New York Times* complains that the Soviet State is unable and unwilling to wither away. . . . But really, their anxiety is groundless. Developments are running the precise course predicted by the classics of Marxism." (*New York Times*, October 5, 1977, p. A5, col. 3.)

initiative and variety of approaches to social and economic problems, for instance, the impressive statement of Keynes, "Individualism, if it can be purged of its defects and abuses, is the best safeguard of personal liberty in the sense that . . . it greatly widens the field for the exercise of personal choice. It is also the best safeguard of the variety of life, which emerges precisely from this extended field of personal choice, and the loss of which is the greatest of all the losses of the homogeneous or totalitarian state. For this variety preserves the traditions which embody the most secure and successful choices of former generations; it colours the present with the diversification of its fancy; and, being the handmaid of experiment as well as of tradition and fancy, it is the most powerful instrument to better the future."[21]

The anti-utopias of Huxley and Orwell are thus to be seen as dramatizations of a body of criticisms that had long been accumulating. Besides these criticisms, constructive suggestions had been advanced for combinations of planning and personal choice that might meet the serious objections to the present system without being exposed to the more serious dangers of totalitarianism. This is not the place to consider such suggestions in detail; in sum they show a realization of the problem and at least reasonable hopes of solving it. The general principle was well enunciated by Mannheim: "At the stage of planning, freedom can only be guaranteed if the planning authority incorporates it in the plan itself. . . . The various historical interpretations of freedom—freedom of movement, freedom of expression, freedom of opinion, freedom of association, freedom from caprice, and tolerance—are all special obligations which must be met by the new society."[22] Obviously any society that meets these obligations must provide for large areas of uncertainty which will be fields for hope.

[21] J. M. Keynes, *A General Theory of Employment, Interest and Money* (1936, repr. London, 1960), p. 380.
[22] K. Mannheim, *Man and Society in an Age of Reconstruction* (London, 1940), pp. 378 f.

VIII

Another line of utopian thought has also, by disillusionment, issued in anti-utopianism and in so doing has created a new form of hope—the hope of perpetual revolution. The most obvious roots of the disillusionment were the impossible goals set by the revolutionary tradition, above all, equality. That all men are created equal is a self-evident falsehood of which the American revolutionists saw the potential popular appeal. It appealed as a tacit compromise: the revolutionary aristocrats would no more give up their slaves than would the workers and farmers be content with equality—they wanted to rule. The compromise was so successful that the slogan "equality" was taken over by the leaders of the revolution in France. There the philosophic tradition soon began to reveal its implications and some leaders declared themselves willing to accept these. "Let all the arts perish, if need be, so long as we still have true equality!" wrote Gracchus Babeuf.[23] It remained for the theoreticians of the Russian Revolution to push this principle to the extreme of absurdity by throwing in the crafts and the sciences: "Under capitalism, if a man is a bootmaker, he spends his whole life in making boots . . . if he is a pastrycook he spends all his life baking cakes. . . . Nothing of this sort happens in communist society. Under communism people receive a many-sided culture, and find themselves at home in various branches of production: today I work in an administrative capacity . . . tomorrow I shall be working in a soap factory, next month perhaps in a steam laundry and the month after in an electric power station. This will be possible when all the members of society have been suitably educated."[24]

[23] "Manifeste des Égaux," in V. Advielle, Histoire de Gracchus Babeuf et du Babouvisme (Paris, 1884), vol. I, p. 198.

[24] N. Bukharin and E. Preobrazhensky, The ABC of Communism, tr. E. and C. Paul (Ann Arbor, 1966), pp. 71 f. This balderdash should not be thought the consequence of a brain operation by a surgeon who had been a bootmaker the week before. Actually it is a development of Marx and Engels, The German Ideology, in K. Marx, F. Engels, Collected Works (London, 1976), vol. V, pp. 87 ff.

Of course such nonsense was not taken seriously by the men in power. (When Bukharin outlived his utility he was understandably executed—a means of vocational mobility in communist society that he had left unmentioned.) But many who did believe it were painfully undeceived, while outside the Communist Party, even before the Russian *reductio ad absurdum,* what Henry Adams called "the degradation of democratic dogma" was becoming generally apparent. "All governments use force . . . ," Pareto had written before 1916, "whether universal suffrage prevails or not, it is always an oligarchy that governs, finding ways to give to the 'will of the people' that expression which the few desire."[25] This generalization based on prior history has not been contradicted by subsequent events, in spite of the pretense of democracy kept up alike by communist and western countries. Consequently a few enthusiasts emotionally committed to equality have rejected all society, including the established communist states, in favor of a perpetual revolution, which must be perpetual because it has an unattainable goal. As soon as any state is established, inequalities necessarily develop; therefore the only way to preserve equality is to prevent the establishment of any stable government. But this supposes there is "equality" to "preserve." There is not. In social chaos, too, men are grossly unequal. The physically fit, well armed, well organized, daring, unscrupulous, cynical, and clever have enormous advantages. Professional revolutionists contemptuous of equality often have these characteristics and do very well in their profession.

The most prosperous and important of professional revolutionists, Mao Tse-tung, had personal reasons for his policy. The best years of his life had been those he lived as a guerrilla and leader of revolutionary forces in the field. There, too, he had been most successful. The necessary limitations of his power—or, at least, his open exercise of it—imposed by the

[25] V. Pareto, *The Mind and Society,* ed. A. Livingstone (New York, 1935), Vol. IV, p. 1526, No. 2183.

role of an official in a civilian state were little to his liking; he liked even less the complex social and economic problems posed by the administration of a great country and the necessity of dealing with these through a complex structure of civilian offices in which the heads of the various departments became centers of power in their own rights and tended to conceal and might even come to threaten his preeminence. More and more, as he grew older and began to feel his powers slipping from him, he turned back in memory to the good old days of the open, violent revolution of his early manhood, and both from sympathy and from policy he used his influence to back a new generation of young, violent revolutionaries against the older generation, now established administrators and his potential rivals or, even worse, successors.[26]

The hope for perpetual revolution, however, has other roots, deeper than an old man's jealousy and the disillusionment and ambition of the young. Those are emotional and subjective, but at the heart of the matter lies an intellectual, therefore objective, problem, the perennial difficulty of defining the object of hope, "the good society." From the communist side Rosa Luxemburg put her finger on the sore spot: "The practical realization of socialism as an economic, social and juridical system is something which lies completely hidden in the mists of the future. What we possess in our program is nothing but a few main signposts which indicate the general direction in which to look for the necessary measures, and the indications are mainly negative in character, at that. . . . The negative, the tearing down, can be decreed; the building up, the positive, cannot. New territory. A thousand problems."[27] This is the confession of a believer still confident as to the possibility of the ideal state, although she doesn't know what it looks like or how to realize it. Was her

---

[26] This is not to imply that Mao's reasons for the "Cultural Revolution" were solely personal. For a discussion of his theoretical and practical motives, see M. Meisner, "Utopian Socialist Themes in Maoism," in *Peasant Rebellion and Communist Revolution in Asia*, ed. J. Lewis (Stanford, 1974), pp. 207 ff.

[27] *The Russian Revolution and Leninism or Marxism* (Ann Arbor, 1961), pp. 69 f.

commitment to the cause based on her vision of what she did not know, or on her rejection of what she did? As to "the negative, the tearing down," she was clear. But her lack of any clear picture of the positive was not her fault. It resulted from the fact that Marx and Engels had no clear vision, either. When one goes to them for a picture of the society they hope to create, one gets mainly a collection of phrases in which the key words are disguised negatives—"a class*less* society," one in which government "will *wither away,*" in which private property "will *be abolished,*" the expropriators "will *be expropriated,*" and so on.[28] Bertrand Russell summed up the cause and consequences with his usual clarity: "Marx . . . is not concerned with justice, but only with resentment. . . . The motive of . . . his system is . . . the purely negative principle of hatred. I do not think that out of such a principle a good social system can be created. As we have seen in Soviet Russia, when men whose motive power is hatred acquire authority, they still from habit continue to hate, and will therefore turn on each other. The only possible issue of such a psychology is dictatorship and a police state."[29] This is a trifle unfair to Marx. It is true that he almost wrecked the International in order to regain control. Others were to be equals, but he was to be boss. However, he did have another positive hope besides that for personal power—it was the aspiration of a nineteenth century ex-Jewish intellectual and ex-European alien to be accepted, accepted in a society, accepted for what he was

[28] This holds, too, for most fellow travelers down to the present time. E.g., J. Moltmann, "Religion, Revolution, and the Future," in *The Future of Hope,* ed. W. Capps (Philadelphia, 1970), pp. 102 ff. After eventually defining what is hoped for as "the negation of what is experienced" (p. 113) he does go on to concede (p. 119) that "positive visions and concrete utopias" are needed to change the world (which he wants to change because he hates it), and he finally finds these positive visions (on p. 126) in the hopes for: (1) the all-embracing vision of God, (2) *liberation* of man *from* physical hunger, (3) *freeing* man *from* oppression by other men, (4) *emancipation* of man *from* racial humiliation. The last three are negatives. What men will *do* when no longer hungry, enslaved, and humiliated is something he never considers. "The all-embracing vision of God" is a phrase of religious window-dressing that has no indicated content; its vacuity is made conspicuous by the essay's total lack of concern about God, of whom Moltmann seems to have had no vision.

[29] *New Hopes for a Changing World* (London, 1951), pp. 86 ff.

and for what he wanted to do and could do. It was this hope for acceptance, romanticized as "brotherhood," that made him and his work the core of an ever growing society of social rejects. But it is also this hope that accounts for his bitterness at rejection, for the hatred of which Russell rightly pointed out the terrible consequences.

The currently idealized reaction to dictatorship and a police state is conspiracy for revolution, so the primary hope of communism, for destruction of capitalist society, carries within itself a lethal chromosome that will produce antibodies to attack whatever structure may grow from it. To attack—not to destroy. Disillusioned alike with democracy and with communism, the new revolutionists have found a new ideal—revolution as a way of life. The title, *Revolution for the Hell of It*, [30] perfectly sums up this theory and practice of pure rejection. But rejection requires an offer, violence needs a victim. So the new "rebel without a cause"[31] "is careful," as Sartre observes, "to preserve intact the abuses from which he suffers, so that he can go on rebelling against them. . . . He does not want to destroy or transcend the [existing] order, but only to rise up against it."[32] We have here the political equivalent of the sadist. At the core is rejection for the sake of rejection, the hope of opportunities for violence and cruelty. This hope requires that the playpen—the parental society, whether communist or capitalist—must be preserved. The James Bond props, costumes, and episodes are straight from television. But within these limits the play is in deadly earnest. The murders and cruelties are real; now, at long last, even the risks are becoming real. The reactionary trend towards capital punishment poses a serious threat to *avant-garde* murderers. But even this has one advantage. The game can now be played with a fine claim to self-sacrifice, self-righteousness, and dedication to a high (if not quite clearly defined) cause. That

[30] By "Free" (New York, 1968).

[31] A psychopathic type well analyzed by R. Lindner in the book with this title (New York, "1944." *Sic.* Properly 1955).

[32] J. Sartre, *Baudelaire*, 2nd ed. (Paris, 1947), pp. 58 f.

makes it all the more fun—a real kinky variation of the Cynic-anchorite paradox: rejection of moral obligations as a form of virtue. For the psychology, see the literature in defense of Manson and in praise of De Sade and Genet. Perhaps it may be a further consideration, to these pseudohumanitarians, that social revolution is probably the surest means of making most people most unhappy most quickly. Happiness commonly results from hopes and their gratifications, and most men's hopes (for work, advancement, home, children's careers, etc.) are shaped in terms of the prevailing social pattern. Destruction of the pattern not only disappoints the particular hopes, but may even destroy the capacity to form new ones.

IX

The history of utopianism sketched in the three preceding sections has illustrated the political side of the history of hope in the modern world, especially the growth of the hope (or threat?) to reshape men by controlling their social environment. Now we turn back to the other prophetic dream of the Renaissance, that of the alchemists, to reshape men by controlling their physical environment, the dream of which the realization has been the development of the physical sciences and engineering.

The causes of this development were incalculably complex. High among them, certainly, must be ranked the hope for wealth that launched the explorations of the fifteenth and sixteenth centuries, gave men for the first time correct knowledge (at least in outline) of the world they lived on, and led to the long history of European and American conquests and to the unprecedented concentration of wealth in Europe, the United States, and Canada. This wealth provided the capital to finance and the markets to justify the development of all sorts of practical conveniences, from steam engines and knitting mills to vulcanized rubber and automobiles, each one the result of some individual vision and particular, personal hopes, but together the means of transforming both society and scientific knowledge in a way neither envisioned nor hoped for. *A fortiori* the same has been true of the purely scientific advances financed by the same wealth, which have so changed our knowledge of nature and our ability to control it that even scientists cannot fully envisage the consequences. This ignorance is the most important scientific achievement. The present limits of the possible are beyond our ken. So, consequently, are the limits of hope, defined as "desire combined with expectation." We are, in a sense quite other than Wordsworth conceived, "moving about in worlds unrealized," but worlds of which the realization impends upon us, though it may be hastened or delayed, formed or disfigured, by our coming history. This unpredictability of the potentials of our new knowledge guarantees at least one of the essential conditions of hope, so long as we are able to continue to realize these potentials and to extend the knowledge further.

The importance of scientific progress for the nature of hope, not just for the achievement of particular objectives, can best be seen by comparison of the modest hopes that Bacon thought utopian (above, p. 128 f.) with the sorts of choices that are open to us now, thanks to the increase of our powers by the physical sciences. The increase is so great that the problem of hope has changed fundamentally. It is no longer how to achieve particular goals, nor even how to rank them (which to prefer and which to sacrifice). These questions of course continue to arise and are sometimes difficult, but they are always superficial. The fundamental problem of hope today is to decide *what* we hope to be. We glimpse now the possibility of modifying almost indefinitely human genetic characteristics, longevity, social structures, habitat, diet, of changing the requirements of the body and the possibilities of the mind so as to adapt both body and mind to conditions and tasks hitherto thought impossible. Granted that the possibility is still far from realization—farther, perhaps, than we are from Bacon—and that such changes may never in our generation become objects of practical hopes, they still lie on the horizon like clouds that promise a far-off storm. With such possibilities open, humanity is now faced with the awful question usually put to children, "What do you want to be when you grow up?" What sort of world do we want to make? What sort of creature do we want to become? The pious anticipation of St. John, "Beloved, now we are children of God, and it has not yet been revealed what we shall be" (I John 3:2), has now come to an unexpected fulfillment. The new, incalculable element in modern history—which means, in the history of the scientific age, the last century and a half—is the latent hope of a new kind of being living a new kind of life in a new world.

Besides confronting us with this fundamental problem, scientific advance has contributed a "principle of uncertainty" to every field from atomic physics to international politics. What will be possible ten years from now? Yet more, it has opened a great number of areas for research, that is, for the hopes of individual scholars. Each new discipline and science both expresses and makes possible new hopes, and the same is true of the extension of earlier disciplines to new fields. Taken together the resultant changes have amounted to a change in the character of the consciousness of the educated class and even, to some extent, of that of the average man. Jaspers rightly pointed out the enormous extension of modern man's apprehension by microscope, telescope, radio, television, recording, printing, etc., and consequently the creation of a new consciousness of the world by extending our knowledge of all parts of it.[33] But the change goes beyond this, and again it was foreshadowed by dreams, though in this case they were the dreams of reason.

Early nineteenth-century German philosophy, taking up the ideas of Origen and the later Neoplatonists, dreamed of the world as a single process, the progressive unfolding of the spirit. *"Es ist der Geist,"* said Goethe, *"der sich den Körper baut."*

[33]K. Jaspers, *The Origin and Goal of History,* tr. M. Bullock (London, 1953), p. 117.

("The spirit forms bodies for itself.") Gradually, through the subsequent century and a half, the dream has approached realization (with "matter" being substituted for "spirit" and "energy" for "matter") as the progress of the physical and social sciences has revealed in more and more detail the causes and nature of their interdependence. We now seem to be actually on the verge of a unified system of knowledge in which chemistry will be seen as a branch of physics, biology as a branch of chemistry, and anthropology as a branch of biology, while human psychology, linguistics (including mathematics), sociology, economics, history, and the studies of the various literatures, arts, and crafts, will all be seen as special fields of anthropology—studies of ways in which the human animal has reacted or will react in certain circumstances to certain stimuli. Since the past circumstances and stimuli can never be determined with complete accuracy, the account will always remain, in such fields as history, to some extent conjectural. But as the outlines of the main structure become increasingly clear, the parameters they provide will more and more limit conjectures in the particular areas and will bring into being a scientific understanding of the world and the self, in effect a new type of mentality. As applied to the future, the grasp of this new mentality will always be limited by the principle of uncertainty, the recognition of the incalculable variables that may arise. Students will therefore have a much clearer vision of possibilities, a better justified range of hopes, while retaining the uncertainty as to realization that makes hope possible.

These optimistic predictions depend on the supposition that political and social problems will be solved in such a way as to preserve the possibility of free research, and this means not only the permissibility but also the financing, for research of the sort now needed is enormously expensive and therefore mainly dependent, either directly or indirectly, on governments and great corporations that finance much of the work done in universities, hospitals, etc. The classical picture of the isolated scholar pursuing his studies in contented independence of the surrounding world is now out of date; few physical scientists now can work without equipment beyond their private means. Insofar as intellectual freedom depends on correct understanding of the physical world, our hopes for intellectual, political, and economic freedom must go together.

The political conditions for scientific research are especially precarious in communistic countries. If the USSR is in fact gradually growing out of its period as a police state—and one hopes against hope that it may be—this is because the positive achievements of Soviet science and social and economic studies have raised new questions, given rise to new hopes, and so enabled many of the intelligentsia to escape from the desert of political dogma. This escape, like that of imaginative artists, results in their alienation from the dismal orthodoxy of Russian society; hence the long series of trials, imprisonments, and expulsions of artists and scientists by the communist authorities. Artists can be safely liquidated or expelled; to the administrative mind they seem important, at most, for propaganda; but scientists may be both valuable and dangerous. Thus so long as competition with the free world continues, the communist rulers face a dilemma: if they encourage scientific research they encourage the escape of more and more of their intellectuals into private worlds of thoughts and hopes which, being rational, can be communicated and undermine the official system; but if they shut off scientific research they will fall behind in the international competition. This dilemma would not exist if they ruled the whole world; then society could be stabilized—at least for centuries—in approximately its present form and there would be no need for scientific advance. The communist rulers' perception of their dilemma may be a major factor impelling them to try their chances soon in a third world war. We may reasonably hope, however, to keep their chances poor.

If peace can thus be maintained we may indulge in the hopes for scientific progress sketched above. For research scholars and for those who devise applications of discoveries

there will be the repeatedly renewed challenge of novelty. For
most men the consequences will be perceived in changing
conditions of daily life, continuing and extending the availability of conveniences (and inconveniences) of all sorts, which
have already so far altered our circumstances that even those
who lived in the age before electricity was in common use can
hardly remember the limitations of that existence, and those
born after it can hardly conceive them. Will the life of 2078
differ from ours as greatly as ours differs from that of 1878
(when the electric light was invented)? Will the educated
man's understanding of the world change in the future century as greatly as it has in the seventy-five years since Einstein
received his doctorate? It may. Fundamental problems, for
instance, that of the nature and cause of consciousness, still
await solution. Will they be solved? We cannot tell, but we can
hope.

X

Looking back over this chapter's attempt to review in seventy-five pages the changes that a hundred centuries have produced in the hopes of western man, we can outline briefly
those most closely connected with the growth of society. Primitive men, living as families or groups of families in a "culture"
that offered a very small range of hopes, gradually, by slow
accumulation of experience and equipment, were led to the
development of civilization. With civilization came alienation:
rulers and priests, artists, writers and philosophers were led to
peculiar hopes for distant or special objectives, hopes that
most of their neighbors or subjects did not share, and these
hopes distinguished them from "the ordinary man." For ordinary men, with comparatively stable society came a certain
amount of security that their everyday needs would be satisfied. For the rulers and planners, security provided the
leisure necessary for developing larger hopes and the plans to
implement them. Their implementation—larger hunting expeditions, expansion of cultivated areas, journeys for trade,

colonization, conquests—resulted in some successes, some failures, and dissatisfaction arising from both, and shared by the ordinary men as well as the leaders. The dissatisfaction manifested itself in two sorts of hope: social, for reform of the society according to the wishes of the reformer, and antisocial, for individual escape from, exploitation of, or mastery of the society—e.g., the hopes of the anchorite, the criminal, the philosopher, the magician, the tyrant. Hopes for reform necessarily presuppose the idea of a society different from the existing one, at least in respect of the elements to be reformed; therefore they must be to some extent "utopian." If they fail wholly or in part, as they commonly do, the elements not realized may persist as a utopian tradition in the society and are apt to be connected with other sorts of utopianism resulting from suppressed infantile drives, fear of death, and the like. The almost universal refusal to accept the fact of human mortality commonly produces some sort of postmortal utopia; this is often matched by a legendary, prehistoric one, the lost infancy that never was. The utopian tradition produced by one or another combination of these elements may then influence further pretendedly practical plans for reform (as, for instance, the notion of the noble savage contributed to the liberal and leftist belief in the essential goodness of man and the consequent supposition that all human evils can be eliminated by proper socioeconomic arrangements—a supposition that has had disastrous consequences in shaping American foreign policy, to say nothing of its fundamental role in Marxist pictures of the future state.)

This *carte de l'espérance*, like the *carte du tendre* of the seventeenth century, has the advantages of simplicity and clarity, and the disadvantage that it does not always fit the facts. The most conspicuous discrepancies are those due to omission, and these were inevitable. My attempt was only to sketch the main features of the territory—as it were, the courses of the largest rivers—the great jungles and swamps have deliberately been passed by. Among the greatest of these is certainly the sub/unconscious (for convenience' sake let me say "sub-

conscious" without attempting to distinguish). Almost everyone would now admit that, alongside conscious hopes, subconscious ones, expressed in preferences, impulses, and patterns of behavior have probably done as much or more to
shape the course of events, and may have been no less shaped
by them. The disproportion in this treatment is understandable: the course of conscious history is well known, relatively
easy to describe, and there is so much of it that even a drasti-
cally summarized account, like the preceding, takes all the
space available. The history of the subconscious, on the contrary, is almost totally unknown and generally neglected. Indeed many of the psychologists most concerned with the subconscious would deny that it had a history. For them it is an
aspect of "human nature," and "human nature," like the dog-
mas of the Holy Catholic Church, is "in all times, all places,
and all men," forever the same.

Here anthropology and history are important correctives.
If the structure of the subconscious is determined by family
relations, it must have changed with the changes in the structure of families, changes that have occurred in many societies,
often within historical times; e.g., the dying out of the harem
in the near east, within the present century, should have produced a profound change in the psychological structure and
therefore in the subconscious hopes of the population, so
should the changes in family life that have taken place in the
west as cottage industry changed to centralized manufacture,
taking the fathers away from home, and again in our own time
as it became common for women to find outside employment
and the mother early moved out of the child's environment.
Not only changes in family structure, but changes in artifacts
must have produced profound changes in psychological
structure—notably so the development of clothes and the
different taboos about wearing them. *The Locomotive God*[34] is
a brilliant study of the role of even a relatively peripheral
artifact in the shaping of an individual psyche. (Is the current

[34]By W. Leonard (New York, 1927).

explosion of homosexuality in part a consequence of the spread of bottle feeding instead of breast feeding?) Again the development of purity laws, rules of politeness, and the like, should be studied not only as consequences of subconscious drives, but also as causes altering and perhaps even generating such drives, and in general further study of hope should give more attention to subconscious hopes and should try, so far as the evidence permits, to trace their changes.

Besides neglecting the subconscious, the preceding survey, to remain a survey, has had to omit important aspects of the history of conscious hopes. Nothing has been said of the sources, but their varieties, ranging from trivial details of everyday life to the most important elements of the greatest social structures, would tell us much about the varieties of hope. Consider, for instance, the history of popular songs as a record of the hopes of common people, how they changed as women came to do more of the family buying and so acquired more economic power—a change represented by "Little Grey Home in the West" and "My Blue Heaven"—and how they changed again when adolescents became affluent. Coinage, by contrast, records the hopes of the rulers, but also what the rulers thought their people hoped, since the claims made on the coinage, like those made in royal inscriptions, were intended to be popular. Yet another side of the picture is presented by the history of investments, loans, and deposits. "Creditor" means "believer," but faith without hope is not sufficient for investment. Thus a quantified study of hope as the basis of capitalist society should be possible.

Charities, too, are indicative of hope, and sometimes of quite important changes in it. For instance, ancient charities largely went to make life more enjoyable for those who could enjoy it—to cities, especially, for games, theaters, plays, gymnasia, temples, sacrifices, and public ceremonies and festivals, which were great shows and feasts for the public. The hope was to improve the quality of the present life. Christians rejected their cities in favor of the Christian conventicles they joined. Their charities went to these and their hopes were, first, to be rewarded in the next world for their self-denial in this one, and second, to take care of the dependent members of their group—the children, sick, invalid, aged, insane, and professionally religious. Except for the children, the religious, and those of the sick and insane who might recover, the beneficiaries were incapable of living healthy lives; they could at best hope for continuance of the unsatisfactory. Hence Christianity came to canonize those who denied themselves in order to prolong the miseries of others. A similar change in charity has taken place during the present century. In the early 1900s benefactors gave generally to projects that would improve the quality of public life: libraries, opera houses, museums, universities, parks and public gardens and concerts headed the list. Then came the social gospel. Now large gifts most often go to projects for the care of the incompetent: social work, hospitals, nursing homes, schools and other institutions for the handicapped. The hideous is generously financed and therefore flourishes.

Particularly important for the history of hope is the history of legislation. The legislator says people are to do what he hopes they will do. However, the fact that he has to lay down the law on the matter is usually an indication that some people, at least, are doing otherwise, or are likely to do so. Accordingly, almost all legislation, even the codification of customs, is to some extent a reaction to as well as an expression of hope. Often the gap between law and practice has been wide, this even in the earliest known period: the so-called cuneiform "codes" from Mesopotamia are often contradicted by preserved documents of particular cases. Similar discrepancies are indicated by Biblical, rabbinic, and Roman law. In sum, legal history is a history of hopes compromised, more or less, by practical considerations.

Even more intriguing is the question of the relation of hope to the history of the arts and the sciences. The great ages of art, literature, and learning coincide, for the most part, with the peaks of political and economic power of the countries concerned. (When they do not coincide, the discrepancy commonly results from the continuance of an artistic or scholarly tradition after the collapse of a political power.) Thus the great periods of Egyptian art are those of the great Pharaohs and of the revival of national power under the Saite dynasty; Assyrian art reaches its peak during the greatest extension of the late Assyrian empire; Persian art, with the Achaemenid empire and again with the rise of the Sassanids; the first great age of Greek art (as distinct from Minoan) begins and ends with the flowering of Mycenae; the next begins with the great expansion of Greek colonization and the composition of the Homeric poems in the late eighth century, and ends with the conquest of Greece by Macedon. Hellenistic art and learning flourish in Alexandria and Pergamum precisely when those cities enjoy their greatest wealth and power. The greatest art and literature of the Roman republic dates from the period of its greatest extent, and that of the empire comes from the age of Augustus. It is needless to continue. Anyone familiar with modern literature will immediately think of examples; those of Spain, Italy, and the Netherlands are conspicuous. But how is this correlation to be explained? Is it simply that the peak of political and economic power financed works of art and scholarly studies which otherwise could not have been undertaken? Sometimes this is surely the case; had there been no Athenian empire there would have been no Parthenon. Or is the distribution due to the subjectivity of criticism? Only the works produced in great powers are given great attention; nobody will ever hear of the foremost poet of Andorra, whatever his merits. But may it not also be the case that in great powers men feel themselves of importance, look to the future, and have hope? This is true especially of the leaders, but the leaders give the tone to the whole society. Conversely, too, the stagnation of intellectual life in powerless countries may be seen as a consequence of the deprivation of hope. Hence the insignificance of Greece after the Roman takeover, of the Arab world after the Turkish conquest, of Spain in the late seventeenth and the eighteenth centuries (Goya is a lighthouse on a barren reef), and of Turkey after the industrial revolution in the west. The upper classes had plenty of money and leisure, but no hope to lift them above personal relations, private pleasures, and religious fantasies.

All such explanations that begin with objective "historical" facts (i.e., those of political, military, and economic history) and go on from them to "explain" artistic developments, religious movements, and the like appeal to historians, who are primarily trained in political, military, and economic history, are well supplied with documents to demonstrate "objective" events, and like to believe that the history of culture is determined by such documented causes. But it may be that both the "historical" and the artistic achievements were consequences of psychological changes that manifested themselves first in the social activities of drastic and dynamic men, but later affected also the more reflective and creative characters. One unfortunate consequence of rationalism has been that our justified disbelief in *daimones* has led to unjustifiable neglect of the demonic, the tidal waves of passion and power which, as Longfellow said, "come to us at times from the unknown and inaccessible solitudes of being,"[35] and not to individuals only, but to societies. The economic interest of shepherds has made *panic* a pejorative term, but Pan was the god of fertility and could seize men as well as animals. Perhaps such great seizures as those which occurred at Athens in the fifth century and at Florence in the fifteenth may best be understood as manifestations of the power indicated by his name.

At the opposite emotional extreme from panic, but comparable to it as a cause of enormous changes in popular hopes, is fashion, another phenomenon of which the preceding survey has said nothing, though it has often played a role of the utmost importance in cultural history, for instance, in the popularization of gymnasia in ancient Greece and the changes that followed from their frequentation. Another, comparably important, example of its influence can be seen in the change

[35] "The Sound of the Sea," in *A Book of Sonnets.*

from the ancient to the modern attitude toward children, in their parents' hopes for them, and consequently in their own hopes and notions of themselves. This example is the more impressive because it directly contradicts the guidelines for hope that are given by "objective facts." Objectively children are inferior because they are small, weak, and ignorant. These facts are constantly rubbed into them by other children who are bigger, stronger, and more experienced than they. Therefore the normal child wants to become bigger, stronger, and more experienced, in sum, "to grow up." Poor parents and ambitious parents also commonly hope their children will grow up quickly and, if poor, become more useful, if rich, realize their ambitions. The ancient world was one of extreme poverty, by our standards, and of extreme ambition in the upper classes, because of the competitive tradition strong in both Greece and Rome. Therefore ancient pictures and statues of children and plans for their education commonly represent the ideal child—the child as nearly adult as possible. Children are shown in the arts with adult proportions, their clothes are adult garments in smaller sizes, their reading consists of those books which adults believe every adult ought to know—first of all, Homer. The life of the child is thought of as differing from that of the adult mainly by being inferior, undeveloped, preparatory, not yet serious. Therefore no books describe or perpetuate—let alone, teach—childrens' life for its own sake. Only with the development of a rich middle class, in the seventeenth and eighteenth centuries, when parents have money for leisure and sentimentality, but assured and at the same time limited social positions, that make ambition relatively unimportant, does the life of the patrons of the arts and the makers of fashion begin to revolve around the home, so that the children *as children* become important decorations, and parents no longer want them grown up. Italy led the way in this development of bourgeois luxury and sentimentalism. The realistic observations of infant stature, by the artists of the Renaissance, are developed in the seventeenth and eighteenth centuries into caricatures of balloon-headed babies. Every picture is invaded by the population of *putti*. The fashion of infantilism spreads to literature and education; childhood is discovered to have values of its own (innocence, virtue, proximity to the gods—all of these lost in adult life), literary works are written to glorify it and are used in education to keep the little readers childish. Hence *Peter Pan*. In such children's books there is no long-term hope. The future, growing up, is inevitable, but undesired. The implicit teaching is, live for the present, and the understandable consequence is the crop of adult babies in our bars.

Between fashion and panic lies a third topic we have mostly left unexplored, that of the obscure commerce between conscious hopes and anticipations. We remarked that dreams, daydreams, and visions, whether philosophic, scientific, or otherwise abnormal, have repeatedly presented objects of hope that were not yet known. Such dreams and visions, too, have often determined the direction of scientists' research and consequently the ways in which human powers were extended. It should now be remarked that when research does result in an extension of human powers, it is often the dreams already occupying men's thoughts that determine how the new powers are to be used.

Thus from time immemorial men dreamed of changing their sex, and of visiting the moon. The ancient Greek myth of Tiresias' change of sex was shaped by wishful thinking, and trips to the moon go back to Lucian and Menippus, and probably to prehistoric daydreams. But now these dreams have become hopes—and have become so because they first were dreams. There was no "practical reason" for research to be directed to change of sex; no major therapeutic need was met by the techniques developed to imitate this change; they were developed simply because there was a market for them, because there was a dream that became a hope as soon as opportunity appeared. Similarly, although landing on the moon enabled us to perform various experiments of interest to astronomers, the immense expenses of the lunar landing programs were undertaken primarily, not for the sake of scientific knowledge, but because of their publicity value for the propaganda contest we were then carrying on with Russia. Their publicity value was due, again, not to the scientific, political, military, or economic importance of landing men on the moon, but to the landing's ability to capture popular interest and therefore television audiences. This it could do because most of those audiences had been brought up on Buck Rodgers and because Buck Rodgers' popularity in turn was derived from the age-old dream of travel to the heavens.

Such dreams and visions are of particular importance for social policy as indications of the areas and directions of unsatisfied hopes. From unsatisfied hopes come the seismic upheavals that shake the foundations of governments and civilizations. These unsatisfied hopes are mainly those of the central nervous system. From the hopes generated by the muscles and the other bodily organs come the practical activities calculated to satisfy them—hunting, fishing, agriculture, milling, cooking, pottery, building, weaving, the techniques that are the bases of stable civilization. Populations concerned only with these hopes and occupied with these techniques are conspicuously stable. So far as I can recall, no major revolution has ever been carried through by a peasant population—this in spite of their numbers and of the hardships and oppression to which they have been exposed. Peasants have often provided the manpower and sometimes some of the leaders (e.g., Mao), but I do not know of any instance in which committees of peasants actually managed the proceedings. The notion that revolutions result from poverty is false; revolutions result from hopes generated by the brain. "Liberty, equality, and fraternity" has been a successful slogan; "Bread, beef, and beer" has not. The goblet on the banner of the Hussites represented their demand for communion in both kinds, not for cheaper wine. Even the Russians chose as their emblems a hammer and sickle, not a pair of shoes and a loaf of bread (and again the images were premonitory of what their subjects were to be given). The most widely advertised of unsatisfied hopes at present is probably that for equality, but "equality," as we have seen, is a euphemism for "rule." "Rule" means power, and power means nothing save what the aspirants plan to do with it. The many aspirants are at odds with each other and have no generally accepted, positive plans. As usual, the kingdom of heaven is undescribed.

Between the demands of the body and the dreams of the central nervous system lie the complex desires generated by the sexual organs and the senses, and ranging from purely physical pleasures to the hope of love and the vision of beauty. Notions of beauty and love have changed profoundly in and because of the course of history, and have often sufficed to change even the quality of sensible experiences. Actions once alluring have become revolting, what was beautiful in one age has been found garish or colorless in another, and so on. Now that the relation of sexuality to dreams has been established, that of taste to dreams should be investigated. In the earliest times "poet" and "prophet" were one. Hesiod and Amos were members of this common category; Greek and Roman poets continued until imperial times to affect prophetic dignity. The affectation should not be wholly discredited; Shelley resumed it in earnest with his claim that "poets are the unacknowledged legislators of the world" *(In Defense of Poetry),* an exaggeration that conceals an element of truth: the visions first expressed by artists and prophets, when they gain acceptance, shape the hopes and ultimately the legislation of succeeding generations. Much poetry of the Old Testament prophets has been recast in federal legislation and Supreme Court decisions of this century. Further, the artist's vision is prophetic because it is a perception of a type of order, of which the work of art, and especially its beauty, is the expression. But the perception of order is the essence of understanding. Therefore, as Plato perceived, beauty is an introduction to the intellectual world. The expression of order as beauty is not directly translatable, but has an irresistible charm for the young whose sensations are still most vivid.

Perception of beauty is the understanding of the young; understanding is the beauty of the old. This holds for works of nature, as well as art. A beautiful person or animal is the creation and expression of a biochemical order that has moulded the limbs in its own image. Every beautiful object offers a promise of understanding; if it were not understandable, it would not be beautiful. What the brain, as a product of nature, perceives as harmonious, is the order of nature that produced it. As the body hardens and the senses lose their sensitivity, the mind's eye focuses on the intellectual order, and by understanding realizes the hope that the senses aroused. This was summed up by Yeats in *Sailing to Byzantium:*

> Soul . . . [has no] singing school but studying
> Monuments of its own magnificence.

If we look at these monuments—the expressions of the hopes of men through the five thousand years and more of occidental history—we find them, insofar as they transcend the immediate objectives of their times, constantly centered on two hopes which are essentially one: the hopes for life and power. Not qualified life or power—as we have seen, the pictures of heaven, the world to come, the classless society, and so on, from time immemorial have been amazingly devoid of positive characterization save in the most general terms; the Middle Ages insisted on beauty, modern visionaries insist most often on love (e.g., Marx's "brotherhood"). Both these are promises of understanding, and Plato saw deeper than both when he chose "intelligibility." Jaspers echoes him in arguing that, with the appearance of history, reality as a process becomes conscious, and if history is a true breakthrough, not merely a transitory phenomenon, "it will lead to Being's becoming manifest through man and to man . . . [with] potentialities of which we can have no foreknowledge."[36] Again the conception of utopia as a creative environment, not a fixed, describable creation! "The last enemy that

---

[36] K. Jaspers, *The Origin and Goal of History,* tr. M. Bullock (London, 1953), pp. 47 ff.

shall be overcome is death," said Paul (I Cor. 15:26). This victory is the ultimate goal of the hopes of western man, and those hopes have been shaped in the course of history not only by the particular influences, reviewed above, of historical events on the visions of particular ages, but more profoundly by the progressive revelation of history itself—men's increasing perception of a continuous, intelligible course of events in which they, and all humanity, are involved, in which significant changes can be produced by human actions, and in which, although the individual participants are transitory, the process of understanding, the intellectual life, continues and increases.

IV

The Hope for Hope

I

Now that we have seen something of the psychological roots from which hopes grow and the historical ramifications they have formed, does this knowledge help us understand our present predicament, the crisis of hope described in Chapter I? If we do understand it better, what can we do about it?

Our predicament, as the reader will remember, was brought into focus by realization that the extension of human settlement was probably near its end. For the predictable future we shall be limited to the earth and its resources, some already almost exhausted. Hence we have to choose what to do with the means that remain. Choice is made difficult by lack of accepted standards, neglect of traditional morality, rejection by many social groups of basic values of western civilization, defense of such groups by cultural relativism, private escape by the irresponsible into various adult playpens, and the frequency with which the responsible turn to philanthropy and so strengthen the sickly elements of our society at the expense of the healthy. All these difficulties might be represented as consequences of the lack of a common, adequate hope; hence investigation of the history of hope might be expected to yield relevant results.

It does. It indicates that no common hope will be adequate. Between such generalities as "the common good" and such personal wants as health, food, and a good night's sleep, there are few hopes that everyone in our society can be expected to share. This follows from the connection observed between the growth of society and the alienation of most of its members from each other and from the society as a whole. As the hopes possible to cultivated men become more extensive and require more out-of-the-way knowledge, they also become more remote from the personal hopes of the average man, who is himself alienated from his fellows by the formation of personal hopes, as distinct from the common concerns of earlier tribesmen. Primitive society did not enable its members to form their own households, indulge their own tastes, and live private lives; our society does, and the penalty of privacy is selfishness.

We have written hitherto of a crisis of hope, but the historical survey has shown us a crisis of hopes. There is no one great hope of salvation common to everyone. Several brands are on the market—Christianity, Islam, Communism, psychoanalysis (Freud and Marx ran true to type in proclaiming gospels for all mankind)—but none can claim universal acceptance or invariable success. Rather than such panaceas, the needs of most individuals seem determined by their peculiar characters. For the intellectual, the only hope is a life of intellectual exploration; towards the other end of the spectrum, the stupid hope for a life of physical comfort and animal affection, with a little televised violence for excitement. And so on, variations are innumerable.

II

Given this range of hopes, many people suppose the best society to be that which offers the widest range of gratifications. Some hopes, however, had better not be gratified. The rapist, the sadist, and their respectable analogues, the ruthless accumulators of capital or of administrative power, should not be left to play at will. Either their liberty and pursuit of happiness should be so curtailed as to condemn them to perpetual frustration, or their characters should be remoulded by "reeducation," as the Communists call it, to which many of the Communists' pupils prefer death. It would be more economical and effective, and probably more merciful, to curtail their lives. Death is the one sure cure for sadistic impulses, and the grave, the one house of detention from which nobody can escape (or get out on parole) to commit another murder.

Besides these individual aberrations, historical review has shown several areas in which problems of hope lie at the bases of contemporary social crises. First there is the economic-ecological, from which we began in Chapter I. This is clear. Western civilization has developed a pattern of hopes—for survival of offspring, medical care, diet, housing, controlled environment, education, clothing, gadgetry, etc.—which, if continued by the West alone, would soon run through the world's known resources, and if extended to the rest of mankind would bring almost immediate disaster. If all adult Chinese, Indians, and Africans were given automobiles and allowed to run them freely, the air pollution and increase of temperature would soon make most of the world uninhabitable. Yet "the western way of life" has become the great white hope of many orientals and Africans. Moreover, important aspects of it—particularly the hope for the survival of children —have been so far realized that many in third world countries are close to starvation. Either (1) the western pattern of hope must be changed, or (2) its extension must be limited to certain peoples and social classes, or (3) new sources of materials and energy must be found for its gratification, and new techniques, to prevent its gratification from making the world uninhabitable. All these possibilities will probably be realized to some extent. (1) The pattern of western hopes will change as prices rise and materials become unavailable. (2) The extension of upper class western ways of life to the rest of the world will slow down or cease. (3) These changes will be somewhat cushioned by scientific and technological developments and discovery of resources. The immediate dangers are the political consequences of a declining standard of living in the West, disappointment of vocal elements in undeveloped countries, and exploitation of the discontented by Russia, China, and the United States in their competition for resources and power.

Competition for resources and power will continue and increase, not only because of its roots in human nature, but also because of the increase of population and the hope for western ways of life. Consequently budgets will continue to tighten, more careful planning will be necessary, and harder choices (like God's on new year's day—Who is to live, and who to die?) will have to be made. Insofar as our rulers exercise their divine right systematically (not very far) their choices will be guided in part by their notions of societies they hope to produce, i.e. by plans more or less utopian. This brings us to the second area in which contemporary social crises arise from problems of hope, viz. social planning. Our review of the history of utopianism showed that the weakness of most utopias was to overlook psychological problems: they supposed that, if a society could assure economic sufficiency for its members, the members would be happy and virtuous. The unlikelihood of this was foreseen by Genesis and demonstrated by Freud, not to mention the horrors of communist, nazi, and fascist societies. Henceforth the dangers of social planning will be clear to all informed and intelligent persons except those who hope to benefit from it. Nevertheless, it is necessary. The question is one of degree. We find ourselves in a range at both ends of which there are danger points. If planning exceeds the safe maximum our society will degenerate into a tyranny; if it falls below the safe minimum, we shall have chaos. Between these uncertain boundaries lies the Vanity Fair of the politicians, where policies are determined by personal interests. Personal interest makes most politicians wary of thorough social planning: by that, they themselves might be liquidated. Nevertheless, increasing economic need is gradually forcing them towards increased planning. Their reluctant progress does leave time for discussion of utopias. The discussion is mostly academic and literary, but may prevent some future utopias from having the more dreadful characteristics of those past.

In all major governments now extant or likely to arise, the participation of most citizens in the process of government is and will be mainly passive and ritualistic. They will participate by doing what they are told, and not doing what they are told not to, by filling out income tax forms, observing traffic regulations, receiving relief checks, going to polls and pulling levers beside names of persons about whom they are almost wholly ignorant, and so on. While their societies remain relatively stable and satisfactory, matters of governmental theory and practice will not rank high among their hopes. Instead, they will hope for various personal goodies. The inconsistencies between their various hopes, between their hopes, capabilities and opportunities, between their hopes and those of their families, neighbors, and societies, will continue to occupy respectively their psychiatrists, clergy, teachers, and lawyers, not to mention the social agencies involved. As a whole, such private affairs make up the third area in the current crisis of hopes. We touched in Chapter I on major aspects of this area: disintegration of home life, increase of loneliness and selfishness (degenerating into sadism and violence), increase of crime, disintegration of the educational system, and increase of private escapism in many forms, among which drug addiction and superstition have recently been conspicuous. The social background and interconnection of these phenomena have been described; the importance in them of intellectual myopia and terminological confusion should also be noticed. Many of the great hopes of our society turn out on inspection to be great equivocal terms of which the meanings are imperfectly understood. Three examples (of many) are "progress," "wealth," and "pity."

"Progress" begs the question, "progress towards what"? The usual answers are "human happiness," "the greatest good of the greatest number," and so on. But these may not be compatible. Attainment of "the greatest good" as defined by the greatest number would probably result in a society of television entertainment and plastic vulgarities, where nobody would be happy. Both "good" and "happiness" need definition. The difficulty of defining "good" is notorious, but many still think "happiness" an emotional condition well defined by common usage. Any child old enough to talk can tell you whether or not it's happy; if unhappy, it's likely to insist on telling you. Plato pointed out that such happiness is apt to be self-destructive. You can make an average baby happy by giving it a piece of candy, and then another, and then another, and . . . You can make an average man happy by giving him a new automobile, and then . . .? The hope of keeping humanity happy by feeding it an interminable succession of new gadgets (the hope implicit in the advertising and social policies of much of the business world) will lead to ecological indigestion. Even worse, it leads to decreasing emotional returns. As gadgets become more common, they cause less happiness. The nausea of the sixties, which affected chiefly children of the well-to-do, can plausibly be seen as the result, in part, of technological overfeeding. Give them too many toys and they start to break them. So what, if it makes them happy? So they go on from toys to people. What was a nuisance becomes a danger. Both nuisance and danger make the rest of us unhappy; our reactions make the little darlings unhappy; the pursuit of human happiness by subhuman devices ends in a failure predictable by everyone but the executives of manufacturing corporations and their advertising companies.

Most of those who admit that they hope for "wealth" go on to claim that they want it "as a means, not an end." The number of real misers, persons who actually loved and hoarded money for its own sweet sake, was probably never large and must have been reduced by the introduction of paper currency and the development of stock agencies. To love a Merrill Lynch Pierce Fenner & Smith monthly statement is something like loving the First Cause—an exercise in passionate abstraction of which few are capable. Nevertheless, the hope for "wealth" goes far beyond the hopes for "the things money can buy," because some of the more important things money can buy are those acquired by not spending it—security, power, prestige, a standing higher than one's neighbors. Being thus a matter of comparison, wealth is threatened by its general increase; when other people become wealthy, those of the wealthy whose fortunes do not increase become relatively poorer, the more so because wealth is commonly measured in terms of money. Concentration of hope on this single form leads to intense competition and perpetual disappointment (exemplified in the familiar wage-price spiral and its too familiar consequences of inflation, depreciation of the currency, and so on). Hence to collect statistics proving greater "wealth" does nothing to demonstrate an increase of "the wealthy" (*pace* Mr. Wattenberg).[1] As the standard of living rises, the poverty level rises, too. The "experts" in the social services push it up, to demonstrate the continued need for their service, but popular psychology pushes it faster, because "poverty," like "wealth," in the western world is more often a psychological than an economic condition. When the Watts riots occurred in Los Angeles, "fully 65%" of the families in the areas that produced the rioters owned automobiles.[2] The main grievance of one of the looters was that she had been forced to pay for a television set she had bought on credit. To make up for this outrage she stole three more. These and similar thefts were described by a liberal historian as consequences "of acute and chronic material deprivation."[3] Since the standard of living of the poor, especially in America, has recently risen beyond all precedent, we are now faced by vast increases in the numbers of the dissatisfied and the intensity of the dissatisfaction. That the standard of living of the middle class has correspondingly declined (in quality, as distinct from dollar cost) has further increased these increases. Thus one consequence of the general hope for wealth seems to have been a great extension of psychological poverty.

[1] B. Wattenberg, *The Real America* (New York, 1974), an invaluable collection of data.

[2] A. Fogelson, "White on Black," *Social Studies Review,* IV (1966), p. 356.

[3] A. Fogelson, "The 1960's Riots," *Report to the Commission on Law Enforcement,* pp. 41 and 48.

THE HOPE FOR HOPE

"Pity" is another generally admired term of which the general admiration is likely to be lethal. We hope to be, and to be thought, compassionate. We hope to be so because we are so. As already observed, the "compassion" of parents for their offspring is basic for the survival of most mammals, including man, and in all animal society groups whose members sacrificed themselves for each other were most likely to survive—a rule exemplified in history by the successes of early Christianity and of modern Judaism. Both the lady in *The Choirboys*[4] who had her baby in the ladies' room and left it in the trash can, and the policeman who commented that she should not be prosecuted—"she did the taxpayers a favor"— defy a compulsion that rises from the depths of our emotional structure, the compulsion Kant called "the categorical imperative" and thought the voice of God. However, the other side, too, has its philosophers, not only Nietzsche, but Plato as interpreted by the Neoplatonists. For them compassion, defined as a consequence of love for something inferior, is a form of the primal sin, the mind's turning away from the contemplation of perfection to the enjoyments of the lower world. If we turn away from these metaphysical speculations to the actual situation as perceived by a sensitive observer, we find Pound writing:

> Compleynt, compleynt I hearde upon a day,
> Artemis singing, Artemis, Artemis
> Agaynst Pity lifted her wail:
> Pity causeth the forests to fail,
> Pity slayeth my nymphs,
> Pity spareth so many an evil thing,
> Pity befouleth April,
> Pity is the root and spring.
> . . .
> All things are made foul in this season.
> This is the reason, none may seek purity

---

[4] J. Wambaugh, *The Choirboys* (New York, 1976), p. 307.

> Having for foulnesse pity . . .
> Nothing is now clean slayne
> But rotteth away.[5]

Only it doesn't. It pullulates. To say nothing more of the undeveloped countries, in America and Europe professional criminals, protected by organized pity, increase daily. So do professional welfare recipients, our new leisure class. So do the insane. Pity makes discipline difficult, protects lazy workers and students, and, for their sakes, penalizes good ones who are denied the opportunities and consequences of rising in their employment or mastering their studies because the lazy will not. Wherever one turns in this culture one finds rot protected by pity.

III

Discussion of the dubious nature and dangerous consequences of such "great common hopes" has taken us away from the problem with which we began: If the search for some common hope to unify and motivate our society has proved vain, what can we do about the current crisis of hopes? Let us try another tack, and begin by asking, "Who are we?"

"We" are a literary convention behind which lies the society that made it conventional, the "good society" of the essayists of Victorian England, a relatively uniform and, as to social ideals, unanimous group. "We" knew what "we" hoped to maintain: a society in which business would prosper, government would be just, honest, and economical, but sufficient to maintain good order at home and protect our interests abroad; a society free, as far as possible, of corruption and crime; a society where no one would starve or go without clothes and shelter, and where, beyond these minima, everyone would be rewarded according to his works; a God-fearing society, pious, but tolerant, free of superstition, universally

---

[5] E. Pound, *The Cantos* (New York, n.d.), Canto XXX, p. 147.

literate, its leaders men of education and good breeding, aware of current intellectual developments, open to new ideas, but also devoted to the best elements of western European civilization and to the characteristics of our own tradition. This was the common *ideal.* When, as often, there were deviations in practice, the offenders could be exposed with the expectation that "everybody" (who mattered) would disapprove. When writers disputed as to how "we" could attain or preserve the ideal, and what "we" should do to remedy particular abuses or achieve specific goals, the disputes were, so to speak, within the family. They took for granted "our" common concern. They also set a literary pattern perpetuated in newspaper editorials, and convenient. I have often fallen into it, and shall fall again.

Nevertheless, this pattern is now an anachronism. The assumption of basic agreement can no longer be made. Instead of writing about what "we" should do to maintain the traditional order, one can only discuss what might be done by unspecified persons who might somehow or other attain the power to do it. To quote a recent sociological study, "Post-industrial society will be a society of subcultures with different values and preoccupations.... There is increasingly no 'compact majority,' only a steady proliferation of divergent minorities.... Social policy ... may increasingly have to learn how to manage diversity."[6] If there is no "compact majority" those who "manage" "social policy" must also be a minority. But which? Not only members of different social circles, but also representatives of different psychological types want different ideal societies. When the French Revolution came, the Salpêtrière mental hospital was cleared out as if by magic: the patients saw outside a ready-made drama offering them heroic identity and self-transcending action. When society went insane, the insane found themselves at home. Too many of them still are.

In this situation "we, the people" actually means "we, the

---

[6] R. Mills, *Young Outsiders* (New York, 1974), pp. 189 f.

members of the ruling cliques." To talk of "government by
the people" is ludicrous. Practically, the average citizen is
almost utterly powerless. What can you do about any political question? Write your senator? I am tempted to insert
sample letters and replies for comic relief. Or tragic? The
power of election permits "the people" to choose between
candidates selected by rival cliques, and the need of election
leads most cliques and candidates to avoid open advocacy of
unpopular measures and also, especially before elections, to
advocate popular ones. Thanks to this "true democracy" al-
coholic beverages and cigarettes, two major causes of death,
are still widely advertised and readily available; there will be
no great increase of the tax on gasoline, nor on the oil im-
ported to produce it; in general, no candidate for office
openly advocates any increase of taxes, except on "the
rich." Such phenomena do attest the people's vague veto
power, but to describe the system subject to this restraint as
"government by the people" is typical of political orators
and high school "civics" teachers. In fact we are governed
by what C. Wright Mills called "the power elite," though he
should have extended the term to include, e.g., the heads of
pressure groups which persons anxious for power have organized to oppose government by other groups of the
power elite. In a government so constituted all laws must be
the work of one or another clique or alliance of cliques acting, as Plato said, in what they believe to be their own interest (and may also sometimes believe to be the interest of the
rest of the people).

IV

What are the cliques, what are their powers, and what do
they want? These questions should be preliminary to any
account of what we may hope from government action. They
are far easier to ask than to answer. Exact delimitation of the
cliques is impossible. They are neither mutually exclusive nor
internally consistent. Important individuals commonly be-

long to several cliques, and many cliques contain bitter rivals and members of considerably differing views. As to what they want, their long-term hopes, these are matters of speculation on which, most often, they do not speculate. One does not usually organize a successful pressure group by discussing social theory or ultimate objectives, but by "lining up" friends, acquaintances, and outsiders likely to be interested, so as to get this measure through or stop that one. Cooperation in such *ad hoc* enterprises is often based on particular personal interests; sometimes it has no further consequences; more often it is the consequence or beginning of a political friendship that may become consistent, and may eventually lead to some private discussion (tactfully restrained) of further objectives. For the public, the clouds of rumor, the camouflage of deceit, the confusing battle cries of competing parties, make the whole process like Tennyson's description of Arthur's "last, dim, weird battle of the west" where "friend and foe were shadows in the mist."[7]

Out of the mist loom up vaguely five giant figures, big government, the big poor, big labor, big business, and big crime. As might be expected in Arthurian legend, they are all monsters with multiple heads. That is to say, none is controlled by a single group nor follows invariably a consistent program, and they ally with or attack each other by turns, as convenience dictates. Nevertheless, their typical hopes are roughly discernible.

The core of big government is its beneficiaries: the enormous federal and state civil bureaucracies, the enormous military establishment, and the professional politicians (except those in the pay of other interests). A second circle of beneficiaries are those nominally independent but employed by government: a vast number of contractors and subcontractors, not to mention lawyers for whom the extension of government regulations has been a godsend. These circles have a large following of believers in bureaucracy who think the

---

[7] *The Passing of Arthur,* 94 ff.

best way to deal with any social problem is to impose more government regulations and set up a new bureau to administer them. The first hope of a bureaucrat is to keep his job, the second, to get a raise. As altruists, they hope to expand the system, so as to get jobs for their relatives and friends. The theoreticians among them often hope for achievement of complete socialism, that is, subordination of all business and labor to governmental managers, and abolition of substantial private wealth, so that all citizens will be dependent on the governmental managers for food, housing, pre-natal and maternity care, baby watching, education, employment, entertainment, medical care, care in old age, and burial. Since the managers do not produce wealth, this hope of saddling the workers with the cost of an enormous, indolent directorate would seem ridiculous were it not near realization.

The most reliable allies of big government are the big poor, since they are its pensionaries. "The big poor" must be distinguished from "the poor," of which they are only a part. Most communities contain some poor and help them with wise economy. In the cities, however, more generous welfare programs have attracted vast numbers of determined recipients. The poor have taken over entire districts and sometimes control the government. Such groups are "the big poor," a major political power. Their hopes are clear. Having established themselves as a new leisure class, they hope for more money to enable them to enjoy their leisure, and less supervision to interfere with their enjoyment. Better medical care would be welcome, so would better housing—though they reserve the right to break it up or burn it down, just for fun. These hopes they rarely formulate with clarity, but express by their actions, their choice of representatives, and their resistance to resettlement projects, not to mention opportunities of employment (which might require work).

Big labor is even more sharply distinguished from "labor" than "the big poor" from "the poor." "Big labor" is the unionized minority of the American labor force. The unions were formed primarily to get better wages, shorter hours, and better working conditions; they have raised their sights to include security of employment, support during unemployment, insurance for sickness and old age, many minor "fringe benefits," maximal pay for minimal labor, and an assortment of sinecures for union organizers. The members also hope to get their friends and relatives into the union and find jobs for them. The leaders commonly hope to keep their union positions and increase their already large salaries. Traditionally allied with big government in its battle against big business, the unions have now been so successful that their members, by income, are an important part of the middle class; their political hopes are changing accordingly and the change is complicated by the fact that their leaders, now wealthy, often have interests in big business and/or big crime. Accordingly the ambivalence of this central figure is one of the factors that makes the course of the battle most dubious.

Big business and big crime sometimes seem to be Siamese twins, crime, as already observed, being one of our biggest businesses, and many big businesses (entertainment, hotels, transport, etc.) having important links with criminal interests. Like the preceding groups, both are distinct from the larger totalities, "business" and "crime," though here the distinctions are less sharp and less often perceived. The hopes of big business and big crime are hardest to identify because here one has to do less with uniform classes having uniform interests than with a great number of highly capable, extremely various, and variously situated individuals, most of them free of immediate economic needs, and many imaginative, original, capable of important action on their own without regard for the apparent interests of their group. They are most nearly at one in their opposition to big government, though the government activities to which they most object are not identical. For big business they are those entailing what the editors of *Fortune* described as,

> Social drag . . . the combined effects of the excessive costs, inefficiencies, and disincentives that government imposes

on . . . the private sector. . . . Social drag includes such
things as:

Welfare payments and unemployment benefits so generous that they erode incentive to look for work and to accept
work that is offered.
Busybody regulation not disciplined by rational cost-
benefit calculation.
Bureaucratic overstaffing.
Statutory minimum wages, which reduce employment
opportunities for unskilled workers, especially young people.
Government-granted privileges that enable labor unions
to establish unreasonable work rules and to force wage
increases far in excess of productivity gains. . . .
Social drag is both inflationary and depressive. Extra
costs translate sooner or later into higher prices. What's
more, the growing scope and size of welfare-state entitle-
ments unrelated to work help create an excess of claims
upon the output of the economy. . . . On the supply side,
social drag diverts resources from investment to consumption, dulls incentives to work and to invest, and channels
enormous numbers of working hours into such unproduc-
tive activities as administering unsound regulations and trying to comply with the same.[8]

This should be read as a piece of (truthful) propaganda
written, not to attract popular following (how many of the
populus read *Fortune?*) but to rally members of the group, win
their support for this common platform, and give them a
common set of objectives and arguments. If the defenders of
big government set forth a counter catalogue of "business
malpractice" it would probably include such things as:

Needless exploitation of natural resources so as to destroy both them and the environment.

[8] *Fortune,* XCVI (November 1977), p. 103.

Neglect of the dangers of manufacturing processes both to the workers employed and to the neighbors of the plants.

Neglect of the dangers of products to those likely to use them.

Misrepresentation of inferior products.

Promotion of inferior, perishable products so as to drive good, lasting ones off the market.

Needless changes of products and failure to stock parts of earlier models, so as to render those obsolete and un-repairable.

Increases of price not justified by increase of cost.

Exportation of American capital, skills and machines to start firms abroad that will employ sweatshop labor, pro-duce cheap goods, put Americans out of work, and yield profits exempt from American taxes.

Retention of profits without regard to the stockholder's right to a fair return.

Distribution of profits without regard to stockholders' interests, in huge bonuses to board members and upper administrative employees.

Extensive bribery of public officials.

Clearly both these lists are negative. They tell us what these parties hope to get rid of, but say nothing of what they hope to produce. The hopes of the big government party are fairly predictable from European and Chinese examples; those of big business and big crime are unpredictable as a whole be-cause of the variety and unpredictability of the individuals involved. To make matters worse, big government is the best customer of big business; important business executives regularly take high posts in the government, while generals, admirals, secretaries and undersecretaries of departments re-tire to take posts in corporations. What can be made of a battle in which the engaging giants exchange their heads? The evidence suggests that there may be a "power elite atti-tude" shared by businessmen, bureaucrats, gang leaders, labor leaders and politicians alike. If so, the chief hope common to all of them is probably that their present comfortable situation will continue.

V

The preceding sketch of America's most influential groups has of course omitted many. Religious groups have not been included, though they have much influence and it will increase as public education gets worse—the poor children sent to public schools will lack the intellectual training to see through religious propaganda, and more of the well-to-do will send their children to private schools which are usually religious. So church and synagogue membership will probably increase, but I see little likelihood of any great increase in religious observance. Religious persecution through civil legislation—e.g., laws against abortion, divorce, homosexuality, etc.—we have always had. At present the *dévots* seem little more than holding their own.

More important was the omission of the middle class—farmers, small businessmen, skilled workmen (non-unionized), artists and professional people (except for government and corporation lawyers and lawyers with corporations as clients). This class was the backbone of the early United States. As J. Karabel observed, "To a greater extent than any nation before and perhaps since, white America in the period before the Civil War was a society of independent producers—consisting overwhelmingly of farmers, shopkeepers, and craftsmen who owned the property they worked."[9] Moreover, long before its role in American history the educated middle class had been the distinguishing characteristic of western society. It has provided many political leaders and most inventors, engineers, and scientists, has been, when strong and secure, the backbone of the resistance to totalitarian government, and so has made possible the freedom of thought, expression, and

[9] "The Reason Why," *The New York Review*, XXVI (1979), February 8, p. 23.

action by which the present intellectual and economic preeminence of the western world has been achieved.

That a class once so important should have been omitted from the above list is evidence of the change that has taken place in America during the past century and a quarter. This change was due to many causes: immigration introduced cheap, landless labor; mechanization with cheap labor produced cheap goods and drove most small craftsmen out of business; mechanization of farming, the cheap farmland of the West, and cheap railroad transport ruined many small farmers of the East; cheap goods, transport and labor made possible department stores that outsold the small shopkeepers; manufacturers, railroad magnates, and great merchants accumulated fortunes that dwarfed the small businessman's, while increase of the population and the growth of mass media made insignificant anything he could do to get himself heard.

These changes have reduced what was once the country's characteristic and ruling class to a class of better paid but worse protected laborers, more than half of whose income goes for the support of big government, the big poor, big labor, big business, and big crime. The impact of the changes, however, might have been less had the middle class been clearly aware of its interests. Instead, much of it was devoted theoretically to equalitarianism (the revolutionary tradition and the antebellum society of the north had been strongly equalitarian) and the attempt to maintain an equalitarian society was an important factor in what happened.

Pursuit of the impossible equalitarian goal lowered the middle class, rather than raised the lower. In particular: (1) Equalitarian extension of the right to vote brought into the electorate a mass of ignorant and irresponsible voters and greatly enlarged the class of purchasable vote-getters, notably the news media, advertising and public relations agencies, and leaders of political clubs, labor unions, churches, gangs, racial organizations, etc. These changes reduced the middle class numerically to minor significance and increased the cost of campaigns—both to reach the voters and to hire the vote-getters—so that few save rich men and professional politicians can hope to be candidates. (2) Equalitarian taxation, with inflation sparked by government spending of taxes, has reduced the members of the middle class, as individuals, to economic insignificance and has deprived them of the means for significant political action. (3) Much of the tax money has gone for equalitarian welfare programs and these, with inflation and minimum wage laws (also equalitarian) have pensioned off most of the servant class, priced those willing to work beyond the means of middle class employers, and so stripped middle class life of the many small services that once made it agreeable and left its members time for political and cultural activities. (4) Legislation to enforce and finance "equality" has produced so many legal complications and such demand for lawyers that the cost of legal services has risen far beyond the means of the middle class, whose members have thus been all but stripped of legal protection. (5) The pursuit of equality in education has in many public schools held back classes to the speed of the incompetent, taught by example that learning and good behavior are unimportant, destroyed discipline, and made many junior-high and high schools centers of physical violence, drug addiction, and venereal disease (hitherto at least quarantined in small districts).[10] Those of the

[10] Some intellectual consequences of equalitarianism in education have been pointed out by R. S. Berman, Chairman of the National Endowment for the Humanities, in a statement that deserves quotation at length: "The progress of literacy," he reports, "has been accompanied by a perceptible decline in educational quality. Whether by standards of conventional middle class taste or as seen by statistics and examination, the powers of literacy have been diminished. As it has become broad, it has become shallow. One examination after another convinces us that students know less, although they have been educated more. For example, the elementary school system of Washington, D.C., acknowledges that the grades of students in the 1970's are the lowest in recent history, while college entrance examinations scores elsewhere have undergone a perceptible average decline. Having at last achieved in this country what passes for universal literacy, we note a simultaneous lowering of standards, a lowering of mental capabilities." As a consequence of this and other changes, he goes on to say, "Colleges took on those functions previously left to high schools: they now do the domestic job of socialization, remedial work, prepare students for careers, and in general act not so much as centers for intellectual accomplishment as day care centers for post-adolescents. There may be a necessity

middle class who cannot afford to send their children to private schools are forced to expose them to these dangers and to see them grow up, at best, in ignorance.

In all these respects—in political power, economic means, quality of life, legal protection, and education—the middle class has consistently been deprived of advantages it once enjoyed. By this deprivation the gap between it and the small ruling class has been greatly increased; so has the power of the rulers. Consequently the middle class does not, as a class, rank among the major groups whose hopes—or, the hopes of whose leaders—are likely to shape the future of this country. As individuals its members are an important body of consumers, the management of whose tastes and hopes is a major concern of advertising and of the manufacturers and merchants who buy advertising. This management is usually guided by shrewd estimates of existing tastes and hopes; these it often builds on and reinforces. Thus, by their short-term importance, the private hopes of members of the middle class expert a great influence on economic planning. The class as a class, however, is not a conspicuous figure in decisions on long-term policies.

Not at present. If its deprivation continues it may become dangerous. Modern European history shows that as such injustices accumulate the resultant sense of outrage can transform the temper of the middle class and change its role from the protection of individual liberties to the support of radically reformatory governments that are apt to become totalitarian. The ruin of the German middle class by the great inflation and its subsequent exploitation by the social planners of the Weimar regime made it a stronghold of the Nazis, who came to power as a reform party. The chaos and corruption of postwar Italy won similar support for the Fascists. "The [taxpayer] will turn, being trodden on."

---

for this in an economy without significant apprenticeship or even useful functions for those who are not yet adult." This appeared in his article, "Culture and Society," *American Council of Learned Societies Newsletter*, XXVI (1975), pp. 4 ff.

VI

The turning point, however, seems at present a good ways off. It may never be reached if the campaign for equality cools, and the actual differences in human capacities and needs find more recognition in governmental policy. Meanwhile, we are left with government by cliques and, more specifically, by the politicians who succeed in winning support from one or more cliques.

The liberty of the rest of the people is the liberty to choose sides, but most of the people are not concerned to exercise it. Rare is the election in which the number of votes for the winning candidate exceeds that of the voters who did not vote. Moreover, those who do vote commonly choose their favorites for reasons apparently trivial. One woman of late explained her choice for Governor of New York by admitting, "I don't know what he stands for, but he's got such a nice, friendly face and all those lovely children." At higher levels of competence one gets more sophisticated replies. Some time ago, disgusted by the pin-the-tail-on-the-candidate game played in the voting booth, I called a friend, one of the partners in a large law firm, and asked his advice about the candidates for judicial positions. It was succinct. "They're all ignorant crooks. It's a notorious scandal. The best thing you can do is vote for those least likely to win. Then you won't be responsible for what's done, and you help perpetuate a *pro forma* opposition to the ones in office. Here the Republicans haven't a chance, thank God, so you can vote for them safely."

—"But, good heavens, why is this allowed to go on? Can't the bar association do something?"

—"Who do you think runs the bar association? The lawyers in cahoots with these judges. Excuse me, I've got an overseas call coming in." Click.

Turning to the politicians themselves, we find that most do follow one consistent policy—they consistently try to keep themselves in office. Since most voters are neither aware of nor interested in most of their actions, they can accommodate many fund raisers and vote getters by semiprivate operations, doing them favors proportionate to the favors they can do. They can also indulge their own tastes when doing so will not lose them much support. A few seem to be guided by coherent political theories and social plans. Many have pet causes they favor for reasons other than personal advantage, just as many rich persons have pet charities. But even in favoring these, they must forego consistency when it would interfere with the give-and-take of practical politics.

These being the facts of political life, the question of what can be done about the current crisis of hopes is, "What will the power elite do about it?" There is little likelihood that they will do much. Most politicians think of the hopes of the public primarily as means of getting votes; to manufacturers, advertisers, and the media they are means of getting sales; to labor, crime, and the poor they are of little or no concern. Manufacturers, media, etc., commonly cater to short-term hopes; they will do all they can to keep consumption high and expensive credit available for the purchase of bargain disappointments, each of which will lead the purchaser to hope for something better. The politicians will continue to spend generously for the benefit of popular causes and private supporters (primarily contributors—this keeps money in circulation). As deficits, welfare stipends, and taxes rise, and the dollar sinks in value, the causes working against the formation of homes and for their disintegration, against the accumulation of savings and for hand-to-mouth existence, will operate ever more powerfully to produce the results described in Chapter I.

Many politicians will privately welcome the change. For them, an apathetic and purchasable populace will seem an advantage. The fewer who meddle in public policy, the easier it is to manage. Increase of the various forms of escapism— from masochism and drug addiction to mysticism and philanthropy—diminishes the number of informed voters and the difficulty of winning elections. So do the inefficiency of education and the increase of the uprooted and unattached; isolated and ignorant people are easier to win over, or to push over if they cannot be won. Welfare is admittedly an expense and crime a nuisance; but the expense is almost wholly born by ordinary taxpayers, and members of the power elite rarely suffer from petty criminals. Besides, a number of them are major criminals. The interesting information that one of President Kennedy's lady friends phoned him often from the homes of distinguished gangland figures[11] makes one wonder how far up in our society the management of organized crime is located and the profit distributed.[12] Whatever the answer, we can plausibly suppose that little will be done by our rulers to alter the prevailing insufficiency of hopes. What will be done is what has to be done to deal with pressing practical problems. The deals will add up to some sort of policy, no doubt partially self-contradictory. Barring a great scientific breakthrough, this policy must lie mostly within the range of present possibilities, and will lie mostly within the more limited range of probabilities. These, therefore, provide the preliminary parameters of our political hopes, which can conviently be summed up by a new beatitude: Blessed are those who expect nothing, for they shall not be disappointed.

VII

The distinction between possible and probable is greater than ever before. This fact profoundly changes the problem of hope. Formerly rulers, all-powerful politically, were imprisoned by the narrow limits of what was physically possible. Now scientific discovery has extended the possible beyond imagination, but the limits of the probable are narrowed by

---

[11] *Facts on File,* December 27, 1975, p. 975.

[12] Far, no doubt, above the shabby persons commonly represented as gang leaders; they do not look like the heads of an industry grossing, from drugs, gambling, prostitution, rackets, robberies, etc., thirty or forty billion dollars a year. It is hard to believe that this industry is the last outpost of free enterprise and still in the hands of many relatively small entrepreneurs, a unique survival of the old, independent, American way of life.

social and political considerations. Man is no longer imprisoned by nature, but by man.

This is clearest in the realm of education, which in its largest sense includes the formation of hopes, not only by teaching in schools, but by the many forms of social control available to powerful corporations and governments. Huxley has eloquently described the dangers of propaganda, advertising, brain-washing, chemical and subconscious persuasion, and hypnopaedia,[13] on which public opinion in the West imposes various degrees of control. Similarly, political considerations veto, for instance, the use of homosexuality to slow the growth of populations, though it might be helpful. Other means have had little success. The natives of overpopulated countries do not rush to have themselves sterilized; when given artificial devices for birth control they rarely use them. Many will not even take pills regularly: they decorate cakes with them, thread them for necklaces, and give them to children to play with. But they are acquainted with homosexuality and, often, not averse to it. If the governments of their countries would recommend homosexual practices, finance books, films, radio and TV programs recommending homosexuality, facilitate and reward the formation of homosexual clubs and marriages, and advance homosexuals in government employ, a precipitate decline in the birth rate might result. The project could count on vigorous support from artists and intellectuals; the main interest of the *avant-garde* is the *derrière*. But it could count on even more vigorous opposition from the great religious organizations which, regardless of the private inclinations of their personnel, live by inculcating traditional morality and the sense of guilt that needs their services. Moreover, the governments of many states think surplus population a guar-

---

[13] *Brave New World Revisited*, (New York, 1958), Chs. IV–X. The account may be a bit too pessimistic. The communist governments' control of the media has made their use of them huge experiments in direct "education," with surprising results. Recently the Roumanian government replaced broadcasts of Mickey Mouse with socialist propaganda; so many citizens turned in their radio sets (they cannot be purchased, only leased) that Mickey Mouse had to be restored.

antee of cheap labor and continued relief. These are only the
first considerations that come to mind at the suggestion of
such a project.

Similar calculations of probability must be made for every
major proposal, even those that seem most desirable. For
instance, scientists now talk seriously of finding, within this
century, some method to put off aging.[14] At the same time,
however, the "right to die" movement is spreading in Europe
(where one Frenchman was kept in a coma for twenty years)[15]
and has had some success in the United States. So has the
"right to live" movement, to secure for the old the right to
continued employment. Imagine the adjustments that would
be required by any considerable lengthening of life! Consequently the question, whether or not research for extension
of life will be funded, or even permitted, by the government,
is moot. Violent opposition would certainly be met by any
proposal to produce by genetic alteration a longer-lived
strain of human beings, or one with better intellectual equipment, although this, too, now seems a future possibility.[16] In
view of the probable but incalculable difficulties that confront
most proposals for considerable scientific changes in the
bases of our culture, it seems best, in attempting to calculate
future hopes, to work from the assumption that biological
changes, at least, will be relatively minor for many years to
come. As for political and military changes, a similar assumption seems justified, though the appearance is equally unrelia-
ble; we are frequently assured that the relevant facts are secret. In ignorance of the facts we may be comforted by the

---

[14] See the report of Dr. B. Strehler to the Federation of American Societies for
Experimental Biology, meeting at Atlantic City, 1974, and the paper of G. Feinberg,
"Some Scientific and Social Aspects of Aging Control," *Minutes of the Columbia Univer-
sity Seminar on the Nature of Man,* September 21, 1975.

[15] *New York Times,* December 7, 1975, p. 14.

[16] "We now know," says C. Waddington, "that long continued selection for the
ability to learn a useful lesson from experience will so increase this ability that the
lesson may become to some degree genetically assimilated." Review of N. Tinber-
gen, *The Animal in Its World* (Cambridge, 1974), in the *New York Times Book Review,*
February 3, 1974, p. 3. Waddington is Buchanan Professor of Animal Genetics at the
University of Edinburgh.

common supposition that the consequences of a full-scale war between any two of the three great powers would be so dreadful, and the dangers, not only to the common people, but to the ruling cliques of the countries concerned, would be so great and so difficult to predict, that there will be no such war. This seems likely. Since we cannot refute it, we may as well relax and enjoy it.

To moderate our enjoyment, we turn to current economic predictions, all of which are based on this assumption. Economic production is a growth industry and its products, often supported by wide research, are often widely various. At one extreme (that of ultimate vulgarity) is a 1976 Mobil advertisement, "You ain't seen nothin' yet," predicting a future of yet more gadgetry, with "a 21-minute subway ride between New York and Los Angeles . . . TV sets that automatically record your bowling score; even a scientific measurement for romantic love." Oh bliss, oh rapture! All this will be produced by intensive employment of the populations of the developed nations, to provide the undeveloped ones with these necessities of life (i.e., gadgets). The workers will be paid with currency so far inflated that "the Gross World Product" will rise "from $5.5 trillion to $300 trillion, and the average income of every man, woman and child on earth . . . from the current $1300 a year to $20,000" (of which the purchasing power in current terms will be about $200). That this program would make a shambles of the environment was not mentioned; Mobil has never been sensitive to exhaust fumes.

Turning from such gaseous science fiction to the opposite extreme, we have Heilbroner's prediction that "Only two outcomes [of the present situation] are imaginable. . . . One is the descent of large portions of the underdeveloped world into a condition of steadily worsening social disorder, marked by shorter life expectancies, further stunting of physical and mental capacities," etc., the other being "the rise of 'iron' governments" capable "of halting the descent into hell" by forcible imposition of birth control and similar measures. Even such a development, he concluded, would only tempo-

rarily retard the progress of mankind as a whole toward ex-
haustion of the environment, after which, if men survived at
all, they would do so only in a " 'post-industrial' society" with
limited population, primitive means of production, and probably authoritarian governments.[17] Similar arguments, with
even less comfortable conclusions, have recently been defended with much more detail by E. Mishan.[18]

Between such extremes a more realistic and therefore limited prophecy is that by W. Leontief, reporting on government
research on the relations of resources, environment and
growth. "Our computations showed that . . . it will be possible,
with improved technology and more efficient land use, to feed
the globe's increasing population. [He did not say, how long.]
Mineral resources will be adequate in this century and, if new
reserves are discovered at the rate they have been discovered
in the past, long beyond it. Neither the technology nor the cost
of pollution abatement should present an insuperable barrier."[19] However, it was found that under the present economic system, with optimum performance, the gap of per
capita production between developed and developing countries would probably increase throughout the rest of this century (p. 24). This divergence could be stemmed only by immense transfers of capital to the developing nations, and since
"realistically speaking, one cannot expect a Kansas farmer or a
Detroit blue-collar worker to pay higher taxes, year after year,
in order to help some villagers in Africa" (p. 29—only a Cambridge white-collar worker would be fool enough to do that),
the only possible source of the funds required would be diversion to this purpose of monies now used for national defense.
Leontief did not observe that the continued rivalry between
the United States, Russia, and China, postulated as part of the

[17] R. Heilbroner, "The Human Prospect," *New York Review of Books*, January 24,
1974, pp. 21 ff.; the quotations are from pp. 23 and 33.
[18] *The Economic Growth Debate* (London, 1977).
[19] "Natural Resources, Environmental Disruption, and Growth Prospects," *Bulletin
of the American Academy of Arts and Sciences*, XXX (1977), #8, especially pp. 23 ff. The
quotation is from p. 25.

continuance of the present order, would make any such diversion of defense funds unlikely. (The Pentagon has planned to increase them during the next five years from $117 billion to $173 billion annually,[20] allegedly because of comparable Russian increases. While the continued hostility of our countries continues to support so generously the military, their manufacturers, and their manufacturers' employees—including senators and congressmen?—there is little likelihood that relations will improve.) Nor did Leontief consider the questions whether, or why, it was desirable that "the developing nations" should be helped to develop further. The answer is that their continued development will provide more investment opportunities for international banks, more markets for the manufactures and services of international corporations, more satisfaction for believers in equality, and more taxes, inflation, and pollution for the ordinary taxpayers in the developed countries, the products and earnings of whose labor are being pumped out of their countries to increase the wealth of plutocrats who keep most of their money out of reach of taxation. As usual, big business and doctrinaire democracy work together to despoil the middle class.

Given this state of affairs we should expect a continuance through the predictable future of present economic patterns, modified more or less by the pull and haul of practical politics. The haul now beginning (and it threatens to be a long and painful one) will be that of adjusting our economy to the fuel supplies now available and the prices being charged for them. Our current government deficits (about $45 billion in 1977, $60 billion in 1978) confront us with the necessity of economizing, consequently of deciding—in general, what we hope to keep and what we are prepared to give up, in particular, what we will do to get cheaper fuel. To facilitate these decisions we have the dubious advantage of democracy and the farsighted, incorruptible legislators it provides us, the rivalries of oil, gas, coal, nuclear, water, and regional power inter-

[20] *New York Times,* February 3, 1978, p. 1.

ests, energetic leftist propaganda to prevent our development of nuclear power, a wealthy, vocal clique of sentimental ecologists, media determined to exploit to the full the sales value of any rumored danger, and a public equally excitable, ignorant, and unwilling to forego the use of its gadgets, let alone its automobiles, speedboats, etc. These should add up to national bankruptcy. However, bankruptcy of the United States would ruin its creditors, particularly the Arabs and Europeans who, if we had to withdraw our forces from their countries, would be overrun by Russia. The Swiss are said to dislike bad debts, but probably prefer them to commissars. So long, therefore, as American credit is protected by the Russian army, we shall probably get enough gas and gold to keep us going, but the going will be rough. Barring unforeseen discoveries, we have ahead of us a long period of gradual impoverishment and a steadily declining standard of living as we gradually are forced to make do with less and less.

At least we may be forced to make do with less of the incompetent. Since we must economize, welfare expenditures should be expendable, and first among them the funds we annually export to finance the population explosion in countries already shattered by it. Admittedly such economies will not increase our popularity abroad, while at home the primary consequences of domestic economies will be political disturbances, compounded as usual by antisocial sentimentalism. However, these will probably produce no basic change in our social structure. The necessity of feeding, clothing, and warming our enormous population means that the anti-technology and decentralization movements will most likely be marginal nuisances.[21] The government dare not risk disruption of the big corporations that are providing the essential services. The failure of successive socialist governments in England to achieve substantial and enduring socialization is here significant. Moreover, if we expect the arms race to con-

---

[21] See "Technological Choices in the Context of Social Values," *Bulletin of the American Academy of Arts and Sciences*, XXX (1977), #5, pp. 4 ff.

tinue, we should also expect continuance of its economic results. It has kept many workers and military personnel off relief rolls. It has siphoned off the money, labor, and personnel that might have been used for social changes. It has forced the United States and Russia to compete for support and cater to pressure groups at home and abroad, sacrificing for them the attempt to follow consistent policies. One could hardly find records of more frequent tergiversation than those set by these two great powers during recent years. So there is little likelihood of our government's taking the lead in any general, organized social change. There is less likelihood of any revolutionary group's being able to precipitate one. The variety of individual careers available in western society offers hopes that attract so many of the competent that the capable defectors will be at most a small minority. They disagree with each other and have no concerted program. Few would be willing to go through the drudgery, the years of recruiting, drilling, and petty party politicking necessary to build up the unified and disciplined organization needed for any fundamental political change in a country of this size. Hence the present system will continue.

Finally, these arguments against the likelihood of organized social change are confirmed by consideration of the other side of the case. Apart from the possibility of a major war, the chief reasons for doubting that the near future will be "more of the same, but poorer" are two. (1) New sources of power may be developed and these may radically change the political and economic situation. (2) The triumph of some new political party in the West, or of some new clique in Russia or China, may set one or more of the great powers off on a course of social, economic, and even biological change so extensive as to produce practically a new culture. However, (1) although it is almost certain that new sources of energy will be developed,[22] it is not likely that they will

[22] See, for example, P. Raeburn, "Working toward the Fusion Age," *Columbia Today* (March, 1977), pp. 27 ff.

soon produce vast changes. Probably the new energy will simply give us a new lease on the old life, making possible the perpetuation, perhaps for another century, of the present nonsystem with its combination of contradictory initiatives and pork-barrel projects. Similarly, (2) it is almost certain that new cliques will come to power in Russia and China, and not wholly unlikely that one or more new parties may do so in the United States. But that any of these political groups will be able to change profoundly the immense nonorganizations over which they may attain what is commonly called "control," is not likely. They will depend on the support of many minor groups with varying hopes; therefore they will have to proceed by compromises; and they will have to operate through the existing bureaucracies, which are immensely resistant to change. The story goes that just before Eisenhower's inauguration Truman, waiting in his office for Eisenhower to arrive, looked at his desk and said, "Poor Ike! For the next four years he's gonna' sit there an' issue orders. An' then nothin' will happen. An' he'll never know why." In all superstates run by vast bureaucracies, the advent of a reforming administration marks the beginning of a battle between Hercules and the hydra. The hydra wins. *Plus ça change, plus c'est la même chose.*

VIII

These familiar reasons for expecting more (but somewhat less) of the same, and tailoring one's hopes accordingly, have been given in outline because familiar. Many additions that might be made to the preceding summary will occur to many readers and therefore need not be made. Sometimes, however, familiar patterns result from motives of neglected complexity. This is true of one of the most pervasive but least tangible defenses of the established order, the widespread resistance to utopianism, particularly to those forms of utopianism characterized by increased governmental power and planning. Such resistance by business, labor, and professional

organizations, landowners, etc., is familiar, arises from obvious self-interest, and is clearly effective. But around this well-
recognized center there is a wide penumbra of similar resistance arising from widely dissimilar and sometimes
unrecognized reasons. These can be classified roughly as historical, theoretical, and emotional.

First among the historical reasons, but probably least important, is the long and generally second-rate tradition of
utopianism. Few utopias have been works of great intellectual
distinction. (Plato's *Republic* is an outstanding exception;
More's *Utopia* is more admired than read and if read more
would be admired less.) Yet fewer have been practical—the
term itself disclaims practicality—and most of the few that
came to realization also came to grief. Accordingly, the term
"utopian" is abusive and the judgment implied is commonly
extended to most proposals for planned societies.

A second and more important reason are the awful examples of planned societies that this century has supplied—the
Italy of Mussolini, the Germany of Hitler, the Russia of Lenin,
Stalin, and their successors, and the China of Mao Tse-tung
(not to mention such minor extermination camps as Vietnam
and Cambodia). Not only the horrors reported from these
countries, but the "holocaust industry"—the novels, stories,
plays, movies, and television programs about Nazism—have
irreversibly shaped European and American imagination and
consequently our thoughts on social planning. To the end of
this century most of our contemporaries will probably go
through history backwards, their minds fixed on those atrocities with such loathing and fascination that anything represented as an imitation of policies characteristic of them will be
condemned. The deadly regimes of the communist tyrannies
imposed by the Russians on their subject countries in eastern
Europe and by their allies in Cuba and elsewhere, and the
dismal consequences of socialist policies in Sweden and England, have gone to confirm this attitude. Almost equally
serious has been experience with the inefficiency and corruption of our own government, notably the colossal waste and

dishonesty of the relief and rehabilitation programs. These are perceived as primary consequences of social planning, and we want no more of them.

To reinforce these historical objections, there are theoretical ones. The problem of devising a plan both workable and satisfactory seems almost insoluble. In a state with millions of citizens anything like direct democracy is out of the question. The character of a representative democracy depends on how the representatives are controlled by their constituents; ours are often free to act against public interest, but so dependent on patrons and pressure groups that they cannot consistently act for it. To move towards oligarchy by increasing the independence of the representatives and the power of the central government to control the media and the voters, begs the question of the quality of the controlling officials. Today's paper reports connections of a millionaire pornographer, indicted for murder and arson, with our present Ambassador to the United Nations (Young) who is said to have facilitated his jailbreak, and our former Director of the Budget (Lance), remembered for dubious banking practices.[23] We must face the critical question asked about Plato's *Republic:* If the guards are to oversee the people, who is to oversee the guards?

Even if this objection could eventually be met—say, by infantile conditioning or genetic control to produce individuals or a whole breed of unfailing virtue—proponents of a wholly planned society would still have to face another objection, well stated by Heilbroner: "Socialist governments—the best of them, not the worst—seek to create good societies, not just affluent ones. But the trouble with good societies is that it is difficult for them to tolerate dissent. Disagreements about policies or ideas that can be regarded by morally unconcerned societies as mere choices among expedients tend to be regarded by morally committed societies as choices between good and evil. In this way, aberrant behavior or belief threaten to become identified with moral turpitude. Thus I

[23] *New York Times,* June 15, 1978, p. A 23.

think that a seed of totalitarianism resides even in the best government that pursues virtue for the society it governs."[24] "Virtue" is commonly conceived as conformity to a pattern, so we should recognize ideological selfishness—the love of making patterns, the theoretician's desire to see his plans carried out—as a major source of the demand for social change (when the theoreticians are out of power) and the demand for social conformity (when they are in). The ideological reformer, when successful, as a matter of moral duty becomes a tyrant, witness Robespierre. He also is in danger of becoming a sadist, since his love of making patterns is commonly allied with his love of power, and power is most dramatically shown by forcing people to do what they don't want to do. The sadistic reformer values reforms partly because of, and sometimes even in proportion to, the resistance they generate.

Supposing a hairline could be securely drawn between righteousness and tyranny, there would yet be another theoretical problem: Why? Any proposal for change that is not immediately gratifying must face the question, "Why should the present be sacrificed for the future?" If the present is satisfactory, why change? And even if the future could be improved, would it be better for us, or for its unknown inhabitants? Why should I sacrifice my pleasures for posterity? What has posterity ever done for me? Are we being exploited by social planners for the benefit of potential persons who as yet are not, and may never be? And will they, in turn, be exploited by the planners of their generation, so that humanity goes forever from hope to hope, always sacrificing the present for the future, like Faust in the legend, never able to find a life worth living for its own sake, an age to which it can honestly say, "Stay because thou art so fair"?

These historical and theoretical objections to utopianism commonly conceal, but express, an emotional resistance that also finds emotional expressions and concealments, most

[24] "Trying to Make Sense of It," *New York Times*, October 10, 1977, p. 29.

often when proposals for social planning are attacked as threats to human dignity and freedom. This is not surprising, many of them are.[25] Hence we come to the impasse brilliantly summed up by Mishan: The individual cannot be trusted to pursue his self-interest without doing irreparable damage to society, but society cannot be trusted to pursue the public interest without doing irreparable damage to individuals and hence to itself.[26]

This antithesis depends on different meanings of the word "damage," and neglect of the different types whose interests would be damaged. The damage we think likely to be done by "individuals" (including corporations) is mainly to long-term hopes held by the few humans concerned for the future of humanity: individuals would squander resources, pollute the environment, gradually (but not in our lifetime) make the world uninhabitable. The damage done by a benevolent and well-managed totalitarian society would be primarily to the short-term hopes of most men like ourselves, who care little for the future of humanity and not much for our contemporaries. We should have to toe the line, to obey the rules. Worse, if the government were democratic we should have to participate in making the rules. Our precious leisure and irresponsibility would be replaced by official sessions of the all-holy "democratic process" and the conferences, committee meetings, private discussions, and interminable intrigues that are its substructures. Think of being compelled to become "a good citizen"! The Athenians learned with regret the price of democracy: to make them attend sessions of the assembly and listen to the immortal masterpieces of Greek oratory the marketplace had to be encircled by a rope dusted with red chalk. The rope was hauled in and all those it caught were herded

---

[25] The attack on "the literature of freedom and dignity" by B. Skinner, *Beyond Freedom and Dignity* (New York, 1972), hardly refutes this charge by its implicit denial that freedom and dignity exist. Whether perceptions or illusions, their existence is undeniable and so is our desire for them. A book that advocates social controls, but neither proposes specific ones nor asks who would control the controls and for what purpose, does nothing to reassure the reader.

[26] E. Mishan, *The Economic Growth Debate* (London, 1977).

into the assembly. Anyone found outside with red chalk on his clothes was fined.

The need for such methods shows how far resistance to governmental control is the result of short-term individual hopes, notably laziness (unwillingness to participate in the drudgery of government), selfishness (personal interests, most often economic, counter to public policy), vice (fear of effective moral censorship, unwillingness to conform to the standards of the community), crime (fear of effective supervision of political campaigns and of work done for the state, fear of thorough reform of the police and the judiciary, fear of a thorough check on the relief rolls and of extended surveillance of criminal activities). The "civil liberties" campaign for the protection of "privacy," pushed to ridiculous extremes during the past few years, was presumably financed in large part (though of course indirectly) by organized crime,[27] but its amazing success at the expense of public interest was possible and is tolerated only because so many of us have something to hide. The income tax, in particular, has made us, from our presidents down, a nation of cheats (and the cost in self-contempt and consequent cynicism, as well as money, has fallen most heavily on the middle class—the rich have lawyers to cheat for them, the poor get home free). Given all the private interests that an honest, efficient, and thorough government, even if not totalitarian, would threaten, it is clear why the average American hopes for the continuance of the present corrupt, inefficient, superficial system. After all, laziness, selfishness, and a little vice are usually important elements in life, liberty, and the pursuit of happiness. We have bad government because we want it.

Not only personal failings but corporate abuses and philosophical aberrations contribute emotional opponents to the threat of any rule by reason. The passionate resistance to

[27] What other wealthy group stood to gain so much from it? Political subversives indeed profited from it, but can hardly have done much to foot the bill unless they were supplied with money for that purpose from abroad.

public regulation by large business firms has been more publicized but less successful than that by labor unions and professional societies. In the field of education the defenders of equality view with alarm the growing tendency to subject the public schools to the public's judgment. And so on. Every special interest generates special pleading to defend it and corresponding resistance to the hope for a planned society from which, if the plan were successfully carried through, all such anomalies would be eliminated.

IX

Sketching the hopes that motivate resistance to utopianism has led us, through hypocrisy, to the border of the subconscious. Beyond that border lurks the motive we met repeatedly in reviewing history—man's resistance to the human condition, to finitude, the necessity of choice, the inevitability of death. If the future be planned and if the plan succeeds only one set of our infinite imagined possibilities will be realized. Spontaneous, personal projects, the peculiar expressions of individualism, will become impossible. A completely planned society would be a gigantic cemetery of dreams.

The resistance to utopianism because of its threat to provide a definite and therefore unsatisfactory answer to the question, "What do we hope for?" is paralleled in private life by the resistance to choosing a career, an attitude that often becomes acute in the later years of college. The indefinite possibilities and innumerable hopes of childhood have at last to be sacrificed, for the sake of realizing only one. The time has come to grow up, and growing up is a great leap forward toward death.

Even when the leap has been made, we continue to resent it. This is why so many persons of average or better abilities nevertheless abandon careers already begun. One reason commonly alleged is the fear of monotony. "I don't want to be just an X all my life." "X" may be "housewife," "factory worker," "bank executive," or occupant of any other position requiring relatively repetitive performance. The hope is usually not for some other specific position, but merely for something new, different from the past (compare the millennial and utopian hopes described in Chapter III). To accept a definite, permanent position is dangerous; one may be led to see the whole of one's life in a single, swift glance—education, employment, marriage, children, boredom, the retirement home, the hospital, the undertaker's parlor, and the grave. The hope for change is thus a mask for the reluctance to sacrifice our other hopes, to recognize our unimportance, to encounter death.

The complaint of "monotony" is usually connected with that of "triviality," which arises from the same resentment at the sacrifice of hopes necessitated by the choice of a career, the decision to be some one thing. Thus complaints about "triviality" are usually symptoms of the complainant's rejection of society, not indications of its cause. Usually, too, they indicate that the complainant lacks either the imagination to realize the importance of his work to the people he serves, or the human feeling to care for those people, or both. An executive whose work was to supervise the investment of millions of dollars every day once complained to me of the triviality of it all. He thought it trivial because he had almost no time to consider any of the consequences of the investments except the likelihood of their paying off to his company. Neither the opportunities and hopes that the loans gave to those who received them, nor the financial security that the returns provided for hundreds of thousands of people, could be entered in his books. At least his shortsightedness did no damage, except to him; what mattered most to everyone else, that the money should be securely invested, was seen to. The housewife, however, who complains of the triviality of her work is unconsciously telling you that she doesn't think her husband and children are worth the waste of her exceptional talents on the "trivial" job of making a comfortable, beautiful, peaceful, and loving home for them, and training her children to live in it and to learn to live in the world around it. After all, she might have a career of her own—writing advertisements, or even creating immortal junk jewelry. *Qualis artifex pereo!*[28]

Such complaints are therefore characteristic of the stupid and selfish, but not peculiar to them; they often result from mere inertia—taking a job at its face value without considering its consequences, or following some current fashion—for instance, the feminist campaign to conceal the importance of women as homemakers. The abilities to see through convention and propaganda, to realize the importance of one's function, to care for the people one serves, and, consequently, to delight in doing one's work well—these abilities are necessary for that "love of one's work" which, as Swedenborg said, is the common condition for a happy life.

This holds for dealings with things, as well as people. The basis of hope is the capacity to love. As Baudelaire said, it is the child's love of every single stamp in his collection that keeps the world large, and, against Baudelaire, it is the shrinking of the power to love, not the increase of knowledge, that makes it small.[29] The great archeologist Henri Seyrig had few equals in the extent of his knowledge, but almost none in the delight with which he seized on any new object from the ancient world.

The capacity to love is the only means of escape from the ultimate cause of the sense of triviality, that is, again, the expectation of death. Cause and effect were grasped by the author of Ecclesiastes: "Vanity of vanities; all is vanity. . . . For what happens to beasts happens to men; as the one dies, so does the other"—1:2 – 3:19.

This connection has been profoundly explored by Ernest Becker in *The Denial of Death* (New York, 1973). Becker supposed all perceptions of threats, and consequent fears, to be forms of the underlying fear of death. The infant can only repress this fear, occupy itself with other things, and so create

---

[28] "How great an artist is lost by my death!" Reportedly the last words of Nero. Suetonius, *Nero* 49.1.
[29] See "Le voyage" in *Les Fleurs du Mal*.

a partly illusory world from which at least one aspect of reality is excluded. Hence Becker concluded that the best thing a man can hope for is "the 'best' illusion under which to live" (p. 202). Discovery of this " 'best' illusion" or "most legitimate foolishness" is therefore the goal of "the science of mental health" and Becker found it in devotion to an imaginary deity who, because imaginary, "is hidden and intangible. . . . All the better: that allows man to expand and develop by himself" *(ibid.)*. Devotion to this vague, transcendent lie would enable Becker's patient to enjoy a "compelling illusion that does not lie about life, death, and reality" (p. 204)— except, of course, by its assertion that Daddy is there.

This prescription for salvation by regression to infantilism is based on the belief that no regression is necessary. It takes for granted that the patient has remained emotionally an infant and, like all infants, an egomaniac, with no concern for other people except insofar as they minister to his own comfort. This supposition is probably correct for most patients of psychiatrists—that's why they're patients. For most healthy persons, however, the limits of individualism are broken by love; the area of personal concern is extended to include parents, friends, sexual partners, and children; in children, as Plato's Diotima pointed out, love finds instruments of immortality by which the individual is consoled, to some extent, for his own death (*Republic,* 206c). From the hope of immortality in descendants men have often gone on to think of the survival of tribesmen, countrymen, or men in general, as continuation of their own lives, and not only to hope, but to work for future generations as for themselves. Hence artists hope to produce objects of enduring beauty, and scientists to contribute to the advance of human knowledge. The classical symbol of this hope was an old man's planting trees, an image Cicero made famous.[30] It is this normal and mature transference of loves and hopes to others, not infantile adhesion to theological illusions, that enables mature men to find the

[30] *Tusculans* I.31; *De Senectute* 24 and 59.

significance and importance of their own work in its contribution to the survival of mankind. To the complaint that life is trivial, the proper answer is, "Grow up." Alternatively one might say, "Regress a little further," since the hope for survival was that which we found built into living tissue among animals and even among insects. Such prehistoric living tissue still lives in us and continues to hope as heretofore.

X

From this descent into the underworld of the unconscious, and so to the central mystery of our subject, we now come back to the present crisis of hopes and, particularly, to its characteristic paradox, the rejection of practical hopes because of utopian standards, coupled with the rejection of utopianism. If our analysis be correct, the root of this is selfishness, the failure to develop normal concern for others and hopes for them, hopes that are commonly formed by adults and give to adult life its importance and variety: goals, plans, possibilities of success.

Selfishness, the refusal to grow up, is of many sorts, from the self-determined solitary confinement of the catatonic to the brilliant social career of the gifted egomaniac. An egomaniac whose gifts are sufficient to secure him a steady series of satisfactions may live happy; enjoying his own unbroken, perfectly reciprocated love, he may go from hope to hope and achievement to achievement, in a lifelong triumphal procession to the grave. Most, however, are unable to live up to their expectations and blame their failures on the wickedness or stupidity of the world. Accordingly they hope for a reform of society, but if any one reform became imminent, let alone actual, they would soon shift their hope to another, not only because none could ever give them their due, but also for the reasons outlined above. Selfishness is fostered by the breakup of families, displacement of workers, and other causes outlined in Chapter I, but a further contributing cause has now to be described. It is what we may call the tradition of social rejection, one of the most remarkable elements of western civilization and particularly important in shaping the present crisis of hopes.

This tradition is not uniform. A number of its causes and elements were mentioned at different places in our account of the history of hopes, here they may be rapidly brought together: Denunciation of the rulers of society is preserved alike in the books of the Israelite prophets, the Thersites episode of the *Iliad,* and the poems of Hesiod. Rejection of the prevalent standards and mores of his society was given classic expression by Socrates. The antisocial side of Socrates' teaching was variously developed by Antisthenes, Plato, the Cynics, and the Stoics. Elements from these Greek and Israelite traditions are fused in the teachings attributed by the Gospels to Jesus. The letters of Paul and Acts show us the beginnings of an organized counter culture: the Church. When the Church took over and was taken over by the Empire, the counterculture tradition lived on in monasticism and in Judaism. Moreover it remained latent in the Sacred Scriptures accepted and taught by the Church. Hence sprang a series of popular sectarian movements, rejecting the standards and attacking the officials of mediaeval and renaissance society. This tradition was laicized in the eighteenth and nineteenth centuries, particularly by evangelicals and Jews who turned to "good works" for justification when they lost their faith in God. The growth of rationalistic and humanitarian social criticism in the eighteenth century culminated in the American and French revolutions; the development and systematization of revolutionary thought by nineteenth-century thinkers, particularly Marx and Engels, culminated in the triumphs of the communist parties in Russia, China, and elsewhere.

Thus western culture has at its heart a revolutionary literature sometimes embarrassing to the conservative authorities in Moscow, Washington, and the Vatican. Rulers and revolutionists have essentially the same objective, to make people move. Rulers can use the stick and the carrot. Revolutionists, having neither stick nor carrot, must make do with abuse and promises. Revolutionary literature is thus at once antisocial and utopian, composed of attacks on the definite, existing society and promises of an indefinite good society to come. Thus advocacy of a utopia can be instrumental in promoting the rejection both of present society and of specific plans to reform it; in effect, it can be anti-utopian and should be considered as one of the factors in the resistance to utopian social planning. The same resistance is perpetuated by antisocial elements in the sacred texts of Christianity, Judaism, the bourgeois democracies and the communist states, and the perpetual propaganda issued by the rival authorities of the great powers, attacking the society and standards, as well as the rulers, of the other side. From all this historical root system, through schools, churches, synagogues, libraries, theaters, and discussion groups, springs up an ever new undergrowth of attacks on society, on persons who succeed in society, and on the normal course of a successful life.

These attacks are often unjustified. As Russell observed and as Wattenberg has demonstrated,[31] it is a matter of objective fact that in the United States (as in Canada and western Europe) the great majority of people get enough to eat, are decently clothed, adequately housed, and live relatively normal lives, occupied by their everyday concerns. Their basic hopes for physical needs and social relations are evidently realized. This is indicated by the stability of western society, in which years of persistent propaganda against the prevailing order have generally failed to produce any substantial political upheavals, in spite of the fact that most western countries take few military precautions against mass revolts. The hope of getting the people out to the barricades has consistently failed in these countries, because people wouldn't go. When revolutions did occur, as in Spain, the fighting on both sides had to be largely supported by allies from abroad, while most of the common people were involved only as victims. Significantly, Spain was one of the poorest of all the countries in this

---

[31] Russell, above, p. 130; B. Wattenberg, *The Real America* (New York, 1974).

area. The implication is clear. Given a choice between continuing their daily round and getting out to fight or work for
a cause, most people prefer to continue their daily round.

As further evidence that the tradition of rejection is not
simply a consequence of the injustices of the capitalist system,
we may adduce the similar growth in communist countries. In
spite of the efforts of their governments to destroy the tradition and its representatives, they cannot wholly get rid of it.
It is central to their Sacred Scriptures (the works of Marx and
Engels), as to those of Judaism and of Christianity. But they
can control the exegesis and applications of the authoritative
texts, they can (and do) revise these texts, and they try to
exterminate works without official status that show similar
traits. Hence their hostility to most modern literature, though
it could hardly do much harm in Russia itself where, in spite
of the generally low standard of living and the privileges of
the party members, the majority of the people seem relatively
content. Presumably the government's prohibition of "antisocial" literature results from ideological purism (pattern-
making) and the concern to prevent possible nuisances. As in
the western world, most people seem mainly concerned about
their private lives and satisfied if they can go on living them.

Consequently, in spite of the great names and great works,
the literature of social rejection must be read as a minority
report. In evaluating minority reports, one must first look at
the persons who constitute the minority. In this case, they
often verge on abnormality. Israelite prophecy began as a
form of compulsive behavior among socially marginal individuals. Isaiah for three years went about Jerusalem naked
(20:2 f.). The sanity of Hosea (who felt compelled to marry
a whore, 1:2 f.) and Ezekiel (who baked his bread on dung,
4:15) was even more questionable. Socrates, an extreme eccentric, was ultimately executed, in part because he attributed
divine authority to the voices he heard. Diogenes, the founder
of Cynicism, taught that one should live like a dog, performing *all* animal functions in public; he practiced exactly as he
preached. The Stoics went further, though mainly in theory

—Zeno justified cannibalism. Accordingly, although Cynic and Stoic teachings had considerable influence, Cynics and Stoics were relatively few. Jesus' family thought he was mad (Mk. 3:22). Paul speaks of himself as an outcast from society (I Cor. 4:11 f.; II Cor. 4:7 ff.; etc.). Christianity after the crucifixion was a tiny circle of the followers of a condemned criminal; for almost three hundred years it remained a criminal movement, partially underground. Monasticism, the creation of a minority of Christians, was notorious in its early days for attracting characters of dubious sanity. And so on. In sum, the western literature teaching the corruption of the world, the vanity of human wishes, the dissatisfaction that follows all human efforts to excel in society, has a worse than dubious psychological history. Now, thanks to the successes of Christianity and Communism, it has become part of the official creeds of established governments, but even now the clergy and party members who preach it commonly disregard it in their own practice. The consequent (long notorious) contradictions in Christianity are brilliantly portrayed in Browning's *The Bishop Orders His Tomb at St. Praxed's Church*—a magnificent vignette of an entire culture. If only we had another Browning it could now be matched by a portrait of the present Secretary of the Italian Communist Party: *Marchese Berlinguer Orders His Yacht to Meet Him at Capri.* The disdain of proletarian life that such a portrait would reveal is not limited to party secretaries or to parties in corrupt western European countries. It was deplored fifteen years ago in a letter entitled, "The Polish Bishops to the Polish Priests," which said in part,

> We . . . find it difficult to understand how some party leaders, supposedly representing the working class, show so little solicitude for the real interest of the worker or peasant, pay no attention to the problem of workers' wages or the standard of living of his family. At the same time they try their best to get the highest income, so starkly in contrast to the average wage of an industrial worker, let alone of those who live off their own land in the village. From the

point of view of a democratic economy one cannot but be dismayed by the rise of a new class—of many thousands— whose standard of living far exceeds that of the average physical laborer; nor is it a matter of individual aberration. What is so painful is that for these people a life of luxury, with all its indifference to the average man's level of existence, becomes the rightful norm."[32]

These remarks on the history of the literature of rejection can be supported by others on those segments of society which now chiefly produce, publish, praise, and consume it. Two such segments are conspicuous (though far from mutually exclusive), we may call them, by convenient generalizations, the jealous and the paranoid. Let us follow their own principle and put the last first:

As already observed, social changes sketched in Chapter I have greatly increased the number of isolated individuals. Isolation, especially in large cities, has produced in many a state approaching paranoia. Subconsciously they interpret their neighbors' indifference as rejection, then respond to rejection with hostility and project this by suspecting hostility to themselves, plots against them, injustices, and so on. This hostile, suspicious attitude presently finds expression in their behavior: in fault finding, innuendo, accusation, and the like. Such behavior presently produces real hostility and elicits malicious remarks and actions that are thought to confirm the suspicions. Consequently, the loneliness increases. Being lonely, such people spend much time watching television, many even take to reading. The women make up much of the market for Gothic novels, the men, for murder and spy stories, both are credulous readers of "serious" books exposing sinister and far-reaching political and financial intrigues, threats to human existence from excessive radiation, poisoning of the environment, impending invasions from outer space, and so on. Both did much to account for the success

[32] Quoted by A. Brumberg, "The Open Political Struggle in Poland," *The New York Review*, XXVI (1979), February 8, p. 32.

of Orwell-type utopias. When directed to political affairs this attitude often results in hostility to all persons in authority: established government is a gigantic conspiracy to cheat the common man. Alternatively the forces of law and order may be seen as our last bulwark against a great international communist conspiracy with agents everywhere, especially in Washington. In either event such unfortunates are apt to be implacable opponents of social planning by other people (though they often have drastic social plans of their own). Since their tastes dictate the content of much media material, a number become successful writers or reporters for the media: "It takes one to sell one." As buyers and suppliers in what may be loosely called "the paranoid market" they have done much to create the endemic hostility to social planning that prevails in the United States and guarantees that any public project, from a suburban housing development to a general program for national defense, will immediately be surrounded by a circle of protesters. Lawyers with this type of mentality are especially expensive to the rest of us: we must pay at least half the costs of the suits they initiate, and the laws they sponsor generate innumerable suits. The adversary attitude which the American Civil Liberties Union has adopted towards civil authorities, especially the police, must have cost us billions. It is being extended. The Executive Director of the New York Civil Liberties Union has now gone on to urge that "we should respond to the claims of social service professionals as if they were cops."[33] By "social service professionals" he has in mind the officials and staff of schools, orphanages, welfare agencies, nursing homes, hospitals, insane asylums, and so on. All these he suspects of mistreating their charges who therefore, against any possible abuse of authority, need assurance of full legal protection, to be paid for by the public.

---

[33] I. Glasser, "Prisoners of Benevolence," in *Doing Good*, by W. Gaylin *et al.* (New York, 1978), pp. 99 ff.; the quotation is from p. 124. Notice that Glasser chooses the vulgar, abusive term for "policemen." What would he say of the equivalents that might be used of him?

Even more common than paranoid traits is jealousy. (Napoleon is said to have declared it the chief cause of the French Revolution.) When Thoreau asserts in *Walden* that, "The mass of men lead lives of quiet desperation," we can plausibly say that Thoreau's judgment is a projection of his own desperation at his social and economic failure. Similarly Marx's determination that "All values must be turned upside down" was probably in large part a consequence of his contemporaries' evaluation of his own work. The young Hemingway acidly described the intellectual and artistic society of the left bank as he saw it in Paris after World War I: "The quarter is . . . more a state of mind than a geographical area. . . . This state of mind is principally contempt. Those who work have the greatest contempt for those who don't. The loafers are leading their own lives and it is bad form to mention work. Young painters have contempt for old painters, and that works both ways, too. There are contemptuous critics and contemptuous writers. Everybody seems to dislike everybody else."[34]

Such impressions are confirmed by the explosion of the literature of rejection in recent years. It sells because it gratifies the jealous, fortifies the lazy, consoles the failures, offers excuses in advance to those who fear to fail, arms the dissatisfied, and in general serves the needs of the sizable, uprooted, selfish minority who can neither succeed in society nor live contented without success. The increase of population and the concentration of management in relatively fewer hands have greatly increased the number of such dissatisfied persons; so has the exploitation of the middle class. Most of the victims are literate and want distraction. They form a substantial part of the reading and television-watching public. They are happy to be assured that the rewards they have missed, or fear they will miss, are sour grapes. Consequently

[34] From the original version of *The Sun Also Rises*, now in the Hemingway papers in the Kennedy Library, Boston. Quoted by A. Latham, "A Farewell to Machismo," *New York Times Magazine*, October 16, 1977, p. 99.

they welcome stories of the disappointments of persons, whether historical or imaginary, who sacrificed the easy enjoyment of everyday pleasures in order to achieve some difficult but socially approved goal. It is almost *de rigueur,* in many literary, sociological, and psychological circles, to represent such characters ("workaholics," etc.) as sprung from psychological maladjustment and destined for disaster. If the hero is prominent in business or politics, he must either have achieved his prominence by dishonest means (which will finally ruin his life) or be the victim of a neurotic drive to succeed, and end with a nervous breakdown. His wife must be an adultress, his son must hate him, etc. If by some freak of fate there should be a family both happy and well-to-do, they must be captured by a gang of charming but sadistic sex maniacs, or suffer some comparable misfortune. Much popular history, too, is full of such gratifications of jealousy. Do you plan a biography of a distinguished diplomat who was also a brilliant writer and whose wife was a woman of extraordinary beauty, taste, and intelligence?

—"Perhaps you can place it with a university press."

—"But she was a Lesbian; he was hopelessly in love with her; and despair drove him to homosexuality."

—"Why didn't you say so? You *must* let us have it. We can promise you a first printing of a hundred thousand copies."

Like the lonely and hostile, the lazy, unsuccessful, and jealous have more time for reading and for watching television than do the successful and popular. Accordingly their tastes shape sales, sales shape editorial staffs and reviewers, editors and reviewers shape prestige, and prestige shapes academic appointments, the content of high school and college courses, and thus, eventually, public opinion.

The system is not foolproof, nor genius-proof. Some healthy men of extraordinary intelligence achieve the recognition they deserve. Most healthy adolescents of ordinary stupidity go through high school and college indifferent to pernicious literature and teaching. Stupidity is the Chinese wall protecting civilization from the intellectuals. Besides the stupid, however, there are many intelligent who are extrovert, popular, like society, and from childhood on are mainly concerned with other people. They most often distinguish themselves in business, government, law, medicine, or the physical sciences, and constitute a large percentage of the upper class. They are the people for whose success envious intellectuals console themselves by writing slanted sociological studies and venomous novels, attributing to them the maladjustments from which the intellectuals themselves conspicuously suffer. Fortunately, most of the successful are too busy to notice.

The unfortunates are the sensitive students reached in high school and college when their hopes are not yet formed. For many of these, works from the literature of rejection, presented by persuasive teachers, can result in serious disorientation. The importance of models for the commission of crimes has been mentioned above (p. 19); models for social failure and neuroses are probably even more important. The inexperienced and credulous cannot be expected to discount rhetoric. To say, "Great poets should not be taken seriously," would be false as well as flip. But it should be said that careful interpretation is needed to make clear the subtle ways in which the visions of a perverted genius are of value to the life of a healthy man. Without such interpretation, the literature of rejection can be lethal. Harry Crosby, for instance, seems to have gone from comic posturing to self-destruction in an attempt to live out the poetry of Baudelaire.[35]

A short while ago I was so impolite as to interrupt a conversation. A young man was explaining:

—"It's by that girl who was a star in the last Woody Allen movie. She says that, living in Beverly Hills and going to the studio by limousine, everything was so beautiful that she was cut off from the realities of life . . ."

---

[35] See G. Wolff, *Black Sun* (New York, 1976).

—"How did she know," I interjected, "that beautiful things are unreal and ugly things are real?"

—"She was an Artist," he said loftily, "and Artists have to suffer."

"On my honor I will do my best to do my duty . . ." and be unhappy for my Art. As the hot hymn has it, "I am ready, you can pass the cross to me!" The gospel continues to produce the martyrs. Or, to put it in more fashionable terms, we have lately seen many adolescent victims of the pervasive pollution of the intellectual and emotional environment.

After all this I shall be expected to follow the example of Plato (*Republic* 398a), crown the authors of the literature of rejection (including Plato) with a few laudatory phrases, and send them out of the city. But I am not advocating a planned society, I am merely pointing out the dubious motives and traditions that produce opposition to any practical plan. And if I were to advocate a planned society it would not be one planned to protect the incompetent, nor characterized, in modern style, by prohibition of useful things because the stupid are apt to make bad use of them. If a choice is necessary, I shall give up Harry Crosby rather than Baudelaire. The great works of pernicious literature are too valuable to be sacrificed for the sake of those who cannot read them with understanding. But their danger ought to be recognized. The tradition of rejection, declaring that worldly success is unimportant or worse, that poverty is preferable to wealth, that physical pleasure is a snare, that the wisdom of this world is foolishness and worldly hopes are vanity, is there, enshrined in our sacred literature, taught in our schools, presented with innumerable variations to justify various vices—not the least of them laziness—and to alienate its hearers from the standards and hopes of the surrounding world. The sirens are still singing and the beach before them is piled high with the bones, bikinis, beer cans, paintboxes, and needles of the hundreds of thousands they have destroyed.[36] But for millennia,

[36] *Odyssey*, XII, 37–46.

too, their songs have been the consolation of the unfortunate, the revenge of the oppressed, the encouragement of the neglected, and the citadel of liberty.

XI

Paradoxically, the literature of social rejection and the attacks on society that it engenders contribute to social stability because they often prevent the readers and participants from becoming involved in practical plans for change or attaining positions of power. The conservative should hope that revolutionists will reject society. Those who don't reject it, but get to the top, are the dangerous ones. Marx would have been far less influential without the backing of the rich manufacturer, Engels. Monasticism, by sequestration of many discontented and able-bodied poor, contributed greatly to the stability of later Roman society. Other examples come readily to mind. Thus the increase of the literature of rejection should be added to the symptoms discussed above which indicate that no great changes in the political, economic, or social order are to be expected soon. On the contrary, the rest of this century should produce a bumper crop of gurus.

Nevertheless, this period of comparative social stability is not likely to cause such epidemic abandonment of worldly hopes as occurred in the second and third centuries of the Roman Empire. In the present situation there are irresistible forces making for change, the interplay of these forces is so complex and conjectural, and the possibilities they open for good and evil are so great that, in spite of general stability, political, economic, and social problems will probably continue as the main centers of hope for those whose concerns go much beyond personal affairs. The drama to be played out on the generally unchanging stage is the tragicomedy of free society in the United States and, therefore, in the rest of the free world. Will the hero (with his full complement of heroic flaws!) survive? Supposing fear restrains all major powers from major wars, supposing (with Leontief, above p. 188) that

the population of the free world can be fed till the end of this
century (or, if it cannot, that the resultant famines will be
local), supposing that no scientific or technological break-
throughs, and no unpredictable political upheavals precipitate sudden, violent social changes, supposing, in sum, basic
stability, how will the present politico-socio-economic process work itself out?

We may hope with considerable confidence that the forms
of democratic government will be preserved. So they are
even in the Soviet Union: the election ritual and the legisla-
tive liturgy go on as regularly as the Passover meal and the
Easter mass, but with even less practical significance. In the
free world, as in communist countries, the ceremonial façade masks the struggle between competing cliques of the
power elite, but in the free world the outcome of this struggle is greatly affected by the outcome of the ceremonies,
which no one clique can always control. Hence, as in world
politics the continuance of a divided world forces the governments on both sides to bid for the support of scientists
and secures for learning an importance and consequent
freedom otherwise unlikely, so in domestic politics the rivalry of the major cliques secures for the minor ones considerable liberty and sometimes importance far greater than
the merits of their positions or the numbers of their adherents deserve. We may hope, therefore, that party politics
will continue to occupy their position as the main act in the
central ring of our public circus, so long as our society remains free. The mere fact that they have this position now,
that the great spotlight of the media is consistently focused
on *them*, will also help to keep them where they are. So will
the great actual importance of the government, increasing
as inflation increases taxable income, taxation increases federal receipts, and spending in anticipation of receipts increases inflation. One important political drama to be
played out behind the unchanging stage set will be the attempt to limit deficit spending and consequently the politicians' power to burden their subjects with financial obliga-

tions of unlimited size, and to commit them to economic plans of indefinite duration.

Against such utopianism popular antipathy will be of little avail. It is, in fact, romantic, because in spite of it, and in spite of all appearances of stability, we must choose. We cannot have both the greatest good and the greatest number, nor both progress and security, nor both rising wages and stable money, nor both compassion and justice, nor both quality and equality, nor both unrestrained population growth and a high standard of living—or of human rights, for that matter. (The law of supply and demand holds for men as for everything else; when in oversupply they are cheap, as in India and China.) All these antitheses necessitate choice. Not to choose is also a choice, entailing perpetuation of the present instability, uncertainty, discontent, and national hopelessness, but also of the variety of present opportunities and private hopes.

So much for the short-term view. In the long term, the hopes of human beings are among the main factors working against the survival of humanity. For humanity to survive, planning, discipline, united action, self-control, economy, and sacrifice are necessary. Men, in short, will have to be men. But most men would rather be rabbits; they hope for indefinite continuance and proliferation of the present rabbit-hutch culture fostering affectionate little animals busy with the pursuit of love and lettuce—see the popularity of the rabbit/hobbit type in current literature and illustration. All austere virtues are anathema to rabbits and to those who profit from the rabbit economy of overproduction, overpopulation, continued expansion of the market to make possible more efficient mass production of worse products, and greater profits from less satisfactory services. The few for whom love and lettuce are not enough will continue to hope for other gratifications, societies, powers, or lives. Most such hopes will be moonshine; a few may lead to social, political, and artistic achievements of some importance. The most important and most rewarding in the end will probably be hopes for understanding. If circumstances permit them to be pursued, they may even eventually make it possible to save some of mankind from the destined destruction of this planet. Who knows? Heraclitus said that unless one hopes for the unexpected it can never be discovered, and Francis Bacon, that lack of hope is the greatest obstacle to the progress of science (*Novum Organum*, I,92).

The thought of an end of knowledge, of the cosmos going on like some great, empty machine, the stars wheeling through space with no one to see their beauty, is so terrible that we come back in desperation to our point of departure, the photographs of the surface of Mars that showed it to be uninhabitable and so, apparently, finished the age-old hope for expansion of human settlement. If that hope can never be revived, nothing will remain for mankind but the rest of its ride on this disintegrating spaceship. To this some have already resigned themselves. "Relax," we are advised, "Enjoy the sun. Doomsday is billions of years away, and a billion years is a long time."[37] Whereas the rabbit hutch is here already.

XII

In the rabbit hutch, as in Pandora's box, hope may lie hidden. The rabbits, too, are dedicated to survival, the basic drive of the animal, the fulfillment of the first commandment, "Increase and multiply!" (Genesis 1:28). That's just the trouble. Granted, but it may also prove the ultimate resource. Since the biological process has produced intelligence, it may even go on to enable intelligence to prevail. Zeus was destined to be served by the Titans from whom he was born.

In less poetic language, our exploration of the roots of resistance to the utopian tradition should not obscure the equally deep roots of that tradition itself. A persistent phenomenon of western thought, it springs not only from historical circumstances but also from the primary drives and needs

[37] A. Rosenfeld, "Star of Stars," *Saturday Review*, October 30, 1976, p. 14.

of human nature, of which, like hope in general, it shares the paradoxical power and limitation. Hope is a function of finite life, the interval between inert matter and divine omnipotence. A truly omnipotent and omniscient god could not hope: he would know in advance exactly what would happen, and whatever he willed would at once come to be. Hope is possible only to creatures in a world so orderly as to be predictable, but so complex as to make predictions uncertain, creatures with sufficient power to influence the course of events, but not sufficient power to control it completely. Mythologically we have said that Hope is the brother of Fear (whose other name is Anxiety). Like the brothers in a myth, they are enemies, but the life of each is bound to the life of the other, so that if the one were destroyed the other would also perish. Those who have no hope have nothing to fear; those who have nothing more to fear have nothing to hope for. Accordingly the most famous line on hope in English poetry is the first half of a couplet that expresses despair:

> Hope springs eternal in the human breast:
> Man never is, but always to be, blest.[38]

This is why eschatological speculation customarily stopped short when it came to the Kingdom of Heaven, just as fairy tales stopped with, "They married and lived happy ever after." The Kingdom/Utopia was conceived as a state of perfection, a state in which there was to be no need to hope for anything. Like these, the classless society has written over its door the inscription Dante chose for Hell: "Abandon hope, all ye who enter here."

It was the feat of Vico to react against such static conceptions by emphasizing the nature of history as an unending process of which no stage can be final nor, therefore, unchanging, and by pointing out that the great achievements of each age were the consequences of its peculiar characteristics, e.g., the sublimity of the *Iliad* was a consequence of the sav-

---

[38] Alexander Pope, *An Essay on Man,* I, 95 f.

agery of the world from which it sprang. Accordingly in any age the proper concern of hope is the next, coming age and its potential to correct the failings of the one present. Contrast the common, Aristotelian hopes for final conditions, states of society which, once attained, are simply to go on unchanged forever, "world without end, Amen." The best such state would be like the Museum of Naples with its long lines of classical statues, almost identical, individually beautiful, ultimately boring. How many Venuses can you take? Down all such calculated, classical vistas there floats a whiff of formaldehyde; their beauty is that of a mortician's parlor. The only escape from boredom is change, so if the perfect society is not to be a perfect bore it must be a society organized for change. The change should be for the better. But if perfect, a society cannot change for the better. Therefore "the perfect society" is a self-contradictory concept. What we need now is a society that will win loyalty by offering hope. Hope for what? For whatever we want next.

This was the third brother's reply in the old story of the Devil's wish. Once upon a time there was a righteous man who had three sons. The Devil hated him, but could not hurt him directly, so he tried to destroy his sons as soon as they became independent. When the eldest came of age the Devil disguised himself as a beggar and begged from him. The young man gave him a piece of money. The Devil then took the form of an angel and offered to reward him by giving him anything he wished. He wished to be king and was soon murdered by a wicked courtier. When the next son came of age the Devil played the same trick. The young man wished to be rich and was soon after murdered by a robber. The third son saw what had happened to his brothers and took thought. When his turn came and the Devil made the offer, he replied, "I wish all my wishes would always come true the very moment I wished them." The Devil was bound by his promise; the wish had to be granted. The young man then wished his brothers would come back to life; the wish had to be granted. With the kingdom of the first, the wealth of the second, and the wisdom and wishes of the third, they lived happy ever after.

This is a variant of the Solomon legend, the moral being that the best thing is wisdom, and wisdom being conceived not as knowledge of some system of theology or philosophy, but in the pre-philosophic way, as the ability to solve problems, for it is this ability that enables us to have our wish (to get what we want, so far as is possible) in each new situation as it arises. It was to this old notion of wisdom that Pericles turned when (if we can trust Thucydides) he defined the goal of Athenian education as production of men best able to deal with most various problems (II.41). In this notion of wisdom as capability is the answer to the problem of progress (mooted above, pp. 166 f.). The notion that progress requires a fixed goal is false. We know things we want done now. When they are done, the situation will be changed. In that changed situation, new needs and new possibilities will become apparent. And so on. Infinite progress may be progress towards one after another of an infinite series of goals, of which only the first few are now predictable. In the most general terms: We want to become that which will make us best able to become what we shall next want to become. With this hope, life is oriented towards the future, but enjoys already its reward, the sense of power, the power to adapt the environment to our needs and ourselves to its conditions, the power, in short, of life, for life is such adaptation.

This was the answer found by Marlowe's Faust in perhaps the greatest speech of intellectual drama, the introductory monologue in which he reviews the fields of learning, dismisses logic as merely descriptive, medicine as concerned with the body, law, with trivial disputes, divinity, as leading to fatalism, and finally chooses magic as the way to power:

> All things that mooue between the quiet poles
> Shall be at my commaund. Emperours and Kings
> Are but obeyed in their seuerall prouinces, . . .
> But his dominion that exceedes in this
> Stretcheth as far as doth the minde of man.

The way to power, however, is also the way to danger. Swedenborg, one of the grand masters of psychological observation, held that love of power is the worst of vices. Power for what? The love is everywhere. A blank sheet of paper is perfectly lovely because absolutely submissive. It is also absolutely infuriating because it cannot be blamed at all for our inability to put on it exactly what we hoped to say or picture. With each new sheet of paper we begin with infinite possibilities and end with one limited, therefore unsatisfactory, reality. The transition is a miniature model of the cabalistic account of creation by the self-limitation of the limitless, and the source of evil is the creator's inability (or, in gnostic terminology, "ignorance")—the inability to find a form adequate to the creative impulse which both makes possible the creative effort and requires its constant renewal. At least we can crumple up the sheet of paper and throw it away. Children are far from being blank sheets of paper, but many parents think them so, love them as possibilities for the exercise of power, and blame them for their failure to become what would satisfy the hopes that the parents themselves did not clearly know. The fact that they cannot be crumpled up and thrown away is, for some parents, a further exasperation.

Every beautiful object, and especially a beautiful human body, confronts us with our intense desire to do something with it, and our inability to know what we want to do. The resultant fury is the source of sadism and much vandalism, expressions of a love of power that despairs of knowledge and can vent itself only in crumpling up and throwing away, in humiliating and destroying the objects that attract it. This ignorance is the deepest reason for the principle, "All power corrupts."

Consequently the principle has one exception: The power to know. Knowing (in the largest sense, including reflective thought and understanding) is the only way in which power can be exercised quite innocently. All physical actions have limiting results. Love is always an attempt to hold, and so to shape, someone or something else. Only knowledge requires neither control of others nor submission to them, is in some forms not dependent on physical materials (except the brain) can be indulged without any necessary consequences, and offers lifelong delight. Happily, "The eye is not satisfied with seeing, nor the ear with hearing."[39] There is always something more to be seen and heard. We can go on forever with the hope of Solon, "to grow old always learning more."[40]

"Tomorrow," said the Grand Inquisitor, "you will have to learn some things you do not wish to know."

Of Phasael, brother of Herod the Great, it is said that when captured he thwarted his captors by dashing his own head against a wall and so killing himself.[41] A man of amazing self-control. I wonder if I could do it. I hope I shall never need to try. There are usually easier ways of escaping the Grand Inquisitor.

Until such escape becomes desirable we can accept Aristotle's definition of the good life as "the life of seeing and thinking" (a translation which gives more accurately the meaning of the adjective commonly rendered "contemplative"). It is a life of which the greatest pleasure will be derived from the exercise of our most important organ, the brain. With this conclusion we have our answer to the question, "What can a competent man hope to do?" He can hope to know, which, as Aristotle again said, "All men naturally desire" (*Metaphysics*, I.1).

At the same time we must recognize (still with Aristotle) that we are not disembodied minds nor bodies without societies, that as our minds live in our bodies, our bodies live in the physical and social worlds around us, and therefore the mind's attempt to express itself is necessarily extended by speech and action to the formation of our environment. The myth that God made man in his own image expresses the desire of man to make the world so. From the prehistoric

[39] Ecclesiastes 1:8.
[40] Plutarch, *Life of Solon,* II.2.
[41] Josephus, *Antiquities,* XIV.367; Tacitus, *Annals* IV.45 tells a similar story of a Spanish peasant.

times of the earliest craftsmen and artists we can watch man's steady progress of self-realization in the study, mastery, and remaking of the things around him to serve his needs and so express his nature. It is a reciprocal process: man learns from things; then things learn from (are rearranged and reshaped by) man; then, from the new things he has created, man learns more; and so on.

Thus to the question, "What do you want to be?" the study of history suggests an answer, "I don't want to be, I want to become." We have seen through history, if we have read it correctly—beneath the myriad particular hopes elicited by particular opportunities and expressed in particular projects, achievements, techniques, etc.—beneath all these, as the river runs beneath the ripples, run the deep, undiverted hopes for life, for power, for knowledge, which is formed by life and forms power. Living, knowing, and acting are the forms in which and by which man becomes. Not "becomes this" or "becomes that," but simply, constantly becomes; is not a fixed, bored being, but a living, acting man, an ever-changing consciousness, an understanding steadily extending its reach.

INDEX

Adam and Eve, 127, 128
Adams, Henry, 140
Age, *see* Old age
Alchemy, 123–126, 144
Alexander the Great, 98, 101, 103, 107
Alexandria, 126, 154; Museum, 121
Allende, Salvador, 133
American Broadcasting Company, 19
American Civil Liberties Union, 208
American Revolution, 203
Amos, 159
Anarchy, 85, 137
Anchorites, 112–113, 144
Animals: domestication of, 79–80; evidence of hope in, 37, 38, 54, 55, 58, 80
Anshen, Ruth Nanda, 81
Antisthenes, 203
Apocalypse of St. John, 115–116
Apollonius of Tyana, 108
Aristophanes, 92
Aristotle, 8, 55, 57*n*, 62, 69, 77, 95–97, 99, 121, 218, 221
Arnold, Thomas, 94
Art: Assyrian, 154; Christian, 120; Greek, 89, 90, 92–93, 154; hopes in, 45, 79, 83; in Middle Ages, 121; and national power, 153–155; and perception of beauty, 159–160
Asceticism, 56
Asclepius, 107
Astrology, 27
Athens, 126, 155; architecture, 92–93; downfall of, 73; Parthenon, 120, 154
Attis, 101
Aucassin and Nicolette, 122–123
Auden, W. H., 66

Augustine, St., 115
Augustus, 104, 154

Babeuf, Gracchus, 139
Bacon, Francis, 126, 145, 216; objectives for ideal order, 128–130
Baltic republics, 40
Barrie, J. M., *Peter Pan,* 157
Barron, J., 13
Baudelaire, Charles, 18, 200, 211, 212
Baxter, Richard, *The Saints' Everlasting Rest,* 117
Beat generation, 12
Beauty, perception of, 159–160, 220
Becker, Ernest, 200–201
Behavior, standards of, 13–14, 17–18
Berman, R. S., 180*n*
Bible, 7–8, 29, 121, 203, 204; New Testament, 104, 108, 110, 111, 203; Old Testament, 103, 159
Big business, 175–178, 189, 198
Big crime, 175
Big government, 173–178
Big labor, 174–175
Big poor, 174
Birth, 54
Black Muslims, 25
Blake, William, 27–28, 34
Book of Enoch, 116
Books: as escape from loneliness, 207; literature of rejection, 209–212; violence in, 18–19
Boredom and leisure, 77–78
Bourgeoisie, 23
Brahmins, 97
Brain, pleasures of, 57–64
Brainwashing, 76, 185

Brezhnev, Leonid, 137n
British Empire, 94, 102; see also England
Bronze Age, 85, 89, 98, 101
Browning, Robert, The Bishop Orders His Tomb at St. Praxed's Church, 206
Bukharin, N., 139n, 140
Business: big, 175–178, 189, 198; corruption in, 10–11
Byron, Lord, 55

Cabalism, 115
Cadmus, 23n
Cambodia, 193
Capitalism, 144–145, 152
Care, concern for, 65–66
Castaneda, Carlos, 70–71
Chaldean Oracles, 108
Change: attitudes of youth and age toward, 49–51; hope for, 199–200
Charities, 152–153; see also Social Services
Chaucer, Geoffrey, 120
Children, 167, 220; ancient and modern attitudes toward, 156–157; in art, 156–157; care of, 38, 39; and changing position of women, 15–16; in groups, persecution of differences, 67–69; learning, 58; life patterns, 61; preparation for social environment, 135; prolonged childhood, 157
China, 13, 22, 23, 50, 102, 165, 177, 188, 191, 192, 203; Mao Tse-tung's regime, 140–141, 193
Christianity, 22, 67, 70, 73, 101, 104, 107–122,163,169;charities,152–153; contradictions in, 206–207; as counter culture, 203, 206; early, community services, 109, 128; Egyptian influence on, 86; hope in, 70, 108–111, 114–115, 118–122; hope for salvation in, 108, 111, 113–115; in Middle Ages, 119; resurrection in, 115
Church, 110–112, 119, 121, 122, 203
Churchill, Winston, 9, 133
Cicero, 80, 201
Cities, historical development of, 80–81
City of God, 116
City University of New York, 21

Civil liberties movement, 197, 208
Classes in early societies, 83–84
Cliques, 172–173, 182
Club of Rome, 3
Coleridge, Samuel Taylor, 64
Columbus, Christopher, 99
Communism, 9, 23, 74, 102, 132, 139–143, 163, 165, 214; loss of faith in, 13; reeducation in, 163–164; and social rejection, 203, 205, 206; in totalitarian states, 13, 137n, 193; see also Soviet Union
Communities: early Christian, 109, 128; idealistic, 70–71; religious, 127n; of subcultures, 24–25; see also Utopian communities
Confessors, 111–112
Confucius, 71
Consciousness, 37
Constantine, 101
Counter culture, 11–12, 203, 206
Crassus, 98
Crime, 18–21, 197; big, 175, 184; "family" organizations, 110
Crosby, Harry, 211, 212
Crusades, 34, 73
Cuba, 193
Cultural pluralism, 24, 30
Curiosity, 46–47
Cybele, 101
Cynics (Cynicism), 22, 96, 99, 107, 144, 203, 205; and Christianity, 112–113
Cyprian, St., 67
Cyrus, King of Persia, 102
Czechoslovakia, 40

Dante Alighieri, 114–118, 217
Daydreams, 64, 157
Death: fear of, 104, 150, 200–201; and hope, 55, 56; last enemy, 161; right to die, 186
Democracy, 5–6, 9, 140; future of, 213–214; Greek origin of, 88, 196–197; objections to, 194, 196–197; promises of, 135
Descartes, René, 37
Developing countries: future of, 187–188, 189; hope in, 135–136, 164–165
Dictatorship, 142, 143
Diogenes, 69, 96, 205
Divine man, 106–108
Djoser, King of Egypt, 83

Dobzhansky, T., 44
Drama, Greek, 91–93
Dreams, 45–47, 64; discoveries in, 46; hopes in, 45–46, 157–159; and sexuality, 159; and visions, 157–158
Drug abuse, 20, 21, 25, 26, 30, 65, 166, 180

Ecclesiastes, 57, 200
Ecological problems, 2–5
Economic conditions, prediction of, 187–190
Economic crisis, 3–5, 7, 164–165
Economic security and happiness, 126–128, 131–132, 134–135, 150, 165
Eden, 127, 128
Education, 21–22, 178, 183–185; equalitarianism in, 78, 180–181, 198; and functional illiteracy, 21
Egypt, ancient, 83, 85–86, 103, 154
Einstein, Albert, 149
Eisenhower, Dwight D., 192
Eleusinian mysteries, 103
Elijah Mohammed, 67
Elpistic philosophy, 72
Empedocles, 106
End of the world, millenarian movements, 111; see also Eschatological hopes
Energy sources, 5, 189–192
Engels, Friedrich, 137, 139n, 142, 203, 205, 213
Engineering, see Technological development
England, 12, 127; social criticism in, 133; socialist government, 190, 193
Environment, preservation of, 4
Ephesians, Epistle to the, 53
Epicureanism, 57, 96, 99, 107, 109
Epicurus, 55, 57, 69, 96, 104, 107
Equalitarianism: and decline of middle class, 179–181; in education, 78, 180–181, 198
Equality, 47, 139, 140, 158, 159
Escapism, 26, 30, 183
Eschatological hopes, 101–105; in Christianity, 108, 110–111, 114–115
Ethnic groups, 24, 30
Etruscans, 103
Ezekiel, 205

Faith, 70
Faith healing, 43
Family: changes in, 15–16, 30, 151–152, 166; historical development of, 80–81
Fascism, 165, 181, 193
Fears and hopes, 45–46
Florence, 155
Ford, Gerald, 10
Forrester, J., 39n
Fortune, 175–176
Frankenstein, 124
French Revolution, 22–23, 73, 102, 139, 171, 203, 209
Freud, Sigmund, 163, 165
Fromme, "Squeaky," 12
Fuel supplies, 5, 189–190
Future shock, 50

Genesis, 126, 127, 132, 165, 216
Genet, Jean, 144
Germany, East, 39–40
Germany, middle class, 181; see also Nazism
Ghazzali, al-, 116
Ghost Dance movement, 74
Gnosticism, 86
Goethe, Johann Wolfgang, 146
Gold Rush, 34, 73
Goldwater, Barry, 8
Good, definition of, 166–167
Good society, 170–171; faults of, 194–195
Gothic architecture, 122
Government, 5–6, 182–184; big, 173–178; control by, 194–198; distrust of, 9–10, 193–194; future of, 189–192, 213–215; participation in, 166, 172, 196–197
Goya, Francisco, 154
Great Awakening, 74
Greek civilization, 23, 86–99, 154–155; art, 89, 90, 92–93, 154; athletic contests, 92; colonies, 87, 124; government, 87–89, 94, 196–197; gymnasia, 90, 92; hellenistic period, 100–102, 104, 154; homosexuality, 71, 91, 92; hope in, 86–89, 92–94, 96–100; and life after death, 103–104; literature, 89–90, 93; theaters, 91–93; tyrants, 93, 94; and utopias, 124

Greek mythology, 44–45, 98, 157, 216, 217
Greek philosophy, 69–70, 72, 92, 94–97, 99, 121; and supernatural powers, 105–107
Groups, 24–27; exclusion from, 68–69; persecution of differences, 67–69; religious, 25, 27, 178; social, attachment to, 66–67
Guevara, Che, 137n
Gulag Archipelago, 13
Guyana, People's Temple cult, 25

Hannibal, 107
Happiness, 166–167; and economic security, 128, 131–132, 134–135, 150, 165
Harpocrates, 101
Harrell, D., 43
Health, 55
Heaven, 115–117
Hebrews, Epistle to the, 70
Hegel, Georg Wilhelm Friedrich, 8
Heidegger, Martin, 8
Heilbroner, Robert, 132, 187, 194
Heine, Heinrich, 89
Hell, 117–118
Hellenistic period, 100–102, 104, 154
Hemingway, Ernest, 209
Hercules, 107, 192
Hereafter, see Life after death
Heresy, 22, 111, 114, 121
Hermits, 113
Herodotus, 86–87
Hesiod, 72, 78, 89, 159, 203
Hinduism, 72
Hippodamus, 87, 124
Historical thought and social reform, 132–133
History: conjecture and interpretation in, 32–33; and hope, see Hope
Hitler, Adolf, 98, 133, 193
Home, changes in, 15–16, 30; see also Family
Homeric poems, 154, 156; see also Iliad; Odyssey
Homosexuality, 18, 152, 185; in Greece, 71, 91, 92
Hope: in Christianity, see Christianity; classification of, 51–54; common hopes, 167–172; conscious, 42–43; crisis of, 1–31, 162–170, 202–203; definition of, 36–37; and desire, 36; and dreams, 45–46, 157–159;

Hope (cont'd)
and economic development, 135–136, 164–165; effect on body, 41–43; as expectation, 32, 36–37; and experience, 48–49; and fear, 45–46; for future, 215–222; in Greek civilization, 86–89, 92–94, 96–100; and growth of society, 80–84, 149–161; and historical events, 75–77, 86–87, 100–108, 122–161; historical investigation of, 32–35; for immortality, see Life after death; individual aberrations of, 163–164; for life and power, 160; for new world order, 101–103; personal, 19, 166–168; psychological interpretations of, 42–45; and revolution, 139–144; in scientific and technological progress, 145–149; and social reform, 130–131, 135–136, 138, 150; unconscious, 42, 43; and utopias, see Utopias; in western civilization, 71–74, 164–165; what to hope for, 27–30, 198–202, 218, 219, 222; what we hope to be, 145–146, 219, 222; in youth and age, 50–51
Horror stories, 118
Hosea, 205
Humanitarianism, 27–28, 39, 203
Hungary, 40
Hunt, Leigh, 131
Hussites, 158
Huxley, Aldous: Brave New World, 93, 125, 133, 134, 136, 138; Brave New World Revisited, 61–62, 185n; Heaven and Hell, 117n
Hypnopaedia, 185

Id, 44
Identity crisis, 135
Iliad, 203, 217–218
Illiteracy, functional, 21
Illusions and perception, 59
Imagination, 64; and dreams, 45–46
Imhotep, 83, 89
Immigration, 14
Immortality, hope for, 201–202; see also Life after death
India, 103
Individualism, 38–39, 137–138
Individuals, relationship with society, 196–197

Industrialization, 3, 151
Infantilism, 157, 201
Isaiah, 205; Second, 47, 67, 101–102
Isis, 101
Islam, 67, 73, 163
Isolation, 207
Israel (state), 71
Italy, 154; Fascism, 181, 193

Jaspers, K., 146, 160
Jealousy, 209–211
Jefferson, Thomas, 80
Jeremiah, 101
Jesuits, 76
Jesus Christ, 86, 101, 102, 107, 203, 206
Jews, 70, 71, 97, 102, 119; as compulsive achievers, 135; revolts, 105
Joan of Arc, 114
Job (patriarch), 79, 80
John, Epistles of, 111, 146
Johnson, Samuel, 31, 92
Judaism, 22, 104, 109, 169, 203; hereafter in, 67, 70, 103, 115; prophets, 105–106, 203, 205
Julian the Apostate, 98
Jung, C. G., 44, 124
Juvenile delinquency, 20

Kafka, Franz, 79
Kant, Immanuel, 169
Karabel, J., 178
Kenyatta, Jomo, 24
Keynes, John Maynard, 138
KGB, 13
Kingdom of Heaven, 217
Kings: in early religions, 82–83; growth of power, 84–85
Knights Templar, 126
Knowledge, nature of, 34–35, 220–222

Labor, big, 174–175; see also Unions
Lance, Bert, 194
Laws, 153, 159, 180; Biblical, 7–8; Marxian view of, 23
Leisure: and boredom, 77–78; in Greek civilization, 92–93
Lenin, Nikolai, 137n, 193
Leonard, W. E., The Locomotive God, 151
Leontief, W., 188–189, 213
Lessing, Gotthold Ephraim, 131

Liberalism, 126–127, 150
Liberty, 47, 158
Licinius, 101
Life, prolonging of, 186
Life after death: in Christianity, 108, 114–115; Egyptian beliefs on, 85–86; hope for, 67, 70, 103–105, 108, 150, 201–202
Life patterns, 58, 60–61
Literature, 64; Greek, 89–90, 93; hopes in, 45, 83
Loewi, Otto, 46
Loneliness, 16, 166, 207
Longfellow, H. W., 155
Looting, 168
Love, 159, 160, 200, 201, 220
Loyola, St. Ignatius, 76
Lucian, 157
Lucretius, 104, 107
Luxemburg, Rosa, 141–142

Magi, 97
Magic, 65, 105, 107, 108, 123
Man: divine, 106–108; ideal, 120–121
Manichaeanism, 109n
Mannheim, K., 138
Manson, Charles, 12, 19, 144
Mao Tse-tung, 140–141, 158, 193
Marcus Aurelius, 108
Marie Antoinette, 85
Marijuana, 26, 27
Mark Antony, 98
Marlowe, Christopher, 219
Mars, photographs of, 1, 216
Marx, Karl, 10, 23, 64, 102, 125, 127, 137, 139n, 142, 160, 163, 203, 205, 209, 213
Marxism, 8, 63, 64, 102, 137n, 150
Masochism, 18
Meadows, D., 39n
Medicine, hope of patients in, 41–43
Menippus, 157
Menstrual blood, 43
Messiah (Messianic age), 102, 105, 108, 115
Middle Ages, 119, 121–122, 160
Middle class, 178–181, 189, 197, 209
Middleton, D., 39–40
Military expenditures, 188–191
Mills, C. Wright, 172
Mind-body problem, 41
Mishan, E., 188, 196
Mithraism, 109n
Mohammed, 116

Moltmann, J., 142*n*
Monasteries (monasticism), 70–71, 112, 113, 120, 121, 126, 203, 206, 213
Monotony, fear of, 198–199
Moon, landing on, 157–158
Moral standards, 13–14, 17–18, 60
More, Sir Thomas, 193
Mormons, 25, 26
Moslems, 121
Motion pictures, violence in, 18–19, 118
Motivation, 44, 63–64
Murder, 18–20
Mussolini, Benito, 193

Napoleon, 98, 209
Nash, Ogden, 9–10
National Assessment of Educational Progress, 21
Nazism, 8, 73, 74, 133, 165, 181, 193
Neoplatonism, 38, 108, 146, 169
Neo-Pythagoreans, 126
Netherlands, 154
New Jerusalem, 116
New world order, hope for, 101–105, 110
Nietzsche, Friedrich Wilhelm, 169
Nixon, Richard, 9
Nuclear power, 189–190

Odyssey, 124
Ohio State University, 21
Oil, 4, 189–190; embargo, 2, 5; prices, 7
Old age, 11, 186; attitude toward change, 49–51; societies dominated by the old, 50
Order: love of, 59–60; Will to, 61–62
Origen, 146
Orwell, George, *1984,* 125, 133, 134, 138, 208

Pacifism: Solzhenitsyn's criticism of, 11; and Vietnam War, 6–7
Panama, 7
Panic, 155
Pareto, Vilfredo, 140
Paul, St., 60, 62, 70, 104, 108, 113, 161, 203, 206
Pausanias, 116
People's Temple, 25
Perception: of beauty, 159–160, 220; and illusions, 59; of others, 65–66

Pergamum, 154
Pericles, 93, 94, 219
Persia, ancient, 98, 102, 154
Persona, 65
Personality, magical alteration of, 64–65
Phasael, 221
Philanthropy, 27–28
Philo of Alexandria, 122
Philosophy, 8, 22, 29; and Christianity, 108, 109; Greek, *see* Greek philosophy
Phoenicians, 89
Picasso, Pablo, 47
Pill, the, 16–17, 185
Pindar, 92
Pity, 169–170
Planned society, *see* Social planning; Utopias
Plato, 6, 39, 42, 47, 91, 94–96, 99, 104, 106, 134, 159, 160, 169, 172, 203; *Republic,* 69, 87, 193, 194, 201, 212
Pleasure: of body, 55–56; of brain, 57–64; and purpose in life, 77; of senses, 57
Plutarch, 47, 71
Poets and prophets, 159
"Polish Bishops to the Polish Priests," 206–207
Political problems, 5–6, 165–166, 182–184, 192–194; and hope, 183, 184, 214; *see also* Government
Pollution, 4, 5
Poor, big, 174
Pope, Alexander, 72, 217
Population growth (explosion), 3, 9, 29, 39, 74, 185–186, 190, 215
Population movements, 14
Pound, Ezra, 169–170
Poverty, relative, 168
Power, 159; competition for, 165; and knowledge, 220–221; love of, 63, 220; national, and art, 153–155; sense of, 62–63; supernatural, 105–108
Power elite, 172, 183, 214
Preobrazhensky, E., 139*n*
Priests: Christian, 120; in early religions, 82
Progress, 166, 219
Project Hope, 39*n*
Prophets, 105–106, 159, 203, 205
Proverbs, Book of, 41

Psychoanalysis, 43–45, 163
Psychological influences in history, 73–74
Purpose in life, 77–78
Pythagoras, 97, 106, 126
Pythagoreans, 95, 99

Rabelais, François, 126
Reformation, 22
Refugees, 14
Rejection of social standards, 202–213
Religion, 29, 178; historical development of, 81–82; traditional and modern, 7–8, 22
Religious groups, 25, 27, 178
Renaissance, 22, 122, 127, 144, 156
Resources: competition for, 165; protection of, 4, 29
Revolution, 139–144, 158, 203–204, 213
Revolution for the Hell of It, 143–144
Robespierre, Maximilien, 195
Roman Catholic Church, 10, 121
Roman Empire, 6, 104–105, 107–108, 122, 154; and Christianity, 104, 128, 213
Roman Republic, 154
Ruling class, 181
Russell, Bertrand, 76, 130, 142, 143, 204
Russia, *see* Soviet Union
Russian Revolution, 139, 158

Sade, Marquis de, 144
Sadism, 18, 143, 163–164, 166, 195; and vandalism, 93–94, 220
Saints, 111, 114, 119
Salvation, hope for, 108, 111, 113–115
Sargon, King of Agade, 84, 101
Sartre, Jean-Paul, 143
Science, 144–149; research in, 147–149; unified system of, 147
Scipio Africanus, 107
Self-image, destruction of, 42
Selfishness, 166, 202, 203
Self-sacrifice, 71, 169
Senate Select Committee on Nutrition, 3
Senate Subcommittee on Juvenile Delinquency, 20
Seneca, 80
Sex change, 157

Sexual behavior, 17–18; restricted in communities, 71
Sexuality and dreams, 159
Shabbetai Zvi, 74
Seyrig, Henri, 200
Shadow, destruction of, 42
Shelley, Percy Bysshe, 159
Skinner, B., 42, 196*n*
Slavery, 80, 139
Social change: prediction of, 191–192; resistance to, 195
Social gospel, 131–133, 153
Socialism, 132, 137, 174, 190, 193, 194
Social patterns, 3; conformity to, 194–195
Social planning, 165, 192–198; hostility to, 208, 212; *see also* Utopias
Social reform, 130–136, 138, 150
Social rejection, 202–213
Social services, 27–28, 30, 128, 152–153; opposition to, 208
Social standards: lack of, 3, 8; rejection of, 202–213
Socrates, 69, 92, 94, 95, 106–107, 134, 203, 205
Solomon, 219
Solon, 221
Solzhenitsyn, Aleksandr, 11, 13
Sophists, 92
South Sea Bubble, 73
Soviet Union, 13, 22, 50, 102, 136, 137*n*, 158, 165, 191, 192, 203, 214; culture, 23, 205; power and authority, 142–143; Revolution, 139, 158; as rival of U.S., 188–191; science and social studies in, 148; tyranny, 62, 193
Space exploration, 157–158
Spain, 154; civil war, 204–205
Sparta, 71
Stalin, Joseph, 62, 193
Stoics (Stoicism), 22, 69, 96, 99, 107, 203, 205–206
Stotland, E., 42
Stupidity, 210–211
Subconscious, the, 37, 38, 43–45, 76, 150–151
Subcultures, 20–21, 24–26, 30
Success: hope for, 78–79; jealousy of, 209–211
Superego, 44

Supernatural powers: hope for, 105–108; spiritual, 112–114
Supreme Court decisions, 159
Sweden, welfare state, 12–13, 193
Swedenborg, Emanuel, 63, 70, 115, 200, 220
Swift, Jonathan, *Gulliver's Travels*, 125
Synanon, 25

Taxation, 180, 188, 189, 197
Technological development, 7, 14, 144–149; and family life, 15–16; prediction of, 187
Television: as escape, 207, 209, 210; violence on, 18–19, 118
Tennyson, Alfred, Lord, 173
Theognis, 89
Thomas, L., 41
Thomas Aquinas, St., 19
Thoreau, Henry David, 209
Thucydides, 73, 93, 94, 219
Toffler, A., 50
Totalitarian states, 137–138, 193–196
Triviality, objections to, 199–200
Truman, Harry S., 192
Truth, nature of, 35
Turks (Turkey), 154
Tyranny and planned society, 195
Tyrants, Greek, 93, 94

Unconscious, the, 37, 42, 43, 76, 198
Underdeveloped countries, *see* Developing countries
Understanding, 58, 64, 160–161
Unions, 174–176, 198
United States: democracy in, 9; military expenditures, 188–191; minorities in, 24; in world economy and defense, 4, 165, 188–191
Universities, 121; disorders in 1960s, 11–12; and functional illiteracy, 21
Utopian communities, 25–26, 126–128, 208
Utopias, 69–70, 87, 124–139, 144, 150, 160, 165, 215; criticism of (anti-utopias), 133–134, 138, 139; hope in, 125–126, 134, 136–137; resistance to, 192–196, 198, 202, 216–217; and revolution, 204; and social reform, 130–132

Vandalism, 93–94, 220

Vatican Council, Second, 10
Vergil, 85
Versailles, 85
Vico, Giovanni Battista, 217
Victoria, Queen, 102
Vietnam, 193
Vietnam War, 6–7, 9
Violence, 18–20, 118, 143, 163–164, 166, 180
Visions, 64, 157–159
Voltaire, François Marie Arouet, 8
Voting, 179–180, 182–183

Wambaugh, J., *The Choirboys*, 169
War, possibility of, 186–187
Ward, B., *Spaceship Earth*, 2
Watergate case, 9
Wattenberg, B., 168, 204
Watts riots, 168
Waugh, Auberon, 12
"We," definition of, 170–172
Wealth, 144–145, 167–168
Welfare expenditures, 190, 194
Welfare recipients, 170, 174, 184
Welfare state, 12–13, 39–40, 176, 193
Western civilization: basic suppositions and value judgments, 22–23; extension of, 1–2; hope in, 71–74, 164–165; stability of society, 204
Wilde, Oscar, 130
Will to Order, 61–62
Wilson, Edward O., 44
Wisdom, 64, 219
Witchcraft, 22, 73; killing by, 40–41
Women: change in position of, 14–16, 30, 151, 152; in religion, 120; triviality of their lives, 199–200; working, 15–16, 151
Wordsworth, William, 35, 145
World conquerors, 84, 98, 101
World government, hope for, 84–85
World order, end of, *see* Eschatological hopes; New world order

Xenophon, 106

Yahweh, 101, 102
Yeats, William B., 160
Young, Andrew, 194
Youth: attitude toward change, 48–51; rebellion of, 114

Zeno, 69, 96, 206
Zionism, 74

ABOUT THE AUTHOR

Morton Smith has been Professor of Ancient History at Columbia University since 1962. He holds two doctoral degrees, one in theology from Harvard, and one in philosophy, from the Hebrew University in Jerusalem. Besides many scholarly articles on Greek and Roman history and on Old Testament, New Testament, Patristic, and Rabbinic studies, he has published a number of books, of which perhaps the best known is *Jesus the Magician* (New York, 1978), winner of the Trilling award for that year. Professor Smith has held many distinguished fellowships and was formerly a member of the Institute for Advanced Study; he is now a member of the American Academy of Arts and Sciences and of a dozen scholarly societies. He has been lecturer for the American Council of Learned Societies and for the Archaeological Institute of America and has spoken by special invitation in almost two hundred colleges and universities in the United States and abroad.

ABOUT THE FOUNDER OF THIS SERIES

Dr. Ruth Nanda Anshen—philosopher, author, and editor—founded, plans, and edits *World Perspectives, Religious Perspectives, Credo Perspectives, Perspectives in Humanism, The Science of Culture Series, The Tree of Life Series,* and *Crossing the Frontiers.* She also writes and lectures on the relationship of knowledge to the nature of man and to his understanding of and place in the universe. Dr. Anshen's book, *The Reality of the Devil: Evil in Man,* a study in the phenomenology of evil, is published by Harper & Row. Dr. Anshen is a member of The American Philosophical Association, The International Philosophical Society, The History of Science Society, and The Metaphysical Society of America.